Music in Early America:
A Bibliography of Music in Evans

by

Donald L. Hixon

The Scarecrow Press, Inc.
Metuchen, N. J.   1970

ISBN 0-8108-0374-7

TABLE OF CONTENTS

PREFACE

This bibliography is an index to the music
published in seventeenth and eighteenth century
America as represented by Charles Evans' *American
Bibliography* and the Readex Corporation's microprint
edition of *Early American Imprints, 1639-1800,* this
latter edited by Clifford K. Shipton of the American
Antiquarian Society. Every item containing printed
musical notation, whether published in book, pamphlet,
or broadside form, and whether issued separately or
as part of a larger collection, has been entered;
periodicals, newspapers, and other serial publications
have been excluded.

The book has been divided into six parts,
as follows.

Part I. Alphabetical composer-editor-compiler
arrangement of all items currently available in the
Early American Imprints microprint edition. In
each instance, the serial number assigned by Evans
has been supplied. Title entries are used only in

instances of unknown authorship. In addition, composer-
title analytics for each collection of secular music
have been included; contents of sacred collections
have not been analyzed.

Part II. Alphabetical composer-editor-
compiler arrangement of those items not yet reproduced
in the *Early American Imprints* microprint edition.
Many of these items have not been located, many were
never published, some withheld by the owning library,
and still others a result of inconsistencies or
inaccuracies of entry encountered in *Evans*. The
comments supplied by the American Antiquarian Society
and found on the target cards are reproduced herein.
The microprint edition is continually augmented through
the release of "corrected microprints," and some of
the items currently not available may become accessible
in the future. Until such time, however, Part II helps
provide a more complete picture of music publishing
activities in early America.

Part III. Biographical sketches of the
composers represented. These short notices do not
pretend to give a complete account of the life and
activities of the composers and compilers included,

but they do provide a historical context and lend an idea of the type of music with which each is associated. Biographies of J. C. Bach, Haydn, Mozart, Handel, and others of the same degree of familiarity abound in numerous basic sources of musical biography, and it seemed unnecessary to include them here. In such instances, the reader is referred to Grove's *Dictionary of Music and Musicians*, readily available in even the smallest library. References are occasionally made to sources of national biography (*DNB* and *DAB*) for persons of non-American origin whose direct influence on American music was comparatively slight, or for persons whose chief intellectual endeavors were essentially non-musical (Colley Cibber, etc.) In a very few instances, a particular composer has slipped so completely into the ranks of obscurity that no meaningful biography was possible. The place and date of a composer's birth and death, where available, were based on *Evans*, but modified where discrepancies existed between *Evans* and basic reference sources such as *Grove, Baker, Thompson*, etc. The biographies included in *Sonneck-Upton* and *Wolfe* were also examined, and the most commonly-recurring date was selected for this bibliography.

Part IV. Composer-editor Index. This
index, together with the Title Index forming Part V,
must be consulted in order to derive maximum effectiveness
from this Bibliography. The hundreds of short songs and
instrumental selections included in the collections cited
in Parts I and II, for instance, are accessible readily
only through the use of these indexes. The Evans serial
number is supplied in each instance.

Part V. Title Index. An alphabetical
title arrangement, with composer and Evans serial number
given for each item cited in Parts I and II.

Part VI. Numerical Index, arranged in
numerical order by Evans serial number, with page numbers
indicating citations in Parts I and II.

The form of entry, embracing capitalization,
punctuation, and spelling, often inconsistent with current
usage but occasionally the key to differentiating editions
of the same work, were determined by the title page of the
item being cited. Inaccuracies are identified by the
conventional [sic] in brackets. All editorial remarks
occuring within the citation are enclosed by brackets; those
following the citation are given in *italics*.

By-lines have been omitted, except where they provide biographical information about the composer, or in cases where they help relate the composer or editor to the work. For instance, *The Rudiments of music...By Andrew Law, A. M.* and *Crazy Jane...the words by Mr. Lewis Esqr., set to music by Miss Abrams* were considered to offer sufficiently pertinent information about Andrew Law and Harriet Abrams to justify their inclusion.

Since this is essentially a "finding-tool" index to the music contained in *Evans*, elements of descriptive bibliography (size of volume, price, address of publisher and/or dealer when appearing on the title page, copyright notices, indication of illustrations or cuts, etc.) were omitted. Also, *Evans, Sonneck-Upton,* and *Wolfe* give library locations for each item, and it was not considered necessary to duplicate that information here.

In *Evans*, greater bibliographical significance was attached to the author of the text of musical works than to the composer of the music. Therefore, songs, opera, and musical dramatic works were entered under the name of the librettist or author of the words. In this bibliography, however, the composer was considered pre-eminent. Therefore, certain entries were changed from those found in *Evans*. All changes of entry are indicated in a note following the citation.

In the preparation of this bibliography, it became apparent that there were many instances in which the copy of a particular work reproduced in *Early American Imprints* was not entirely consistent with the item described in Evans. Undoubtedly, the American Antiquarian Society secured for photo-reproduction the most perfect copy available, while at the same time conforming as strictly as possible to Evans's entry. For the sake of uniformity, the bibliography in hand adheres to an entry derived from the title page reproduced, and on occasion this entry may differ slightly from that appearing in *Evans*.

Despite the care with which this volume has been prepared, a completely flawless book is a rare bird indeed. The author would be greatly appreciative if any inaccuracies, inconsistencies, misjudgements, and the like were reported to him at the University of California at Irvine, or in care of the publisher.

Grateful acknowledgment must be extended to many of the staff of U. C. I., and especially to John

Smith, University Librarian, Evelyn Huston, Head of
Public Services, and Margaret E. Kahn, Head of the
Reference Department, for their help in securing
released time for the preparation of this volume.
Thanks must go also to Eric Moon and Ralph Shaw of
the Scarecrow Press for their valuable editorial
assistance and encouragement, and to Don A. Hennessee,
Assistant Social Science Reference Librarian,
California State College at Long Beach, for his
great help in proofreading the original manuscripts.
Most particularly, however, gratitude must be extended
to Charles Evans, who convinced me that, indeed, "What
is hit is history--what is missed is mystery."

Donald L. Hixon

Summer 1970
Irvine, California

REFERENCES CITED IN

THIS BIBLIOGRAPHY

Baker, Theodore. *Baker's biographical dictionary of musicians*. Fifth edition. New York, G. Schirmer, 1958.

Brinley, George. *Catalogue of the American library of the late Mr. George Brinley, of Hartford, Conn.* Hartford, Press of the Case, Lockwood & Brainard Company, 1878-93. 5v.

British Museum. Department of Printed Books. *General catalogue of printed books*. London, Trustees, 1931- .

Britton, Allen P. and Irving Lowens, "Unlocated titles in early sacred American music." Music Library Association, *Notes*, ser. 2, 11 (December 1953), 33-48.

Dictionary of American Biography. New York, Charles Scribner's Sons, 1957. 11v. + index.

Dictionary of National Biography. London, Oxford University Press, 1959-60. 22v.

Evans, Charles. *American bibliography*. New York,
Peter Smith, 1941. 13v. + indexes.

Gaine, Hugh. *The Journals of Hugh Gaine, printer*.
Ed. by Paul Leicester Ford. New York, Dodd,
Mead & Co., 1902. 2v.

Grove, Sir George. *Dictionary of music and musicians*.
Fifth edition, ed. by Eric Blom. New York,
St. Martin's Press, 1955. 9v.

Hildeburn, Charles Swift Riche. *A Century of printing.*
The Issues of the press in Pennsylvania, 1685-
1784. Philadelphia [Matlack & Harvey] 1885-86. 2v.

Metcalf, Frank J., "The Easy Instructor: a bibliographical
study." *Musical Quarterly*, 23 (January 1937),
89-97.

Minick, Amanda Rachel. *A History of printing in Maryland,*
1791-1800, with a bibliography of works printed
in the State during the period. Baltimore,
Enoch Pratt Free Library, 1949.

Sabin, Joseph. *A Dictionary of books relating to America,*
from its discovery to the present time. Amsterdam,
N. Israel, 1961 [reprint of New York ed. of 1868]
29v. in 15.

Sonneck, Oscar George Theodore. *A Bibliography of early secular American music (18th century)*. Revised and enlarged by William Treat Upton. New York, Da Capo Press, 1964.

Thompson, Oscar. *The International cyclopedia of music and musicians*. Ninth edition. New York, Dodd, Mead and Company, 1964.

Wolfe, Richard J. *Secular music in America, 1801-1825; a bibliography*. New York, New York Public Library, 1964. 3v.

KEY TO EVANS SERIAL NUMBERS

The table below indicates the volume number in which
Evans items may be found in his *American Bibliography*.
Items numbered above 39162 are included in the Supplement
to the *Early American Imprints* microprint edition, and
such titles are *not* included in *Evans*.

Item numbers	Volume	Item numbers	Volume
1-3244	1	22298-25074	8
3245-6623	2	25075-28145	9
6624-9891	3	28146-30832	10
9892-13091	4	30833-33261	11
13092-16176	5	33262-35854	12
16177-19448	6	35855-39162	13
19449-22297	7	39163-49197	-

PART ONE

MUSIC IN EARLY AMERICA:

A BIBLIOGRAPHY

ABRAMS, HARRIET, 1760-?. •

Crazy Jane, a favorite song, the words by Mr. Lewis
Esqr., set to music by Miss Abrams. Philadelphia,
G. Willig [1800?] 2 leaves   Evans 48996

ADAMS AND LIBERTY. New York, G. Gilfert [1798?]
Broadside & 2 leaves.   Evans 48557

ADAMS AND LIBERTY. The Boston patriotic song. Written
by Thomas Paine, A.M. [Boston, Thomas & Andrews,
1798] 2p.   Evans 34293
Note: Evans' entry under Thomas Paine, after-
wards Robert Treat, Junior, 1773-1811.

ADAMS AND LIBERTY. The Boston patriotic song. Written
by Thomas Paine, A.M. [Portsmouth, New Hampshire,
1798] 2p.   Evans 34298
Note: Evans' entry under Thomas Paine, after-
wards Robert Treat, Junior, 1773-1811.

ADAMS AND LIBERTY. The Boston patriotic song. Written
by Thomas Paine, A.M. Second edition--corrected.
[Boston, Thomas & Andrews for] Linley & Moore
[1799?] 2p.   Evans 34294
*Note: Evans' entry under Thomas Paine, after-
wards Robert Treat, Junior, 1773-1811.*

ADAMS AND LIBERTY. The Boston patriotic song. Written
by Thomas Paine, A.M. Third edition corrected.
Boston, P. A. von Hagen [1800] 2p. Evans 38177
*Note: Evans' entry under Thomas Paine, after-
wards Robert Treat, Junior, 1773-1811.*

ADGATE, ANDREW, c1750-1793.
Philadelphia harmony and rudiments of music.
Philadelphia, John M'Culloch, 1789. 20p.,
56 plates.   Evans 21629

Philadelphia harmony, or a collection of psalm tunes,
hymns, and anthems, selected by Adgate and Spicer,
together with the rudiments of music, on a new
and improved plan. By Adgate, P.U.A. Philadelphia, Westcott & Adgate [1790] 2, 20, 56p.
                     Evans 22299

Adgate, Andrew (continued)

Philadelphia harmony, or a collection of psalm tunes,
hymns, and anthems, selected by A. Adgate,
together with the rudiments of music, on a new
and improved plan, by A. Adgate, P.U.A.
Philadelphia, Westcott & Adgate [1791]
2, 20, 56, 2, 24p.   Evans 46110

Philadelphia harmony, or a collection of psalm tunes,
hymns, and anthems, selected by A. Adgate,
together with the rudiments of music, on a new
and improved plan, by A. Adgate, P.U.A.
Philadelphia, Carey [1796] 2, 64p.
                                      Evans 29953

The Philadelphia songster. Part I. Being a collection
of choice songs; such as are calculated to please
the ear, while they improve the mind, and make
the heart better. By Absalom Aimwell, Esquire
[pseudonym for Andrew Adgate] Philadelphia,
John M'Culloch, 1789. 16p.   Evans 21628

Contents

p. 3-4	God save America
5	A catch for three voices

Adgate, Andrew (continued)

6-7	Rosy morn
7	Rose tree [from William Shield's The Poor Soldier]
8	Indian chief [alternate title of Alknomook]
9	Anna
10	Myra
11	Graceful move [composed by Signora ____ Galli]
12-13	Friendship. Words by Mr. Bidwell of Connecticut. Tune: The British muse.
14	Glee for three voices [Drink to me only]
15-16	Anna's urn

Rudiments of music. By Andrew Adgate, P.U.A. Philadelphia, John M'Culloch, 1788. 22p.

Evans 20916

Rudiments of music. By Andrew Adgate, P.U.A. Philadelphia, John M'Culloch, 1788. 22p.

Evans 45212

Rudiments of music...Sixth edition. Philadelphia,

Mathew Carey, 1799. 102p.

Second title: Philadelphia harmony, or, a

collection of psalm tunes, hymns, and anthems.

Selected by Andrew Adgate, Part II.

p. 77-102.   Evans 35083

A Selection of sacred harmony, containing lessons

explaining the gamut, keys, and other characters

used in vocal music; also, a rich variety of

tunes approved of by the most eminent teachers

of church music in the United States. Phila-

delphia, W. Young, 1788. 16, 84, 2p.

Evans 45213

-----. The third edition...Philadelphia, William

Young and M'Culloch, 1790. 4, 132p.

Evans 22884

-----. Fourth edition... Philadelphia, William Young

and M'Culloch, 1794. 4, 132p.   Evans 47212

-----. [Fifth edition]...Philadelphia, W. Young,

Mills & Son, 1797. 4, 132p.   Evans 32818

AH WELL A DAY POOR ANNA. A favorite song sung at Vauxhall

Gardens. Philadelphia, B. Carr [1796] Evans 29956

AITKEN, JOHN, comp. 1745-1831.

A Compilation of the litanies and vespers, hymns and
anthems as they are sung in the Catholic Church.
Adapted to the voice or organ by John Aitken.
To which is prefixed, a new introduction to the
grounds of music. Philadelphia, Thomas Dobson,
1787. 6, 136p. Evans 20186

A Compilation of the litanies, vespers, hymns &
anthems as they are sung in the Catholic
Church. Philadelphia, John Aitken, 1791.
181p. Evans 23106

The Scots musical museum; being a collection of the
most favorite scots [sic] tunes: adapted to the
voice, harpsichord, and pianoforte by John
Aitken. Philadelphia, John Aitken, 1797.
2, 175p. Evans 31701

Note: "The unique original is imperfect and
irregularly paged."--American Antiquarian
Society.

Contents

p. 1	The birks of Invermay
2	Roslin castle
3	The broom of Cowdenknows
4	The yellow hair'd laddie
5	Gilderoy

Aitken, John (continued)

6	The blathrie o't
7-8	Duke of York's march
8	Mrs. Frasers strathspey
9	Tweed side
10	The lass of Peaty's mill
11	Logan water
12	An thou were my ain thing
13	Leander on the bay
14	To daunton me
15-16	Shepherds I have lost my love. Adapted by Pleyel.
17	Oh, open the door. Adapted by Pleyel.
18	Gin living worth
19	Braw lads on Yarrow braes. Adapted by Pleyel.
20	One morning very early. Adapted by Pleyel.
21	Chanson ecossoise, adapted for the pianoforte by Pleyel.
22	Mrs. Fleming's strathspey

Aitken, John (continued)

23-24	Danse ecossoise, adapted as a rondo for the pianoforte by Pleyel.
25	The bonnie earl of Murray
26	Here awa', Willie
27	The night her silent sable wore
28	Sweet Annie frae the sea-beach came
29	O laddie, I maun lo'e thee
30	The fife hunt. A favorite reel.
31-32	Scotch air from the Prisoner. Adapted by Attwood [Young Carlos sue'd a beauteous maid]
33-34	Mary Scot
35	Lady Anne Bothwell's lament
36	Auld Rob Morrice
37	When Guilford good, by Burns
38	Pinkie house
39-40	Queen Mary's lamentation
41-42	There's my thumb
43	Auld Robin Gray
44	Bess the Gawkie

Aitken, John (continued)

45	The last time I came o'er the moor
46	Bonny Betsy
47-48	The braes of Tullymet
49-50	I wish my love were in a myre
51	Logie of Buchan
52	The boatman [F. H. Barthelemon]
53	Tarry woo
54	Polwart on the green
55-56	Miss Lucy Campbell's delight
56	Always pleas'd
57-58	Lass gin ye lo'e me
59	There came a ghaist to Margret's door
60	I'll never leave thee
61	When absent from the nymph I love
62	Johnny fa'
63-64	Delvin side. With variations for the piano forte.
65-66	The white cockade. Highland reel.
67	Kath'rine Ogie
68	Allan water

Aitken, John (continued)

69	Woe's my heart
70	There's nae luck about the house
71	Danse ecossoise. Adapted by Pleyel.
72	Dunkeld house
73-74	The Lasses of Dublin. From the Poor Soldier [William Shield]
74	Andrew and his Cuttic gun
75	Ah waking oh!
76	Dusty miller
77-78	To the ewe-bught's [sic, bought's] Marion
79-80	Mary's dream [John Relfe]
81-82	Drumbartons drums
83-84	Shelty's song. Highland reel.
85-88	Scotch medley. Highland reel.
89-90	O Waly Waly
91-92	From thee Eliza I must go. By Robert Burns. Adapted by Pleyel
93	Tulloch Gorum
94	O dear mother what shall I do

Aitken, John (continued)

95-96	Scotch air from the Castle of Andalusia [Samuel Arnold]
97-98	Lochaber
99-100	The bush aboon Traquair
101-102	Lewie Gordon
102	Colonel Montgomery's strathspey
103-104	Etrick banks
104	Let that stand there
105-106	Within a mile of Edinburgh [James Hook]
107-108	Braes of Ballendine. From the Castle of Andalusia [Samuel Arnold]
109-110	The Caledonian laddy [James Hook]
111-112	Low down in the broom
112	Canty body
113-114	Scotch air from Inkle and Yarico [Samuel Arnold]
114	Invernyty's reell [sic]
115-116	Peggy I must love thee
117-118	For lack of gold

Aitken, John (continued)

119-120	Jack of Grissipoly
121-122	Bonny Jean
123-124	Winsome Kate [composed by] Hook.
125-126	O'er the water to Charlie
126	Whisle [sic] o're the love o't
127-128	Bessy Bell and Mary Gray
129-130	Flowers of the forest. From the Castle of Andalusia [Samuel Arnold]
131	When wild wars deadly blast
132	The Marquis of Tullibardine's gigg
133	Davie Rae
134	Captain Mackintosh
135-136	My Nanny O
136-137	Straglass house
137	The Prince's welcome into Inverne
138	Appin house
139-140	The flowers of Edinburgh
141-142	Bonny Charley [James Hook]

Aitken, John (continued)

Aitken, John (continued)

173-174	Jockey to the fair
175	The happy marriage

THE AMERICAN MUSICAL MISCELLANY; a collection of the newest and most approved songs, set to music. Northampton, Mass., Andrew Wright, 1798. 300p.   Evans 33294

Contents

p.	13-16	The lucky escape [From Charles Dibdin's Private Theatricals]
	17-20	The flowing can [From Dibdin's The Oddities]
	21-23	The Alloa house [James Oswald]
	23-25	The dusky night
	26-27	Plato's advice
	28-29	"The echoing horn" [From Thomas Arne's Thomas and Sally]
	30-31	Queen Mary's farewell to France
	31-33	Poor Tom, or the Sailors epitaph [Charles Dibdin]
	33-34	"Never till now I knew love's smart"

The American Musical Miscellany (continued)

The American Musical Miscellany (continued)

70-71	"When bidden to the wake" [From Shield's Rosina]
71-73	Alone by the light of the moon [James Hook]
74-76	"Ah. Why must words"
76-78	"When first I slipp'd my leading strings" [From Shield's The Woodman]
78-80	Nancy, or the sailor's journal [Charles Dibdin]
81-82	Sterne's Maria [John Moulds]
82-84	I sold a guiltless Negro boy [John Moulds]
84-86	The Hobbies
86-88	Ah Delia see the fatal hour [Franz Kotzwara]
89-93	Golden days of the good Queen Bess
93-95	The golden days we now possess. A sequel to the favorite song

The American Musical Miscellany (continued)

	of Good Queen Bess. To the foregoing tune [Words only]
96-98	"Bright Phoebus" [James Hook]
98-99	The Rosary [William Shield]
100-102	Diogenes surly and proud
103-105	Rise Columbia. An occasional song written by Mr. Thomas Paine of Boston.
106-107	The Sweet little girl that I love [James Hook]
107-109	New Anacreontic song
109-111	"There was a jolly miller" [From T. A. Arne's Love in a Village]
111-114	The Twaddle
114-115	The Indian chief [alternate title of Alknomook]
115-116	"How happy the soldier" [From Shield's Poor Soldier]
117	The Lasses of Dublin [From Shield's Poor Soldier]

18

The American Musical Miscellany (continued)

The American Musical Miscellany (continued)

140-141	The heaving of the lead [From Shield's Hartford Bridge]
142-147	An ode for the fourth of July. By Daniel George. Set to music by Horatio Garnet.
147-149	Her absence will not alter me
150-152	"Come rouse brother sportsman" [James Hook]
152-155	The race horse
155-157	Romping Rosy Nell [Chauncy Langdon]
158-159	The graceful move [Signora _____ Galli]
159-161	I sigh for the girl I adore [James Hook]
161-162	How blest has my time been
163-166	The jolly sailor
166-168	The desponding Negro [From Reeve's The Evening Brush]
168-170	Sweet lillies of the valley [James Hook]

The American Musical Miscellany (continued)

The American Musical Miscellany (continued)

204-207	The hermit
207-211	Columbia--by Dr. Dwight [Timothy Dwight]
211-218	Adams and liberty--by T. Paine.
219-221	Hero and Leander
222-224	The beauties of friendship
224-227	Anna's urn
228-230	Corydon's ghost--by Dr. N. [sic, T.] Dwight [Timothy Dwight]
231-232	Within a mile of Edinburgh [James Hook]
233-234	Lullaby [From Storace's The Pirates]
235-237	The primrose girl [James Hewitt]
238-241	Lovely Stella
241-244	The Indian philosopher
245-246	The life of a beau
247-249	A new song for a serenade. By D[aniel] George [Rise, my Delia, from Arnold's Inkle and Yarico]

The American Musical Miscellany (continued)

The American Musical Miscellany (continued)

278-284	How cold it is. A winter song.
285-286	A shape alone let others prize.
	Set to music by H[ans] Gram.
287-291	Bright dawns the day. A hunting
	song. Set to music by a student
	of the University of Cambridge.
291-292	Winter
293-294	Song in the Spoil'd Child [Since
	then I'm doom'd]
295-296	Ye mortals whom fancies
297-300	On music

ANGELS EVER BRIGHT AND FAIR. Sung at the funeral ceremonies
in honor of the memory of the late General Washington.
New York, G. Gilfert [1800] Broadside. Evans 36840

ARNE, MICHAEL, 1740/41-1786.

Homeward bound. A song. New York, B. Carr [1797]
2p.   Evans 32926
Note: Evans' entry under _____ Thompson.

Sweet passion of love. Composed by Dr. Arne. New York,
G. Gilfert [1795] 1p.   Evans 32041
Note: "Not by Dr. Arne as stated in title, but

Arne, Michael (continued)

> *from Cymon by Michael Arne."--Sonneck-Upton,*
> *p. 418. Evans' entry under Dibdin, Charles,*
> *Sweet passion of love. Song from The Padlock.*
> *New York [1797]*

ARNE, THOMAS AUGUSTINE, 1710-1778.

A celebrated duett in Artaxerxes. Fair Aurora...
[Philadelphia, Trisobio, c1796] 2p. Evans 47704

ARNOLD, SAMUEL, 1740-1802.

At the dead of the night, sung by Mr. Johnstone in
Zorinski. Philadelphia, B. Carr [1797] Broadside.
Evans 48040

Cupid benighted. Sung by Mrs. Jordan in the new comedy
of the Wedding Day. New York, G. Gilfert [1796]
1 leaf. Evans 30622
> *Note: Evans' entry under Elizabeth Simpson*
> *Inchbald, 1753-1821.*

The favorite duett sung in the opera of the Children in
the Wood [Young Simon in his lovely Sue] New York,
G. Gilfert [c1795] 2p. Evans 29121
> *Note: Evans' imprint is Philadelphia, G. Willig.*
> *Evans' entry under Thomas Morton, 1764-1838.*

Arnold, Samuel (continued)

Fresh and strong the breeze is blowing [from Inkle
and Yarico] Baltimore, Carr [1800?] 1p.

Evans 49008

Happy tawny Moor. A favorite duett sung by Mrs.
Oldmixon & Mr. Harwood in the Mountaineers.
New York, B. Carr [1796] 3p. Evans 30242
*Note: Evans' entry under George Colman, Jr.,
1762-1836.*

And hear her sigh adieu! A favorite song sung in the
opera of the Shipwreck. New York, J. Hewitt for
Carr, 1798. 2p. Evans 33314

In dear little Ireland, a favorite duett sung by Mr.
Jefferson and Mrs. Oldmixon in the opera of the
Shipwreck. New York, G. Gilfert [1799?] 2p.

Evans 48775

Little Sally. A favorite song sung in the Shipwreck.
New York, J. Hewitt [1797] 2p. Evans 31754

Little Sally, sung by Mrs. Oldmixon in the Shipwreck.
New York, G. Gilfert [1799?] 1 leaf

Evans 48776

Arnold, Samuel (continued)

The Negro boy. A song sung by Mr. Tyler...from Inkle &
Yarico. Philadelphia, Carr [1796] 2p.

Evans 30243

Note: Evans' entry under George Colman, Jr.,
1762-1836.

Pauvre Madelon. A favorite dialogue and duett in
The Surrender of Calais. Philadelphia, Carr
[1793] 3p. Evans 25314

Note: Evans' entry under George Colman, Jr.,
1762-1836.

Pauvre Madelon, a favorite dialogue & duett in The
Surrender of Calais. New York, G. Gilfert
[1798] 2p. Evans 33536

Note: Evans' entry under George Colman, Jr.,
1762-1836.

The rush light. An additional song introduced and
sung by Mr. Bates in Peeping Tom. The words by
G. Colman Junr. Esqr...Philadelphia, Carr [1794]
2p. Evans 27661

Note: Evans' entry under The Rush light...

Arnold, Samuel (continued)

See brother see. A favorite song sung in the opera of
the Children in the Wood. New York, G. Gilfert
[c1795] 2p. Evans 29119
Note: Evans' entry under Thomas Morton,
1764-1838.

The way worn traveller. In the Mountaineers.
Philadelphia, Carr, 1794. 3p. Evans 26783
Note: Evans' entry under George Colman, Jr.,
1762-1836.

The way worn traveller, in the Mountaineers.
Philadelphia, Carr [c1796] 4p. Evans 47705

When on the ocean, sung by Miss E. Westray in the
opera of the Shipwreck. New York, G. Gilfert
[1799?] 2p. Evans 48777

When the hollow drum. In the Mountaineers.
Philadelphia, Carr [1797] 3p. Evans 31954
Note: Evans' entry under George Colman, Jr.,
1762-1836.

ATTWOOD, THOMAS, 1765-1838.

The convent bell. A favorite song sung by Miss
Broadhurst at the Old City Concert.
New York, G. Gilfert [1795] 1 leaf

Evans 47343

ATWELL, THOMAS H.

The New York collection of sacred harmony, containing the necessary rules of music with a
variety of psalm & hymn tunes, set pieces &
anthems, many of which are original.
Compiled for the use of worshipping assemblies
& singing societies from the most approved
ancient & modern authors. Lansingburgh
[William W. Wands?] 1795. 102p. Evans 28216

BABCOCK, SAMUEL, fl. 1795.

The Middlesex harmony. Being an original composition
of sacred music in three and four parts. Boston,
Isaiah Thomas & Ebenezer T. Andrews, 1795.
55, 1p.   Evans 28221

BACH, JOHANN CHRISTIAN, 1735-1782.

Cease a while ye winds to blow. A favorite rondo
by Sr. Bach. Composed [arranged] by Raynor
Taylor. [Philadelphia] G. Willig [1795]
2p.   Evans 28222

BARNARD, JOHN, 1681-1770.

A New version of the psalms of David. Fitted to
the tunes used in the churches; with several
hymns out of the old and new Testament. By
John Barnard, pastor of a church in Marblehead. Boston, J. Draper for T. leverett,
1752. 4, 278, 1p., 16 plates.   Evans 6820
*Note: Evans' entry under Biblia. Old Testa-
ment. Psalms.*

BARTHELEMON, FRANCOIS HIPPOLITE, 1741-1808.

> Three favorite duetts for two performers on one
> piano forte, composed by Mr. Barthelemaw
> [Barthelemon] New York, Peter Erben [1800?]
> 9, 2p.   Evans 49016

BAYLEY, DANIEL, 1725?-1799.

> The Essex harmony. Containing a collection of
> psalm tunes composed in three & four parts,
> suited to the several measures of either version
> set in score by Daniel Bayley, Philo Musico.
> Newburyport, Daniel Bayley, 1770. 2, 22p.
>   Evans 11560

> ---------. Newburyport, Daniel Bayley, 1771.
>   2, 18p.   Evans 11979

> ---------. Newburyport, Daniel Bayley, 1772.
>   2, 18p.   Evans 12319

> The Essex harmony, or musical miscellany. Containing,
> in a concise and familiar manner, all the
> necessary rules of psalmody. To which are annexed
> a variety of plain and fugeing psalm and hymn
> tunes, selected from different authors, both
> ancient and modern. Newburyport, Daniel Bayley,
> 1785. 8, 40p.   Evans 18925

Bayley, Daniel (continued)

A New and compleat introduction to the grounds and
rules of musick, in two books. Book I. Containing the grounds and rules of musick, or an
introduction to the art of singing by note,
taken from Thomas Walter, A. M. Book II.
Containing a new and correct introduction to
the grounds of musick, rudimental and practical,
from William Tans'ur's Royal Melody: the whole
being a collection of a variety of the choicest
tunes [34] from the most approved masters.
Newburyport, Emerson, 1764. 6, 25, 4p.,
23 plates.   Evans 9598

Note: "No copy found with the imprint given
by Evans."--American Antiquarian Society.

----------. By Daniel Bayley, chorister of St. Paul's
Church, Newbury-Port. [The second edition, containing 48 tunes] Newburyport, Daniel Bayley,
1764. 24p., 28 plates.   Evans 9599

----------. [Boston] Daniel Bayley, 1765. 24,
28p.   Evans 41518

Bayley, Daniel (continued)

   ---------. Boston, Thomas Johnson, 1766.

     24, 28p.   Evans 10236

   ---------. Boston, Daniel Bayley, 1768.

     24, 36p.   Evans 10829

The New harmony of Zion; or complete melody.
Containing, in a plain and familiar manner,
all the necessary rules of psalmody. To which
is added a choice collection of a number of the
most approved psalm and hymn tunes, selected
from various authors, both ancient and modern--
also several anthems. Newburyport, Daniel
Bayley, 1788. 6, 96p.   Evans 20956

The New universal harmony, or a compendium of
church-musick: containing, a variety of
favorite anthems, hymn-tunes, and carols,
composed by the greatest masters. Carefully
set in score by Daniel Bayley, Philo Musico.
Newburyport, Daniel Bayley, 1773. 4, 104p.
                       Evans 12664

Bayley, Daniel (continued)

The Psalm singer's assistant; containing I. An
    introduction, with such directions for
    singing, as are necessary for learners.
    II. A collection of choice psalm-tunes,
    suited to the several measures both of the
    old and new version; engraved in a correct
    manner, and is designed for the improvement of
    psalmody, in the congregations, both in town
    and country: all being composed in three
    parts, collected from the best masters.
    Newburyport, Daniel Bayley, 1785. 8, 16p.

                                            Evans 18926

    *Note: "Copies are found bound up in psalm
        books from 1770 to 1785."--American
        Antiquarian Society.*

--------. Boston, M'Alpine, 1767. 8p.,
    16 leaves.   Evans 41691

BEISSEL, JOHANN CONRAD, 1690-1768.

    Paradisisches Wunder-Spiel, welches sich in diesen
        letzten Zeiten und Tagen in denen Abend-
        Ländischen Welt-Theilen als ein Vorspiel der
        neuen Welt hevor gethan. Bestehende in einer

Beissel, Johann Conrad (continued)

> gantz neuen und ungemeinen Sing-Art auf weise
>
> der englischen und himmlischen Chören eingerichtet.
>
> Da dann das Lied Mosis und des Lamms, wie auch
>
> das hohe Lied Salomonis samt noch mehrern Zeug-
>
> nÜssen aus der Bibel und andern Heiligen in
>
> liebliche Melodyen gebracht. Wobey nicht weniger
>
> der Zuruf der Braut des Lamms, sammt der Zube-
>
> reitung auf den herrlichen Hochzeit-Tag trefflich
>
> Praefigurirt wird. Alles nach englischen
>
> Chören Gesangs-weise mit viel MÜhe und grossem
>
> Fleiss ausgefertiget von einem Friedsamen, der
>
> sonst in dieser Welt weder Namen noch Titul
>
> suchet. Ephratae Sumptibus Societatis, 1754.
>
> 1, 212, 1p.   Evans 7147

BELCHER, SUPPLY, 1751-1836.

> The harmony of Maine: being an original composition
>
> of psalm and hymn tunes of various metres,
>
> suitable for divine worship. With a number of
>
> fuging pieces and anthems. Together with a
>
> concise introduction to the grounds of musick

Belcher, Supply (continued)

and rules for learners. For the use of singing
schools and musical societies. By S. Belcher of
Farmington, County of Lincoln, District of Maine.
Boston, Isaiah Thomas & Ebenezer T. Andrews,
1794. 103, 1p.   Evans 26636

BELKNAP, DANIEL, 1771-1815.

The Evangelical harmony. Containing: a great
variety of airs, suitable for divine worship,
beside a number of favourite pieces of music,
selected from different authors: chiefly
original. To which is prefixed, a concise
introduction to the grounds of music. Boston,
Isaiah Thomas & Ebenezer T. Andrews, 1800.
79, 1p.   Evans 36939

Contents (secular music only)

p. 9   Summer [How soon alas must
                summer's sweets decay]
                [Daniel Belknap]

10   Autumn ['Twas Spring, 'Twas
                Summer all was gay] [Daniel
                Belknap]

Belknap, Daniel (continued)

11	Winter [Now clouds the wintry skies deform] [Daniel Belknap]
30	Disconsolation [As on some lonely building's top] [Joseph C. Stone]
31	Milton [When verdure clothes the fertile vale] [Daniel Belknap]
46	East Needham [The little hills on ev'ry side] [Daniel Belknap]
65	Funeral ode [Deep resound the solemn strain] [Daniel Belknap]
66-68	A view of the Temple--a Masonic ode [Sacred to heav'n behold the dome appears [Daniel Belknap]

The Harmonist's companion. Containing a number of airs suitable for divine worship, together with

Belknap, Daniel (continued)

>an anthem for Easter, and a Masonic ode never
>before published. Composed by Daniel Belknap,
>teacher of music in Framingham. Boston,
>Isaiah Thomas & Ebenezer T. Andrews, 1797.
>31, 1p.   Evans 31792

BENHAM, ASAHEL, 1757-1805.

>Federal harmony; containing, in a familiar manner,
>the rudiments of psalmody, together with a
>collection of church music; (most of which
>are entirely new.) New Haven, Conn., Abel
>Morse, 1790. 12, 36p.   Evans 22340

>---------. The second edition. New Haven, Abel
>Morse, 1792. 4, 7-58p.   Evans 24092

>---------. The fourth edition. Middletown, Moses H.
>Woodward [1794] 4, 7-58p.   Evans 26640

>---------. The sixth edition. Middletown, Moses H.
>Woodward [1796] 16, 15-58p.   Evans 30054

Benham, Asahel (continued)

Social harmony: containing first, the rudiments of
psalmody made easy. Second, a collection of
modern music, calculated for the use of singing
schools and worshipping assemblies. [New
Haven, 1798] 56p.   Evans 33398

----------. n.p. [1799] 56p.   Evans 36331

BENJAMIN, JONATHAN, fl. 1799.

Harmonia Coelestis: a collection of church music
in two, three, and four parts. With words
adapted to each, comprehending not only the
metres in common use, but the particular
metres, in the Hartford Collection of Hymns;
the tunes correctly figured for the organ and
harpsichord--with an introduction to music.
Chiefly collected from the greatest masters in
Europe, and never before printed in America.
Northampton, Mass., Andrew Wright for Oliver D.
and I. Cooke, 1799. 79, 1p.   Evans 35179

BILLINGS, WILLIAM, 1746-1800.

The Continental harmony, containing a number of
anthems, fuges [sic] and chorusses, in
several parts. Never before published.
Boston, Isaiah Thomas & Ebenezer T. Andrews,
1794. 1, 199, 1p.   Evans 26673

The Massachusetts harmony. Being a new collection
of psalm tunes, fuges [sic] and anthems,
selected from the most approved authors,
ancient and modern. By a lover of harmony.
Boston, John Norman [1784] 3, 101p.

                                      Evans 18366

---------. [Second edition] Boston, John Norman
[1786] 2, 101p.   Evans 18933

Music in miniature. Containing a collection of
psalm tunes of various metres. Set in score
by W. Billings. Boston, William Billings,
1779. 32p.   Evans 16205

The New-England psalm-singer: or, American chorister.
Containing a number of psalm-tunes, anthems, and
canons in four and five parts [never before

Billings, William (continued)

published.] Composed by William Billings,
a native of Boston, in New-England. Boston,
Edes & Gill [1770] 10, 22, 109, 2p.

Evans 11572

The Psalm-singer's amusement, containing a number
of fuging pieces and anthems. Boston, 1781.
103, 1p.   Evans 17104

The Singing master's assistant, or key to practical
music, being an abridgement from the New-England
Psalm-Singer, together with several other
tunes never before published, composed by
William Billings, author of the New-England
Psalm Singer. Boston, Draper & Folsom [1778]
32, 104p.   Evans 15744

---------. Boston, Draper & Folsom, 1778.
29, 1, 104p.   Evans 43416

---------. The Third edition. Boston, Draper &
Folsom, 1781. 32, 104p.   Evans 43943

The Suffolk harmony, consisting of psalm tunes, fuges
and anthems. Boston, John Norman, 1786.
2, 56, 8, 8p.   Evans 19512

THE BOOK OF COMMON PRAYER, and administration of the

sacraments, and other rites and ceremonies, as

revised and proposed to the use of the Protestant

Episcopal Church, at a convention of the said

Church in the states of New-York, New-Jersey,

Pennsylvania, Delaware, Maryland, Virginia, and

South-Carolina, held in Philadelphia, from

September 27th to October 7th, 1785. Phila-

delphia, Hall & Sellers, 1786. 373, 10p.

Evans 19940

Note: Only the last eight pages contain music.

Evans' entry is Protestant Episcopal Church

in the United States of America.

THE BOSTON COLLECTION: containing, I. An introduction to

the grouds of music; or, rules for learners. II.

A large collection of the most celebrated psalm and

hymn tunes, from the most approved ancient and modern

authors; together with several new ones, never

before published, suited to all metres usually sung

in churches. Selected by a committee from the

singing societies of every denomination in Boston.

The Boston Collection (continued)

Boston, William Norman [1798?] 1-10, 15-16,

2, 17-112p.   Evans 48377

BROTHER SOLDIERS ALL HAIL! A favorite new patriotic

song in honor of Washington. To which is added

a toast written & composed by J. Hopkinson,

Esqr. Philadelphia, B. Carr [1799] 4p.

                                          Evans 35637

BROWN, WILLIAM, fl. 1783-1787.

Three rondos for the piano forte or harpsichord.

Composed and humbly dedicated to the honourable

Francis Hopkinson, Esqr. by William Brown.

Philadelphia, William Brown [1787] 4, 6p.

                                          Evans 20246

BROWNSON, OLIVER.

A New collection of sacred harmony. Containing a

set of psalm tunes, hymns and anthems: likewise

the necessary rules of psalmody. Simsbury, Conn.

[Thomas & Samuel Greek] 1797. 56p.

                                          Evans 31884

Brownson, Oliver (continued)

Select harmony. Containing the necessary
rules of psalmody, together with a
collection of approved psalm-tunes, hymns
and anthems. [New-Haven, Thomas and Samuel
Green] 1783. 2, 8, 84p.   Evans 17857

-----. New Haven, Thomas and Samuel Green
[1791?] 7, 1, 84p.   Evans 23227

BULL, AMOS, 1744?-?

The Responsary; containing a collection of church
musick. Set with second trebles, instead of
counters, and peculiarly adapted to the use
of the New England churches. Together with a
few useful rules of psalmody. Worcester,
Mass., Isaiah Thomas, 1795. 100p.

                                Evans 28370

CAPRON, HENRI, fl. late 18th century.

Come genius of our happy land, a favorite patriotic
song composed by H. C. Philadelphia, B. Carr
[1798?] Broadside.   Evans 48386

CAPTAIN TRUXTON, or Huzza! for the Constellation.
Sung by Mr. Tyler at the Theatre with the greatest
applause. New York, N. Hewitt [1799] 2p.

Evans 36246

*Note: Evans' entry under Susanna Roswell Rowson,
1761-1824.*

---------. Huzza for the Constellation. Sung by
Mr. Fox at the Theatre. New York, B. Carr
[1799] 3p.   Evans 36247

*Note: Evans' entry under Susanna Roswell
Rowson, 1761-1824.*

CARR, BENJAMIN, 1768-1831.

Dead march & monody. Performed in the Lutheran
Church, Philadelphia, on Thursday the 26th
December 1799, being part of the music selected
for funeral honours to our late illustrious

Carr, Benjamin (continued)

> Chief, General George Washington. Composed for
> the occasion and respectfully dedicated to the
> Senate of the United States, by their obet.
> humble servt. B. Carr. Baltimore, J. Carr
> [1800] 2 leaves.   Evans 37105

Ellen arise. A ballad written by J. E. Harwood,
composed by B. Carr. As sung at the Philadelphia and New York theatres by Mr. Oldmixon &
Mr. Hodgkinson. Philadelphia, B. Carr [1798]
2p.   Evans 33855

> *Note: Evans' entry under John Edmund Harwood,*
> *1771-1809.*

Four ballads, three from Shakespeare and one by
[Edward] Harwood, composed & respectfully inscribed
to Mrs. Hodges by Benjamin Carr. Philadelphia,
B. Carr [1794] 9p.   Evans 46998

> Contents

>> No. 1, p. 2-3   When icicles hang by the wall,
>>   from Shakespeare's Love's
>>   labour lost

Carr, Benjamin (continued)

2, p. 4-5   Take oh! take those lips away,
             from Shakespeare's Merchant
             of Venice

3, p. 6-7   Tell me where is fancy bred, from
             Shakespeare's Measure for
             Measure

4, p. 8-9   When nights were cold, a favorite
             song, the words by Mr. Harwood,
             set to music by B. Carr.

The Little sailor boy. A ballad. Sung at the
theatres & other public places in Philadelphia,
Baltimore, New York, &c. by Messrs. J. Darley
Williamson, Miss Broadhurst, Mr. Hodgkinson and
Mr. Oldmixon. Written by Mrs. Rowson. Composed
by B. Carr. Philadelphia, B. Carr [1798] 2p.

Evans 34489

Note: Evans' entry under Susanna Haswell
Rowson, 1761-1824.

The Musical journal for the flute or violin. Volume I.
[Baltimore, Joseph Carr, 1800] 48p.

Evans 37106

Carr, Benjamin (continued)

Contents

Carr, Benjamin (continued)

Carr, Benjamin (continued)

The Musical journal for the piano-forte [Volume 1.

Baltimore, Joseph Carr, 1800]   29 numbers,

misc. paging.   Evans 37107

Contents: vocal section

No. 1   p. 2-3   Rosa, sung with great applause

                       by Mrs. Merry in the comedy of

                       the Secret, composed by

                       A[lexander] Reinagle

         4   Pretty maids all in a row, a

                       favorite nursery song composed

                       by Mr. [James] Hook, for one or

                       two voices

   3   6-7   Poor Lima, a favorite ballad

                       composed by At[t]wood & sung

                       by Miss Broadhurst

         8   Cupid benighted [Samuel Arnold]

   5   10-12   Death and burial of Cock Robin

                       [Samuel Arnold]

         14-16   Courteous stranger, the favorite

                       polonaise sung by Miss Broadhurst

                       in Zorinsky [Samuel Arnold]

Carr, Benjamin (continued)

No. 9	p. 18-19	Poor Mary, sung by Miss Broadhurst in the Italian Monk, composed by B[enjamin] Carr
	20-21	Little Boy Blew, nursery song for two voices, composed by B[enjamin] Carr
	22	Shakespeares willow, composed by B[enjamin] Carr
11	23-26	The wood robin [Reginald Spofford]
13	28-30	Two original Russian airs, adapted to English words No. 1, Inconstant spring thy morn No. 2, Lend me thy saffron robe
15	32-33	Ye ling'ring winds [John Moulds]
	34-35	Never doubt that I love, composed by R[aynor] Taylor

Carr, Benjamin (continued)

Contents: instrumental section

Carr, Benjamin (continued)

	No. 10 p. 18-19	Lord Alexander Gordons reel, arranged as a rondo for the piano forte by I. G. C. Schetky
	20	March in Blue Beard
12	22-23	Minuetto, by Pleyel
	24	Minuetto & Trio, by Pleyel
14	26-28	Six favorite German waltzes
16	29-32	Andante d'Haydn [Minuetto from Surprise Symphony]
18	34-36	3 Divertimentos, by B. Carr
20	38-40	Six imitations of English, Scotch, Irish, Welch [sic] Spanish & German airs, by B. Carr
22	41-44	Rondeau de Viotti
24	46-47	Rondo by Pleyel
	48	Index to instrumental section

Three ballads. Viz. The new somebody--Mary will smile and poor Richard. Philadelphia, B. Carr [1799]

7p.   Evans 35283

Carr, Benjamin (continued)

Contents

p. 2-3   The new somebody.

    4-5   Mary will smile, sung by Miss Broadhurst.
          Written by a gentleman of Phila-
          delphia, composed by B. Carr.

    6-7   Poor Richard. Written by Mr. John Carr,
          composed by B. Carr.

When nights were cold, a favorite song, the words
    by Mr. Harwood, set to music by Mr. B. Carr.
    Philadelphia, B. Carr [1794] 8-9p. Evans 46999

CHERUBINI, MARIA LUIGI CARLO ZENOBIO SALVATORE, 1760-1842.

    Overture de Demophon. Arrange pour le forti-piano
        par Jacques Hewitt. New York, B. Carr [1795]
        4p.   Evans 28412

A COLLECTION OF THE PSALM AND HYMN TUNES used by the
    Reformed Protestant Dutch Church of the City of New
    York, agreeable to their psalm book, published in
    English. In four parts, viz. tenor, bass, treble,
    and counter. New York, Hodge and Shober, 1774.
    7, 54, 54, 3p.   Evans 42655

COSTELOW, THOMAS, fl. 1792.

> The Cherry girl, a favorite song composed by
>
> > T. Costelow. New York, B. Carr [1796?]
> >
> > 2p.   Evans 47761

THE COTTAGE BOY, a favorite song. New York,

> G. Gilfert [1797?] 2p.   Evans 48100

CRAMER, JOHANN BAPTIST, 1771-1858.

> Marche-Turque par Crammer [sic] New York,
>
> > J. Paff [1798?] 2p.   Evans 48405

DANCE FOR WALTZING. Philadelphia, G. Willig [1795]

    2p.   Evans 28535

THE DAY OF MARRIAGE, sung by Mrs. Jones. Baltimore,

    J. Carr [1797?] 2 leaves.   Evans 48102

DEAR MARY, or adieu to old England. New York, Hewitt.

    [1798?] 2p.   Evans 33613

DEARBORN, BENJAMIN, 1754-1838.

    A schedule for reducing the science of music to a
        more simple state, and to bring all its
        characters within the compass of a common
        fount of printing-types; especially calculated
        for the convenience of learners. Portsmouth,
        N. H., 1785. 16p.   Evans 44674

DE CLEVE, V., fl. 1790.

    The Poor blind girl. A favorite song written by
        Mr. C. I. Pitt. Composed by Mr. V. Decleve.
        New York, G. Gilfert [1798] 2p.   Evans 34383
        Note: Evans' entry under C. I. Pitt.

DEVIENNE, FRANCOIS, 1759-1803.

> The Battle of Gemmappe. A sonata for the forte
> piano. New York, G. Gilfert [1796] 14p.
>
> Evans 30341

DEVONSHIRE, GEORGIANNA SPENCER CAVENDISH, DUCHESS OF,
1757-1806.

> I have a silent sorrow here. Sung with great
> applause in the Stranger. The words by
> R. B. Shiridan [sic] Esqr. The air by the
> Dutchess of Devonshire. New York, Hewitt
> [1798?] 2p.   Evans 48410

DIBDIN, CHARLES, 1745-1814.

> Father and mother and Suke, written and composed
> by Mr. Dibdin and sung by him in his new
> entertainment called Castles in the Air.
> Baltimore, Hupfeld & Hammer [1797?] 4p.
>
> Evans 48105

> The lucky escape. Written and composed by Dibdin.
> Philadelphia, Carr & Rice [1794] 2p.
>
> Evans 26878

Dibdin, Charles (continued)

Mounseer Nongtonpaw. A favorite song. Boston
[1799] 2p.   Evans 35848

Nancy, or The Sailor's Journal. As sung by Mrs.
Williamson, at the Hay-Market Theatre, Boston,
with universal applause. Boston, Thomas &
Andrews [1797?] 3p.   Evans 32040

The Patent coffin, written & composed by Mr. Dibdin.
New York, Hewitt [1797] 2p.   Evans 48106

Poor Tom Bowling, or the sailors epitaph. Philadelphia, Carr [1794] 2p.   Evans 26879

The Sailor's journal. New York, B. Carr [1797]
2p.   Evans 48107

The Soldier's adieu. Philadelphia, Carr [1794]
2p.   Evans 26881

The Token. [Philadelphia] Carr [1794] 2p.
                                            Evans 26883

Dibdin, Charles (continued)

'Twas in the good ship Rover, or the Greenwich
pensioner. Philadelphia, Carr [1794] 2p.

Evans 26884

The Waggoner. Written and composed by Dibdin.
Philadelphia, Rice [1794] 2-3p. Evans 26885

DIGNUM, CHARLES, 1765-1827.

Fair Rosal[i]e. A favorite song. Sung by Miss
Westray. The melody by Charles Dignum. New
York, G. Gilfert [1797?] 2p. Evans 32104

DISCOURSE, introductory to a course of lectures on the
science of nature; with original music, composed for,
and sung on, the occasion. Delivered in the hall of
the University of Pennsylvania, Nov. 8, 1800.
By Charles W. Peale. Philadelphia, Zechariah Poulson,
Jr. 50p., 5 folding plates. Evans 38203

Contents

Dirge. Words by Rembrandt Peale, set to music
by John J. Hawkins, Nov. 1800.

Discourse (continued)

> Ode on the death of Titian Peale. By Rembrandt
>
> Peale, set to music by John J. Hawkins, 1800.
>
> The beauties of creation. The words by Rembrandt
>
> Peale, set to music by John J. Hawkins,
>
> Nov. 1800.

DONALD OF DUNDEE, a new song sung by Miss Milne.

New York, G. Gilfert [1795] 12-13p.   Evans 47410

Note: "Separate issue from some unidentified

collection."--Sonneck-Upton, p. 111.

DUBOIS, WILLIAM, fl. 1795-1800.

> Free Mason's march. Composed by Mr. Dubois, arranged
>
> for the piano forte by Mr. Genin [sic, Guenin]
>
> [Philadelphia] Willig [1798] 1 leaf.
>
> Evans 33649

THE DUKE OF YORCK'S [sic, York's] MARCH. Philadelphia,

G. Willig [1799] Broadside.   Evans 35426

DUSSEK, JAN LADISLAV, 1760-1812.

> Good night, a favorite song in the new opera of

Dussek, Jan Ladislav (continued)

the Captive of Spilberg, composed by I. L.
Dussek. Baltimore, R. Shaw [1799]
Broadside.   Evans 48836

Heigho! In the new opera of the Captive of
Spilberg, composed by I. L. Dussek.
Baltimore, R. Shaw [1799] Broadside.
                                          Evans 48837

DWIGHT, TIMOTHY, 1752-1817.

Columbia: an ode. [Philadelphia, 1794?]
Broadside.   Evans 26923

ELEGANT EXTRACTS FOR THE GERMAN FLUTE OR VIOLIN, selected
from the most favorite songs &c. sung in the theatres
and public places. Baltimore, I. Carr for B. Carr
[1794] 36p.   Evans 26936

Contents

Elegant extracts (continued)

18-19	The Sweet little girl that I love [James Hook]
20-21	The Sailor boy capering ashore [From No Song No Supper by Stephen Storace]
22-23	Alone by the light of the moon [James Hook]
24-25	My heart is devoted dear Mary to thee [alternative title of The Indigent Peasant by James Hook]
26-28	The Lucky escape [Charles Dibdin]
29	The Mansion of peace [Samuel Webbe, Sr.]
30-31	Death or victory [From The Wags by Charles Dibdin]
32-33	The Sailors consolation [From Private Theatricals by Charles Dibdin]
34-35	Bachelors hall [From The Oddities by Charles Dibdin]

Elegant extracts (continued)

36   The Lullaby [composed by Stephen
                      Storace in his The Pirates]

Book the second of ELEGANT EXTRACTS FOR THE GERMAN FLUTE
    OR VIOLIN. Selected from the most favorite songs
    sung at the theatres and other public places.
    Philadelphia, J. Carr [1796] 32p.

                                        Evans 30383

Contents

   p. 3-5   Tom Tackle [composed by Charles
                      Dibdin in his Castles in the Air]

   6-7   A Sailor lov'd a lass [composed by
                      Stephen Storace in his The
                      Cherokee]

   8-9   Dear little cottage maiden [com-
                      posed by James Hook]

   10-11   The Soldiers adieu [composed by
                      Charles Dibdin]

   12   Oh say simple maid [composed by
                      Samuel Arnold in his Inkle and
                      Yarico]

Elegant extracts (continued)

Elegant extracts (continued)

The Third book of ELEGANT EXTRACTS FOR THE GERMAN FLUTE OR
    VIOLIN. From the most favorite songs sung at the
    theatres and other public places, among which are
    several of Dibdins and some of the most favorite sung
    at the Philadelphia Vauxhall. Philadelphia, B. Carr
    [1798] 32p.   Evans 33667

Contents

Elegant extracts (continued)

4	Within a mile of Edinboro' town [James Hook]
5	A smile from the girl of my heart, in the Woodman [William Shield]
6-7	Sweet lavender, sung by Miss Broadhurst at Vauxhall
8	Anne Hatheaway by Dibdin
9	The little gipsey, sung by Miss Broadhurst at Vauxhall [presumably composed by Samuel Arnold]
10-11	Old Towler, sung by Mr. Tyler [William Shield]
12	Primroses, sung by Mrs. Pownall [James Hewitt]
13	No 'twas neither shape nor feature, as a duett [J. C. Bach]
14-15	The Caledonian maid [John Moulds]

Elegant extracts (continued)

16	Sweet Martindale, sung by Mr. Darley Junr. at Vauxhall
17	A favorite duett [In thee each joy possessing]
18	The Sailors journal, by Dibdin
19	When nights were cold, sung by Mrs. Hodgkinson [composed by Benjamin Carr and interpolated in Samuel Arnold's Children in the Wood]
20	The Smile of benevolence, by Dibdin [From his Great News]
21	Lucy or Selim's complaint [James Hook]
22-23	When Nicholas, for 3 flutes or voices [William Shield]
23	Dibdin's fancy
24	Little Ben
25	Tom Trueloves knell, by Dibdin
26-27	I never lov'd any dear Mary but you, sung by Mr. Darley Junr. at Vauxhall [James Hook]

Elegant extracts (continued)

28	The Irishman, sung by Mr. Darley
	Junr. at Vauxhall
29-31	Homes home, by Dibdin
32	Index

EMBLEMS OF MEM'RY ARE THESE TEARS. Sung by Mrs. Warrell
in the New Theatre in commemoration of General
Washington's birth-day after his decease, 22d Feby.
1800. Philadelphia, G. Willig [1800] 4p.

Evans 37365

ENCYCLOPAEDIA; or, a dictionary of arts, sciences, and
miscellaneous literature; constructed on a plan,
by which the different sciences and arts are digested
into the form of distinct treatises or systems, comprehending the history, theory, discoveries and
improvements; and full explanations given of the
various detached parts of knowledge, whether relating
to natural and artificial objects, or to matters
ecclesiastical, civil, military, commercial, &c.
Including elucidations of the most important topics
relative to religion, morals, manners, and the
oeconomy of life. Together with a description of

Encyclopaedia (continued)

all the countries, cities, principal mountains,
seas, rivers, &c. throughout the world; a general
history, ancient and modern, of the different
empires, kingdoms, and States; and an account of
the lives of the most eminent persons in every
nation, from the earliest ages down to the present
time...the first American edition, in eighteen
volumes, greatly improved...vol. XII, Mie-Neg.
Philadelphia, Thomas Dobson, 1798. 2, 799, 1p.
35 plates.   Evans 33687

Note: Plates 324-328 are examples of musical
notation as related to modulation, scales,
intervals, etc., as mentioned in the article
entitled "Music," pp. 483-522.

EVENING AMUSEMENT. Containing fifty airs, songs, duetts,
hornpipes, reels, marches, minuett's [sic], &c. &c.,
for 1 or 2 German flutes or violins. Philadelphia,
J. Carr [1796] 1, 14-32p., irreg.   Evans 30396

Contents

p. 14   Le Reveil du Peuple [Pierre
                     Gaveaux]

Evening amusement (continued)

	God save great Washington
	Stoney Point
	What a beau your Granny was
15	When the rosy morn appearing.
	As a duett.
	College hornpipe
	Fishers hornpipe [J. C. Fischer]
16	Soldiers joy
	Plow boy
	Roslin Castle
	Savage dance
17	The new bow wow
	Thou soft flowing Avon
	Money musk
18	Yanke [sic] Doodle
	Tho prudence
	Carmagnole
	Russian dance
19	General Washingtons march
	The rose tree [William Shield]

Evening amusement (continued)

               The white cockade

20   The highland reel

               When bidden to the wake or fair

               Haydns minuet

21   The Kentucky volunteer [Raynor

                  Taylor]

               Air in the Critic

               Ah caira

22   The Marseilles hymn

               Dans votre lit [From Love in a

                  Camp by William Shield]

               Astleys hornpipe

23   The Duke of Yorks march

               Air by Haydn

24   America, commerce and freedom

                  [From The Sailors Landlady

                  by Alexander Reinagle]

               Mrs. Frasers strathspay

               The Irish washer woman

25   Scots air from the Highland Reel

                  [Boys when I play, cry oh crimini,

                  by William Shield]

72

Evening amusement (continued)

	French tune
	March in the Battle of Prague
	[Franz Kotzwara]
	Finale to Inkle and Yarico
	[Samuel Arnold]
26	[How happily my life I led] Sung
	by Mr. Darley in No Song No
	Supper [Stephen Storace]
27	Bride bells
	La Storace
28	O dear what can the matter be
	Slow march [from the Battle of Prague
	Franz Kotzwara]
29	Malbrook
	Spencers fancy
	Mrs. Casey
	Madrigal
30-31	Martini's march in Henry the IV
31	Minuet de la cour

Note: Pp. 27-28 missing from microprint copy;
contents for these pages supplied from Index
and from Sonneck-Upton, pp. 128-129.

FAIR MARIA OF THE DALE, a favorite song. New York,

  G. Gilfert [1796] Broadside.   Evans 47773

A FAVORITE SONG [Thou dear seducer of my heart]

  Translated from the Irish. New York, J. Hewitt

  [1799] Broadside.   Evans 35467

FLAGG, JOSIAH, 1737-c1795.

  A collection of the best psalm tunes in two, three,

    and four parts. From the most approv'd

    authors, fitted to all measures and approv'd

    of by the best masters in Boston, New England;

    to which are added some hymns and anthems, the

    greater part of them never before printed in

    America. Boston, Paul Revere and Josiah Flagg,

    1764. 66 leaves.   Evans 9659

  Sixteen anthems, collected from Tans'ur, Williams,

    Knapp, Ashworth & Stephenson. To which is

    added a few psalm tunes. Proper to entertain

    and improve those who have made some proficiency

    in the art of singing. Boston, Josiah Flagg

    [1766] 60p.   Evans 41612

FRENCH, JACOB, 1754-?

The New American melody. In three parts. Containing, I. An introduction to the grounds
of musick: or rules for beginners. II. A
new and complete body of Church musick
suited to all metres usually sung in churches.
III. A number of new anthems adapted to
social occasions. The whole entirely new
and composed for the use of singing societies.
Boston, John Norman and Jacob French, 1789.
2, 7-100p.   Evans 21841

The Psalmodist's companion, in four parts. Containing, I. The rudiments of musick, in a
concise and easy method. II. A complete
collection of psalm tunes, suited to all
metres and keys, usually sung in churches.
III. A number of favourite chorusses, fuges,
&c. suited to many occasions. IV. A number of
anthems. The whole in alphabetical order, in
each part. Many of the pieces never before
published. By Jacob French, Philo Musicae.
Worcester, Leonard Worcester and Isaiah Thomas,
1793. 100p.   Evans 25513

FRITH, EDWARD.

The Contented cottager, a favorite new song.

New York, G. Gilfert [1796] 2p.

Evans 47789

FROM THEE ELIZA I MUST GO. New York, I. and M. Paff

[1799] 2p. Evans 35524

A GAMUT; OR, SCALE OF MUSIC, for the use of schools.

Lansingburgh, Luther Pratt, 1796. 4p.

Evans 47432

GAULINE, JOHN BAPTISTE, 1759-1824.

So sweet her face. Philadelphia, G. Willig

[1798] 2 leaves. Evans 48453

DAS GESAENG DER EINSAMEN UND VERLASSENEN TURTEL-TAUBE

Nemlich der Christlichen Kirche. Oder geistliche

u. Erfahrungs-volle Leidens-u. Liebes-Gethöne,

als darinnen heydes die Vorkost der neuen Welt als

auch die darzwischen vorkommende Creutzes-und

Leidens-Wege nach ihrer Würde dargestellt, und in

geistliche Reimen gebracht von einem Friedsamen und

nach der stillen Ewigkeit wallenden Pilger. Und nun

zum Gebrauch der einsamen und Verlassenen zu Zion

gesammlet und ans licht gegeben. Ephrata, Druks der

Bruederschafft, 1747. 22, 359, 5p. Evans 5958

---------. 2te Auflage. Ephrata, 1747. 22,

495, 21p. Evans 5959

GILMAN, JOHN WARD, 1741-1823.

A New introduction to psalmody; or the art of
singing psalms. With a variety of psalm
tunes, hymns, & choruses; in three & four
musical parts, the whole engrav'd on
copper-plates. Exeter, John Gilman,
1771. 22p.   Evans 42240

GIN YE CAN LOO ME LASS, a favorite song sung by Mr.
Dignum at Vauxhall Gardens. New York, S. Howe
[1799?] 2 leaves.   Evans 48860

GIORDANI, GIUSEPPE, c1744-1798.

Loose were her tresses. As sung by Miss Broadhurst.
From Collins' Ode on the Passions. [New York]
B. Carr [1796] 2p.   Evans 30239
    *Note: Evans' entry under William Collins,
    1721-1759.*
Loose were her tresses, from Collins' ode on the
passions. [Philadelphia] G. Willig [c1795]
2p.   Evans 47434

THE GIRL WITH A CAST IN HER EYE. New York, J. Hewitt
[1799] Broadside.   Evans 35551

GLUCK, CHRISTOPH WILLIBALD VON, 1714-1787.

Ouverture d'Iphigenie [en Aulide] Philadelphia,
G. Willig [1795] 5p.   Evans 28751

GRAEFF, JOHANN GEORG, c1762-?

Lisbia. A new canzonet. New York, J. Hewitt

[1799] 2p. Evans 35559

GRAM, HANS, fl. 1793.

The Death song of an Indian chief. (Taken from
Ouabi, an Indian tale, in four cantos, by
Philenia, a lady of Boston). Set to musick
by Mr. Hans Gram, of Boston. [Boston,
1793] 2p. Evans 25848

Note: "Philenia" has been identified as
Sarah Wentworth (Apthorp) Morton.
Evans' entry is under Sarah Wentworth
Apthorp Morton, 1759-1816.

Sacred lines for Thanksgiving-Day, November 7, 1793.
Written and set to music by Hans Gram,
organist to Brattle-Street Church, in Boston.
To which are added, several psalm tunes, of
different metres, by the same composer.
Boston, Isaiah Thomas & Ebenezer T. Andrews,
1793. 16p. Evans 25562

Gram, Hans (continued)

> ---------. Boston, Isaiah Thomas & Ebenezer T.
> Andrews, 1793. 16, 8, 8p.   Evans 47066

GRAUN, CARL HEINRICH, 1703/04-1759.

> Sonnet. For the fourteenth of October, 1793.
> When were entomb'd the remains of His
> Excellency John Hancock, Esq; late Governor
> and Commander-in-Chief of the Commonwealth of
> Massachusetts. The music taken from an oratorio,
> by the famous Graun, of Berlin. The lines
> written and adapted by Hans Gram, organist of
> Brattle-Street Church, in Boston. [Boston,
> Isaiah Thomas & Ebenezer T. Andrews, 1793]
> 4p.   Evans 25563

GRISWOLD, ELIJAH.

> Connecticut harmony. Containing a collection of
> psalm tunes, anthems, and favourite pieces
> many of which were never before published, to
> which are added concise rules of singing.
> Designed for the use of worshipping assemblies

and singing societies. By Elijah Griswold
and Thomas Skinner. [n.p., 1796] 62, 8p.

Evans 30521

[H., S. M.]

The Wretched slave. Sung in the new opera of Paul and
Virginia. New York, G. Gilfert [1797] 2p.

Evans 32374

----------. New York, G. Gilfert for P. A. von
Hagen [1800] 2p.   Evans 39151

Note: Evans' ascribes these entries to Jean
Francois Lesueur, 1763-1837. Sonneck-Upton
(p. 327) contains an entry, "Paul and Vir-
ginia...Words by A. A. H. Music by S. M.
H." The British Museum Catalog gives no
clue as to the identity of S. M. H. Wolfe
(v. 1, p. 331) enters this work under
"H., S. M. Unidentified composer, probably
English." Sonneck-Upton has no entry under
the title "The Wretched Slave. Sung in the
new opera of Paul and Virginia."

HAGEN, PETER ALBRECHT VON, SR., 1750-1803.

Funeral dirge on the death of General Washington, as sung
at the Stone Chapel. The music composed by P. A.
von Hagen, organist of said church. Boston,
von Hagen for G. Gilfert [1800] Broadside.

Evans 37009

Note: Also entered as 37481; see p. 245-246.

HAGEN, PETER ALBRECHT VON, JR., 1781-1837.

Adams & Washington. A new patriotic song, the music
composed by P. A. von Hagen, jr. Boston, P. A.
von Hagen, Jr. [1798] 2p.   Evans 34300
Note: Evans' entry under Thomas Paine,
afterwards Robert Treat, Junior, 1773-1811.

To arms Columbia. A new patriotic song, written
for the anniversary of the Massachusetts
Charitable Fire Society by Thomas Paine,
A. M. The music composed by P. A. von Hagen,
jun. Boston, P. A. von Hagen for G. Gilfert
[1799] 2p.   Evans 36033
Note: Evans' entry under Thomas Paine,
afterwards Robert Treat, Junior, 1773-1811.

HANDEL, GEORG FRIEDRICH, 1685-1759.

Handle's [sic] water music. New York, G. Willig
[c1798] 2p.   Evans 33837

HARINGTON, HENRY, 1727-1816.

Damon & Clora. A favorite dialogue. Philadelphia,

Harington, Henry (continued)

B. Carr [1794] 4p.   Evans 27091

Contents

p. 2-3   Damon & Clora [composed by Henry
            Harington]

4   The Reconciliation, being a sequel
            to Damon & Clora. Composed by
            R. Taylor.

HARRISON, RALPH, 1748-1810.

Sacred harmony, or a collection of psalm tunes,
    ancient and modern, containing a great variety
    of the most approved plain & simple airs, taken
    from the Massachusetts harmony, Worcester
    collection, Laws, to which is added, several
    new tunes, never before published, together
    with an introduction to the art of singing.
    Boston, C. Cambridge [1789] 2, 1-4, 7-12,
    2, 6-99p.   Evans 22615

    *Note: Evans indicates publication date of
    1790 rather than 1789, and enters this
    work under Thomas Lee, Jr.*

HAYDN, FRANZ JOSEPH, 1732-1809.

Favorite easy sonata. [New York] P. Erben
[1799?] 5p.   Evans 48872

A favorite rondo in the gipsy style. Philadelphia,
G. Willig [1799?] 5p.   Evans 35606

Overture by Haydn. Philadelphia, G. Willig
[1797?] 2-8p.   Evans 32241

Sonatina...opera 71 [C major] Philadelphia, G.
Willig [1800] 5p.   Evans 33863

HEWITT, JAMES, 1770-1827.

The Battle of Trenton. A sonata for the piano-
forte, dedicated to General Washington. New
York, James Hewitt [1797] 14p.   Evans 33381

The Federal Constitution & Liberty forever. A new
patriotic song written by Mr. [William] Milns
& sung with great applause by Mr. Williamson.
The music adapted by Mr. Hewitt. New York,
James Hewitt for Carr [1798] 2p. Evans 34113
Note: Evans' entry under William Milns,

Hewitt, James (continued)

How happy was my humble lot. A favorite ballad sung
by Mrs. Oldmixon & Miss Broadhurst. New York,
James Hewitt [1799] 2p.   Evans 35618
> Note: Includes arrangements "for the flute"
> and "for the guitar," p. 2.

Three sonatas for the piano forte (op. 5) composed
and dedicated to Miss Temple by Jas. Hewitt.
New York, Carr & Gilfert [c1795] 17p.

Evans 47449

Contents

   p. 1-5   Sonata I [D major]
      6-10   Sonata II [C major]
    11-17   Sonata III [F major]

Time, a favorite rondo. New York, I. & B. Carr
[c1795] 2p.   Evans 47450

When the old heathen gods. Sung by Mr. Williamson in
the farce of Flash in the Pan. The words by
Mr. [William] Milns. Music by J. Hewitt. New
York, James Hewitt for Carr [1798] 2p.

Evans 34115

Hewitt, James (continued)

The Wish, or the sequel to Henry's Cottage Maid.
New York, B. Carr [1795] 2p.   Evans 47805

The Wounded Hussar. New York, James Hewitt,
1800. 2p.   Evans 37614

HODGKINSON, JOHN, 1767-1805.

Let Washington be our boast. Sung with great applause
at the theatre at the conclusion of the "Ode to
the memory of Genl. G. Washington." The words
written & music selected by Mr. Hodgkinson.
New York, James Hewitt [1800] 2p.   Evans 37633

HOLDEN, OLIVER, 1765-1844.

American harmony: containing a variety of airs, suitable
for divine worship...By Oliver Holden, teacher of
music in Charlestown. Boston, Isaiah Thomas and
Ebenezer T. Andrews, 1792. 32p.   Evans 24403

A Dirge, or sepulchral service, commemorating
the sublime virtues and distinguished talents
of General George Washington. Composed at
the request of the Mechanics Association of
Boston.--(Words by Anthony Pasquin, Esq.)

Holden, Oliver (continued)

[Anthony Pasquin has been identified as John Mason
Williams] [Boston, Isaiah Thomas and Ebenezer T.
Andrews, 1800] 4p.   Evans 39106
  Note: Evans' entry under John Mason Williams,
  1761-1818.

Laus Deo! The Worcester collection of sacred
    harmony. *See under LAUS DEO! THE WORCESTER*
    COLLECTION OF SACRED HARMONY.

The Massachusetts compiler of theoretical and
    practical elements of sacred vocal music.
    Together with a musical dictionary. And a
    variety of psalm tunes, chorusses, &c.
    Chiefly selected or adapted from modern
    European publications. Boston, Isaiah Thomas
    & Ebenezer T. Andrews [1795] xxxvi, 71, 1p.
                                        Evans 28848

Sacred dirges, hymns, and anthems, commemorative
    of the death of General George Washington, the
    guardian of his country, and the friend of man...

Holden, Oliver (continued)

        an original composition by a citizen of
Massachusetts. Boston, Isaiah Thomas &
Ebenezer T. Andrews [1800] 24, 4p.

                                 Evans 37635

Note: Also entered as 38445; see p. 249.

The Union harmony, or universal collection of
sacred music. In two volumes. Vol. I--
Containing, I. The rudiments of music laid
down in a plain and concise manner. II. A
large and valuable collection of tunes,
suited to all the metres now used in the
various worshipping societies in America,
many of which were never before published.
Vol. II. Containing, a large and valuable
collection of anthems, odes, and psalm and
hymn tunes, in three and four parts. Adapted
to the use of American choirs, and other
practitioners; a great part of which were never
before published. Boston, Isaiah Thomas &
Ebenezer T. Andrews, 1793. 120, 175, 1p.

                                 Evans 25619

Holden, Oliver (continued)

    ---------. Second edition. Boston, Isaiah Thomas
       & Ebenezer T. Andrews, 1796. 120p.

                                      Evans 30573

      Note: There is no record of Vol. II having
        been printed in 1796.

HOLYOKE, SAMUEL, 1762-1820.

    Exeter: for Thanksgiving. By Samuel Holyoke,
       A. B. Exeter, Henry Ranlet, 1798. 7p.

                                        Evans 33893

    Hark! From the tomb, &c. and Beneath the honors, &c.
       Adapted from Dr. Watts, and set to music by
       Samuel Holyoke, A.M. Performed at Newburyport,
       2d January, 1800; the day on which the citizens
       unitedly expressed their unbounded veneration
       for the memory of our beloved Washington.
       Exeter, Henry Ranlet [1800] 12p. Evans 37642

    Harmonia Americana. Containing a concise introduction
       to the grounds of music. With a variety of
       airs, suitable for divine worship, and the use of

Holyoke, Samuel (continued)

musical societies. Consisting of three and
four parts. By Samuel Holyoke, A. B.
Boston, Isaiah Thomas & Ebenezer T. Andrews,
1791. 119, 1p.   Evans 23446

The Instrumental assistant. Containing instructions
for the violin, German-flute, clarionett, bass-
viol, and hautboy. Compiled from late European publications. Also a selection of
favorite airs, marches, &c. progressively
arranged, and adapted for the use of learners...
Vol. 1. Exeter, New Hampshire, H. Ranlet
[1800] 79, 1p.   Evans 37643

Contents

p. 2	Dictionary of musical terms
3-21	Instructions, explanations, &c.
22-24	Introductory lessons
25	Serenade
	God save America
	Foot's minuet
26	Belleisle march
	March to Boston

Holyoke, Samuel (continued)

27	The black cockade
	Boston march
28	Lesson by Morelli
29	Marquis of Granby's march
	Swiss guard's march
30	Durham march
	Quick march
31	Capt. Mackintosh's march
32	The beauties of fancy
33	For there's no luck about the house
	Dog and gun
34	O dear what can the matter be?
	Yankey [sic] Doodle
35	Straffordshire march
	Rakes of London
36	Grano's march
37	La Choutille cotillion
	Canada farewell
38-39	The wood cutters
	Handel's clarionett
39	British muse

Holyoke, Samuel (continued)

40-41	Duke of Holstein's march
	March in the God of love
41	Love's march
42	Gen. Wayne's march
43	Handyside's march
	Malbrouk
44-45	Count Brown's march
45	Prince Eugene's march
46	Suffolk march
	Free Mason's march [William Dubois]
47	Heathen mythology
	When first I saw
48	Dorsetshire march
	Felton's gavot
49	Philadelphia march
50-51	Duke of Yorks march
52	General Knox's march
53	Baron Stuben's march
54-55	Essex march
56	London march
57	President's march [Philip Phile]
58-59	Handel's gavot

Holyoke, Samuel (continued)

59	Favorite air
60	New German march
61	Gen. Green's march
62-63	Handel's water piece
63-64	Air in Rosina [William Shield]
65	Quick march in Cymon [Michael Arne]
66-67	Col. Orne's march
68	Air
69	Washington's march
70-71	March alla militaire
71	Boston quick step
72-73	Stamitz's air
73	Duettino
74-75	Echo
75	March in the Water music [Handel]
76	Garner's air
77-79	Sonata

HOOK, JAMES, 1746-1827.

Alone by the light of the moon. Boston, von Hagen
[1797?] 2p.   Evans 32270

Hook, James (continued)

----------. A favorite song. New York, G. Gilfert,
1796. 2p.   Evans 30581

Anna; or, the adieu, composed by Mr. Hook.
New York, Moller [1797] 2p.   Evans 48147

Bright Phoebus, a favorite hunting song, composed
by Mr. Hook. New York, James Hewitt
[1797?] 2p.   Evans 48148

The Cottage in the grove. Sung by Mr. Tyler.
Philadelphia, B. Carr [1796] 2p. Evans 30582

Donna Donna Donna Della. A favorite song. New
York, James Hewitt [1797] 2p.   Evans 32271

The Flower of Yarrow, a favorite song composed by
Mr. Hook [New York] Hewitt & Rausch [1797]
Broadside.   Evans 48149

He loves his winsome Kate. A favorite Scotch song.
New York, James Hewitt [1797] 2p. Evans 32272

Here's the pretty girl I love. New York, James
Hewitt [1797] 2p.   Evans 32273

Hook, James (continued)

Hither Mary. Sung with universal applause at

Vauxhall Gardens 1793. Philadelphia,

B. Carr [1793] 2p.   Evans 25626

Hoot awa ye loon. A favourite Scots song.

New York, James Hewitt [1797] 2p.   Evans 32274

The Hours of love. A collection of sonnets,

containing morning, noon, evening & night,

properly adapted for the voice, harpsichord,

violin, German flute or guitar. Philadelphia,

B. Carr [1799] 9p.   Evans 35633

Contents

    p. 2-3   Sonnet I [Morning]

      4-5   Sonnet II [Noon]

      6-7   Sonnet III [Evening]

      8-9   Sonnet IV [Night]

If a body loves a body. New York, James Hewitt

[1797] 2p.   Evans 32276

I'll die for no shepherd not I. New York,

G. Gilfert [c1795] 2p.   Evans 47451

Hook, James (continued)

I'm in haste. New York, James Hewitt [1797]

2p. Evans 32275

The Indigent peasant. A favorite ballad sung with
great applause by Mr. Darley at Vauxhall.
Philadelphia, B. Carr [1793] 2p. Evans 25627

Keep your distance, a favorite song sung by Miss
Broadhurst at the New York Old City Concert.
New York, G. Gilfert [1795] 2p. Evans 47452

The Kiss, sung by Mrs. Seymour at the Ladies Concert.
New York, B. Carr [1797?] 2p. Evans 48150

The Linnet. New York, James Hewitt [1798]

2p. Evans 32277

Listen listen to the voice of love, a favorite new
song. New York, G. Gilfert [1795] Broadside.
Evans 47453

----------. Sung with great applause at Vauxhall
Gardens. Philadelphia, B. Carr [1796] 2p.
Evans 30583

Hook, James (continued)

The Little singing girl. A new favorite song.
    Boston, von Hagen [1799] 2p.   Evans 48885

Love shall be my guide, a favorite song sung by
    Miss Milne. New York, G. Gilfert [1795]
    2p.   Evans 47454

Lucy or Selim's complaint. A favorite song.
    Philadelphia, B. Carr [1796?] 2p. Evans 27136

Ma belle coquette. A favorite song. Philadelphia,
    J. C. Moller [1793] 2p.   Evans 25628

---------. A favorite song sung by Mrs. Pownall,
    written by Mr. Swift, composed by Mr. Hook.
    New York, G. Gilfert [1794?] 3p. Evans 47076

May I never be married. A favorite song. New York,
    G. Gilfert [1798] 2p.   Evans 34087

O whither can my William stray. Baltimore, Carr
    [1798] 2p.   Evans 48474

Rise Cynthia rise. A favorite sonnet written by the
    Earl of Oxford. Philadelphia, Carr [1793] 3p.
                                       Evans 26092

    Note: Evans' entry is under title.

Hook, James (continued)

She lives in the valley below, a new song. Sung by
Master Gray at Vauxhall Gardens, composed by
Mr. Hook. New York, S. Howe [1799?] 2p.

Evans 48886

The Silver moon. New York, G. Gilfert [1795] 2p.

Evans 47455

----------. For the piano forte, German flute or
violin. Boston, von Hagen [1798?] 2p.

Evans 48475

----------. Philadelphia, C. Hupfeld [1798] 2p.

Evans 48476

Sweet lillies of the valley. Sung with great
applause at Vauxhall Gardens. Philadelphia,
Carr [1793] 2p.   Evans 25629

The Sweet little girl that I love. A favorite
song. New York, Carr [1796] 2p.   Evans 30584

The Tear. Song by Godian. New York, Carr [1796]
2p.   Evans 30585

Hook, James (continued)

Then say my sweet girl can you love me, or the
pretty brunette. Sung by Mr. Darley at
Vauxhall 1793. Philadelphia, Carr [1794]
4p. Evans 27789

'Tis not the bloom on Damons cheek. A favorite
rondo. Composed by I. Hook [Arranged for
the piano forte or harpsichord by Alexander
Reinagle] Philadelphia, Reinagle and Aitken
[1789] 3p. Evans 22098

To the maid I love best. A favorite song [New
York, G. Gilfert, 1798?] 2p. Evans 34912
Note: Evans' entry under William Upton.

'Twas within a mile of Edinburgh town. Boston, von
Hagen [1797] 2p. Evans 32067
Note: Evans' entry under Thomas D'Urfey,
1653-1723.

The Unfortunate sailor. Composed by Mr. Hook, sung
by Mr. Fox. New York, Hewitt [1799?] 2p.
Evans 48887

Hook, James (continued)

The Way to get married, a favorite song sung at

Vauxhall Gardens. New York, G. Gilfert

[1797] 2p.   Evans 33583

Note: Evans' entry under John C. Cross.

The Wedding day. Boston, von Hagen [1799?] 2p.

Evans 48888

---------. A favorite song sung by Mrs. Hodgkinson.

Philadelphia, Carr [1793] 2p.   Evans 25630

What can a lassy do. Sung by Mrs. Franklin at

Vauxhall. New York, Hewitt [1798] 2p.

Evans 32278

When Lucy was kind. A favorite song sung at

Vauxhall Gardens. Philadelphia, B. Carr

[1796] 2p.   Evans 30586

Where Liffey rolls its silver stream. A favorite

song in the opera of Jack of Newberry. New

York, James Hewitt [1797] 2p.   Evans 32279

Hook, James (continued)

Where's the harm of that. A favorite song.

New York, James Hewitt [1797] 2p. Evans 32280

William of the ferry. Sung with great applause

at Vauxhall Gardens. New York, Carr [1796]

2p.   Evans 30587

Willy of the dale. New York, G. Gilfert [1795]

2p.   Evans 47456

Within a mile of Edinburgh, sung by Mr. Dignum.

New York, G. Gilfert [1795] 2p.   Evans 45457

HOPKINSON, FRANCIS, 1737-1791.

A Collection of psalm tunes, with a few anthems

and hymns, some of them entirely new. For

the use of the united churches of Christ Church

and St. Peter's Church in Philadelphia.

[Philadelphia, W. Dunlap?, 1763] 9p.,

22 plates.   Evans 9406

Seven songs for the harpsichord or forte piano.

The words and music composed by Francis Hopkinson.

Hopkinson, Francis (continued)

Philadelphia, Thomas Dobson [1788] 2,

11, 1p.   Evans 21152

Contents

p. 1	Song I [Come fair Rosina, come away]
2	Song II [My love is gone to sea]
3-4	Song III [Beneath a weeping willows shade]
5	Song IV [Enraptur'd I gaze]
6	Song V [See down Maria's blushing cheek]
7-8	Song VI [O'er the hills far away]
9-10	Song VII Rondo. [My gen'rous heart disdains]
11	Song VIII [The trav'ler benighted and lost]

Note: The eighth song was added after the title page had been engraved. See Sonneck-Upton, p. 403.

HOWE, SOLOMON, 1750-1835.

> Worshipper's assistant. Containing the rules
>> of music, and a variety of easy and
>> plain psalm tunes. Adapted to the
>> weakest capacities, and designed for
>> extensive utility, as an introduction
>> to more critical and curious music.
>> Northampton, Mass., Andrew Wright,
>> 1799. 32p.   Evans 35643

HUNTINGTON, JONATHAN, 1771-1838.

> The Albany collection of sacred harmony.
>> Containing, a plain and intelligible
>> instruction for learners of church music;
>> together with a lesson for every mood
>> of time, and for every key made use of
>> in psalmody. Also, a collection

Huntington, Jonathan (continued)

of psalm-tunes, hymns, and anthems, suited
to all the different keys and metres made
use of in the American churches; both for
the expression of joy and thankfulness, or
for funerals and subjects of grief.
Northampton, Mass., Andrew Wright, 1800.
i-xii, 9-91, 1p.   Evans 37667

HYMNS AND SPIRITUAL SONGS. In three books. I. Collected
from the Scriptures. II. Compos'd on divine subjects.
III. Prepar'd for the Lord's Supper...the twentieth
edition. Boston, Fowle & Draper, 1762. xxiv,
312, 8p., 8 plates.   Evans 41323

----------. The twenty-first edition. Boston, Kneeland
and Adams, 1767. xxiv, 312p., 22 plates.
                                    Evans 41776

I LOVE THEM ALL, sung by Mr. Darley Senr. at the

Vauxhall Gardens. Philadelphia, B. Carr

[1797] 2p.   Evans 48157

INDEED YOUNG MAN I MUST DENY, sung by Miss Milne.

New York, G. Gilfert [1795] 12-13p.   Evans 47465

JACKSON, GEORGE K., 1745-1822.

One kind kiss before we part. A favorite song
composed by Dr. Jackson and sung by Mrs.
Hodgkinson [Philadelphia] Carr [1796]
2p.   Evans 30931

*Note: Evans' entry under James Oswald,
1710-1769.*

JENKS, STEPHEN, 1772-1856.

Laus Deo. The New-England harmonist: containing,
concise and easy rules of music: together with
a number of tunes adapted to public worship,
most of which were never before published.
Danbury, Conn., Douglas & Nichols [1800]
1-8, 17-24, 25-64.
[Second title:] The Musical harmonist: containing concise and easy rules of music
together with a collection of the most
approved psalm & hymn tunes, fitted to all the
various metres most of which were never
before published. By Stephen Jenks, author
of the New England Harmonist. New Haven, Conn.,

Jenks, Stephen (continued)

Amos Doolittle, 1800. 25-64p.

Evans 37707

JOCELIN, SIMEON, 1746-1823.

The Chorister's companion or church music revised.
Containing, besides the necessary rules of
psalmody; a variety of plain and fuging
psalm tunes: together with a collection of
approved hymns and anthems. Many of which
were never before published. New Haven,
T. and S. Green [1782] 2, 18, 2, 64p.

Evans 17567

----------. The second edition, corrected and
enlarged. New Haven, T. & S. Green for Simeon
Jocelin [1788] 2, i-ii, 3, 14-26, 5-12, 120p.

Evans 21177

----------. The second [third?] edition, corrected and
enlarged. New Haven, T. and S. Green [1791?]
2, 26, 2, 120p.   Evans 23472

Jocelin, Simeon (continued)

The Chorister's companion. Part third. Containing
a collection of approved hymns and anthems.
In three and four parts; some of which never
before printed. New-Haven, Thomas & Samuel
Green for Simeon Jocelin & Amos Doolittle
[1783] 16, 32p.   Evans 17988

----------. Supplement to the Chorister's companion,
containing 16 pages of psalm and hymn tunes newly
composed, or not before printed in America.
New Haven, T. & S. Green for S. Jocelin, 1792.
16p.   Evans 24434

A Collection of favorite psalm tunes, from late
and approved British authors: never before
printed in America. New Haven, Thomas and
Samuel Green [1787] 16p.   Evans 20432

KELLY, MICHAEL, 1764?-1826.

The Favorite duett of Tink a tink [From Blue Beard]
New York, G. Gilfert [1799?] 3p.   Evans 48901

When pensive I thought on my love, a favorite new
song sung in the grand dramatic romance of
Blue Beard, or Female Curiosity. New York,
G. Gilfert [1799?] 2p.   Evans 33537
   Note: Evans' entry under George Colman, Jr.,
   1762-1836.

Young Henry lov'd his Emma well, sung with great
applause in the opera of the Outlaws. New
York, Hewitt [1799] 1 leaf.   Evans 48903

KIMBALL, JACOB, 1761-1826.

The Essex harmony: an original composition, in three
and four parts. By Jacob Kimball, Junr. A. B.
author of the "Rural Harmony..." Exeter,
Ranlet for T. C. Cushing and B. B. Macanulty,
1800. 111, 1p.   Evans 37732
   Evans notes that "Samuel Holyoke was
   co-editor with Kimball."

Kimball, Jacob (continued)

> The Rural harmony, being an original composition in
> three and four parts. For the use of singing
> schools and musical societies. By Jacob
> Kimball, Jun. A. B. Boston, Isaiah Thomas and
> Ebenezer T. Andrews, 1793. 111, 1p.
>
> > Evans 25695

KOTZWARA, FRANZ, 1730(?)-1791.

> The Battle of Prague. A favourite sonata for the
> piano forte or harpsichord. Philadelphia,
> J. C. Moller [1793] 7p.   Evans 25698

> ---------. A favorite sonata for the piano forte
> with accompaniments. Boston, Graupner
> [c1795] 8p.   Evans 28938

> Tell me fairest, tell me true. New York, G. Gilfert
> [1798] 2p.   Evans 34636
>
> > *Note: Evans makes entry under title.*

KRUMPHOLTZ, JOHANN BAPTIST, 1745-1790.

> Louisa's complaint, from Mrs. Robinson's novel of
> Nancenza, the music by Krumpholtz. New
> York, G. Gilfert [1794?] 2p.   Evans 47093

LANE, ISAAC, fl. 1797.

An anthem: suitable to be performed at an Ordination
or at the dedication of a meetinghouse.
Northampton, Daniel Wright, 1797. 6p.

Evans 33977

Christmas anthem: the hymn being in commemoration
of the birth of our Divine Saviour, by Dr.
Isaac Watts; set to musick by Isaac Lane.
Worcester, Mass., Thomas, 1795. 8p.

Evans 47671

LANGDON, CHAUNCY, 1763-1830.

Beauties of psalmody. Containing concisely the
rules of singing with a collection of the
most approved psalm-tunes and anthems.
Selected by a member of the Musical Society of
Yale College. [New Haven, Daniel Bowen, 1786]
2, 56p.   Evans 19749

The Select songster, or a collection of elegant
songs, with music prefixed to each. Compiled
by Philo. Musico. [Chauncy Langdon] New Haven,

Langdon, Chauncy (continued)

Daniel Bowen, 1786. 66p.   Evans 19750

Contents

Langdon, Chauncy (continued)

24	To the same tune [As bringing home, the other day]
25-26	The Shepherd's complaint [Timothy Swan]
27-28	Queen Mary's lamentation
29	Collin and Betsey
30-31	The Timely adviser
32	Lovely nymph
33	To the same tune [Lovely nymph, now cease to languish]
34	How imperfect is expression
35-36	The Young lover
37-38	Fare well ye greenfields [Samuel Howard]
39	Ye fair possessed
40	The Fan. To the same tune.
41-42	Colinet and Phebe
43	The Bird
44	The Answer [words only]
45	The British muse
46	Friendship. An ode. By B. B. [words by _____ Bidwell]

Langdon, Chauncy (continued)

47-48	The birks of Invermay
49-50	The harmless shepherd
51	Wisdom's favorite
52-53	The Dauphin
54-55	The death of General Wolfe
56-58	The frog and mouse. A satire on Italian plays.
59-60	The wonderful old man
61	The tipler's defence
62-64	The flowing bowl
65	Plato
66	Index

LAUS DEO! THE WORCESTER COLLECTION OF SACRED HARMONY.
In three parts. Containing, I. An introduction to
the grounds of musick: or, rules for learners.
II. A large number of celebrated psalm and hymn
tunes, from the most approved ancient and modern
authors; together with several new ones, never
before published: the whole suited to all metres,
usually sung in churches. III. Select anthems,
fughes, and favourites [sic] pieces of musick, with

Laus Deo! (continued)

an additional number of psalm and hymn tunes. The
whole compiled for the use of schools and singing
societies. And recommended by many approved
teachers of psalmody. Worcester, Isaiah Thomas,
1786. 4, 200p.   Evans 19752

---------. The second edition, with large additions.
Worcester, Isaiah Thomas, 1788. 4, 120p.

Evans 21193

---------. The third edition, with large additions.
Boston, Isaiah Thomas & Ebenezer T. Andrews, 1791.
4, 143, 1p.   Evans 23490

---------. The fourth edition, with additions. Boston,
Isaiah Thomas & Ebenezer T. Andrews, 1792.
4, 151, 1p.   Evans 24461

---------. The fifth edition, corrected and revised, with
great additions. Boston, Isaiah Thomas & Ebenezer
T. Andrews, 1794. 155, 1p.   Evans 27202

Laus Deo! (continued)

----------. The sixth edition, altered, corrected and
revised, with additions, by Oliver Holden.
Boston, Isaiah Thomas & Ebenezer T. Andrews,
1797. 142, 2p.   Evans 32363

----------. The seventh edition, altered, corrected and
revised, with additions, by Oliver Holden.
Boston, Isaiah Thomas & Ebenezer T. Andrews,
1800. 143, 1p.   Evans 37786

   Note: Also entered as 37636; see p. 254.

----------. Part III. Worcester, Isaiah Thomas, 1787.
                                        Evans 20452

   *Note: This item consists of pp. 113-198 of
   19752; see p. 115 of this Bibliography.*

LAW, ANDREW, 1748-1821.

The Art of singing; in three parts: viz I. The
musical primer, II. The Christian harmony,
III. The musical magazine. Cheshire, Conn.,
1794. 32, 64, 56, 4, 64p.   Evans 27204

Law, Andrew (continued)

   --------. Cheshire, Conn., 1800. 224p.

                      Evans 37787

The Christian harmony; or the second part of the
Art of Singing: comprising a variety of
psalm and hymn tunes; together with a number
of airs and anthems; calculated for schools
and churches. By Andrew Law, A. M. In two
volumes. Vol. I. [Cheshire, Conn., 1794]
6, 9-64p.   Evans 27205

--------. Vol. II. Cheshire, Conn., William Law,
1796. 56p.   Evans 30680

A Collection of hymns, for social worship.
[Cheshire, Conn., 1783] 48p.

                 Evans 17996

Note: Bound with 17571, q.v. next item.

A Collection of hymn tunes from the most modern
and approved authors by Andrew Law, A. M.
Cheshire, Conn., William Law [1782] 2, 36, 2,
48p.   Evans 17571

Note: Bound with 17996, q.v. preceding item.

Law, Andrew (continued)

The Musical magazine; containing a variety of
favorite pieces. A periodical publication.
By Andrew Law, A. M. Number first.
Cheshire, Conn., William Law, 1792.
2, 32p.   Evans 24464

----------. Number second. Cheshire, Conn.,
William Law, 1793. 10-12, 17-32p.
                                           Evans 25708

*Note: The microprint of this item in Early
American Imprints reproduces an imperfect
copy, but only this imperfect copy has
been located.*

The Musical primer; containing the rules of psalmody,
newly revised and improved: together with a
number of practical lessons and plain tunes,
designed expressly for the use of learners.
By Andrew Law, A. M. Cheshire, Conn., William
Law, 1793. 32p.   Evans 25709

----------. Third edition. [Cheshire, Conn.?, 1800?]
2, 9-48p.   Evans 49106

Law, Andrew (continued)

The Rudiments of music: or a short and easy treatis [sic] on the rules of psalmody. To which are annexed, a number of plain tunes and chants. By Andrew Law, A. M. [Cheshire, Conn., William Law] 1783. 8, 4, 24p.

Evans 17997

----------. The second edition. With the addition of a number of pieces never before published. [Cheshire, Conn., William Law, 1785] 3, 1, 48, 30p.   Evans 19057

Note: "The only copy available is in-complete."--American Antiquarian Society.

----------. The third edition. With the addition of a number of pieces never before published. [Cheshire, Conn., William Law, 1791] 4, 68p.

Evans 23491

----------. Fourth edition. With the addition of a number of pieces never before published. Cheshire, Conn., William Law, 1792. 5, 1, 76p.   Evans 24466

Law, Andrew (continued)

    ---------. Fourth edition, with the addition of a
        number of pieces never before published.
        Cheshire, Conn., William Law, 1793. 5, 1,
        76p.   Evans 46806

  Select harmony. Containing in a plain and concise
        manner the rules of singing: together with a
        complete collection of psalm tunes, hymns and
        anthems. [New Haven, Thomas and Samuel Green,
        1779] 2, 8, 100p.   Evans 16318

  Select harmony, containing in a plain and concise
        manner, the rules of singing. Chiefly by
        Andrew Law, A. B. To which are added a
        number of psalm tunes, hymn tunes and anthems,
        from the best authors. With some never before
        published. Newburyport, Daniel Bayley [1784]
        8, 184p.   Evans 18553

  Select harmony. Containing in a plain and concise
        manner, the rules of singing. Together with a
        collection of psalm tunes, hymns and anthems.
        By Andrew Law, A. B. [Cheshire, Conn., William
        Law, 1791?] 2, 4, 100p.   Evans 23492

Law, Andrew (continued)

A Select number of plain tunes adapted to
congregational worship. By Andrew Law,
A. B. [Boston, Kneeland & Adams, 1767]
16p.   Evans 10662

LEE, CHAUNCEY, 1763-1842.

An Ode for the Fourth of July 1799. Written by
Timothy Todd, esqr. Set to music by the Revd.
Chauncey Lee. Hudson, N. Y., G. Fairman
[1799] Broadside.   Evans 36436
    Note: Evans entry under Timothy Todd,
    1758-1806.

LEE, THOMAS, fl. c1790.

Sacred harmony. n.p., Thomas Lee, Jr. [1800]
8, 57-116, 2p.   Evans 38446
    Note: Evans' entry under title.

LINLEY, FRANCIS, 1774-1800.

A New assistant for the piano-forte or harpsichord.
Containing the necessary rudiments for beginners.

Linley, Francis (continued)

With twelve airs or short lessons progressively arrang'd: to which is added six sonatas, one of which is adapted for two performers, with preludes, rules for thorough bass, a short dictionary of musical terms, &c. N. B. The lessons, sonatas, & preludes have their fingering mark'd. Compil'd, compos'd, and arrang'd, by Fr. Linley, organist of Penton-ville. Baltimore, Isaac & Benjamin Carr [1796] 32p. Evans 30695

Contents

p.	1	[blank]
	2-5	Rudiments
	6-10	Twelve airs, or lessons [Linley]
	11-21	Six sonatas [composed by Benjamin Carr; see note below]
	22	[blank]
	23-26	Preludes [Linley]
	27-29	Second set of preludes [Linley]
	30-31	Rules for thoro'bass
	32	Short dictionary of musical terms

Linley, Francis (continued)

> *Note:* *"The Six sonatas are unquestionably*
> *compositions of Benjamin Carr, and are*
> *as follows: Sonata I (F major), p. 11.--*
> *Sonata II (B-flat major), p. 12-13.--*
> *Sonata III (G major), p. 14-15.--Sonata IV*
> *(C major, 4 hds.), p. 16-17.--Sonata V*
> *(D major), p. 18.--Sonata VI (B-flat*
> *major), p. 19-21. The Dictionary of*
> *musical terms is identical with that*
> *appearing in The Gentleman's amusement,*
> *p. 98, also published in 1796."--*
> *Sonneck-Upton, p. 289. The Gentleman's*
> *amusement, edited by Robert Shaw, begins*
> *in this Bibliography on p. 171.*

Linley's assistant for the piano-forte, containing

the necessary rudiments for beginners, and

twenty-four lessons progressively arranged;

with preludes, rules for thorough-bass, and a

short dictionary of musical terms, &c.; the

lessons and preludes have their fingering

marked. A new edition...Baltimore, I. Carr

Linley, Francis (continued)

[1796] 8, 5-32p.   Evans 47823

Contents

p. 2-5   "Rudiments"

6-19   Lessons

19   Walzer

20   Let life us cherish [by Linley?]

21   Since then I'm doomed [From The
         Spoil'd child]

22   Fresh and strong the breeze is
         blowing [From Inkle and Yarico
         by Samuel Arnold]

23-29   Preludes [by Linley?]

30-31   Rules for thoro'bass

32   Musical terms

Note: See explanatory note on p. 123.

LINLEY, THOMAS, 1733-1795.

Primroses deck. A favorite rondo. Sung by Mr. Carr
at the amateur & professional concerts.
Philadelphia, Carr [1794] 2-4p.   Evans 27562
Note: Evans' entry is under title.

LYON, JAMES, 1735-1794.

A Dialogue on peace, an entertainment, given by the
senior class at the anniversary commencement,
held at Nassau-Hall, September 28th, 1763.
Philadelphia, William Bradford, 1763. 27p.

Evans 9386

Note: Evans' entry under Nathaniel Evans,
1742-1767.

Urania, or a choice collection of psalm-tunes,
anthems, and hymns from the most approv'd
authors, with some entirely new; in two,
three, and four parts. The whole peculiarly
adapted to the use of churches, and private
families. To which are prefix'd the plainest,
& most necessary rules of psalmody. By
James Lyon, A. B. [Philadelphia, William
Bradford, 1761] 2, 5, xii, 198p.

Evans 8908

Lyon, James (continued)

       ---------. A new edition. [Philadelphia, 1773]

            4, xii, 198p.   Evans 12839

MAJOR ANDRE'S COMPLAINT. Philadelphia, Carr [1794]

   Broadside.   Evans 27621

MANN, ELIAS, 1750-1825.

    The Northampton collection of sacred harmony.
       In three parts. Containing, I. A plain and
       concise introduction to the grounds of music.
       II. A large number of psalm tunes, selected
       from the most approved and eminent authors.
       Adapted to all the different metres and keys
       used in churches. III. A number of lengthy
       pieces of several verses each, many of which
       are compositions never before published, and
       calculated for the use of churches and other
       occasions; with a number of universally
       approved anthems. Northampton, Daniel Wright
       1797. iv, 139, 1p.   Evans 32416

THE MARSEILLES HYMN IN FRENCH & ENGLISH. Philadelphia,

   Carr [1793] 3p.   Evans 26106

   Contents

      p. 1-2   The Marseilles hymn

       3   Marche des Marseillois

    Note: Evans' entry under Claude Joseph Rouget de
      Lisle, 1760-1836. The microtexts of items

The Marseilles hymn (continued)

> *26106 and 26107 are identical and each contains both the English and French texts. Neither, however, corresponds precisely with the entry supplied by Evans.*

THE MARSEILLES HYMN IN FRENCH & ENGLISH. Philadelphia,
Carr [1793] 3p.   Evans 26107

> Note: See note above.

THE MARSEILLES HYMN IN FRENCH AND ENGLISH. New York,
G. Gilfert [1796] 3p.   Evans 47904

THE MATCH-GIRL. A favorite song. Composed by a lady.
Philadelphia, B. Carr [1793] 2p.   Evans 25796

MATILDA. A favorite ballad. Sung by Mrs. Chambers in the
comedy of Love's Frailties. Philadelphia,
G. Willig [1799?] 2p.   Evans 35805

MAZZINGHI, JOSEPH, 1765-1844.

> The Maid with a bosom of snow. Sung with great
> applause by Mr. Hodgkinson at the Philharmonic

Society [New York, 1799] 2p.   Evans 35762

MILITARY AMUSEMENT. A collection of twenty-four of the
  most favorite marches adapted for one or two German
  flutes, violins, fifes, or hautboys, &c. Philadelphia, Carr [1796] 24p.   Evans 30795

Contents

p. 2	New French March. L-Reviel du Peuple.
3	Presidents March [Philip Phile]
4	Washingtons March
5	Presidents New March
6	General Knox's March
7	Janizary's March
8	Quick Step in the Battle of Prague [Franz Kotzwara]
8-9	Duke of York's March
10-11	Duke of Yorks Troop
11	Marseilles March
12	Granbys March
12-13	Third Coldstream March
13	Duke of Gloster's March
14	Slow March in the Battle of Prague [Franz Kotzwara]

Military amusement (continued)

15	Archers march
16	March in the Deserter [Dibdin]
17	London march
18	General Waynes new march
19	General Wolfes march
20	Belleisle march
	A Scotch reveilly
21	Mozarts march
22	Dead march
23	Handels march
	Eugenes march
24	Index

THE MILITARY GLORY OF GREAT-BRITAIN, an entertainment, given by the late candidates for Bachelor's degree, at the close of the anniversary commencement, held in Nassau-Hall, New Jersey, September 29th, 1762. Philadelphia, William Bradford, 1762. 15p., 5 folded leaves of music.   Evans 9188

THE MODERN COLLECTION OF SACRED MUSIC: containing the
rudiments of the art and a choice collection of
anthems, and psalm and hymn tunes of every metre;
carefully selected from ancient and modern authors.
Adapted to the use of schools and worshipping
societies. By an American. Boston, Isaiah Thomas &
Ebenezer T. Andrews, 1800. viii, 253, 1p.

Evans 37980

MOLLER, JOHN CHRISTOPHER, d. 1803.

Meddley with the most favorite airs. Philadelphia,
G. Willig [1796] 2-6p. Evans 47835

MOLLER, JOHN CHRISTOPHER and HENRI CAPRON, eds.

The first [-third] number. [Philadelphia] Moller &
Capron [1793] 22p. Evans 25831

Contents

The first number:

p. 2-4   Sinfonia. By I. C. Moller [Arranged for
                piano forte in E-flat major]

5   [Softly as the breezes blowing] A
                favorite song by H. Capron.

Moller, John Christopher (continued)

6	[Hark hark from the woodlands] A favorite hunting song.
7-8	[The cheerful spring begins to stay] A new favorite song by a lady of Phila. [Guitar arrangement, p. 8]

The second number

9-12	La belle Catherine with variations (in wich [sic] is introduced the favorite air of the Yellow hair'd lady) for the harpsichord or piano forte.
13	A lovely rose
14-15	Delia. A new song by H. Capron.

The third number

16-18	Rondo. By I. C. Moller [for piano forte, F major]
19-20	Ye zephyrs where's my blushing rose. A favorite song in answer to the Mansion of peace [German flute or guitar arrangement, p. 20]

[Stevenson]

Moller, John Christopher (continued)

21-22   Asteria's fields. By a lady of
               Philada.

22   A new contredance. By H. Capron.

MOTHER GOOSE'S MELODY: or sonnets for the cradle.

In two parts. Part I. Contains the most celebrated
songs and lullabies of the good old nurses, calculated
to amuse children and to excite them to sleep. Part
II. Those of that sweet songster and nurse of wit
and humor, master William Shakespeare. Embellished
with cuts, and illustrated with notes and maxims,
historical, philosophical, and critical. The second
Worcester edition. Worcester, Mass., Isaiah Thomas,
1794. 94, 2p.   Evans 29122

Note: Only p. vi is music.

----------. Boston, S. Hall, 1800. 95p.   Evans 49118
Note: Only p. vi is music.

MOULDS, JOHN, fl. 1785-1800.

The Caledonian maid, written by Peter Pindair Esquire,
composed by I. Moulds. Philadelphia, B. Carr
[c1795] 2p.   Evans 47495

Moulds, John (continued)

The Much admired song of Arabella the Caledonian
maid, with an harp accompaniment. New York,
G. Gilfert [1795] 2p. Evans 47498

She dropt a tear and cried be true, a favorite
sea song. New York, G. Gilfert [1795]
2p. Evans 47496

MOZART, WOLFGANG AMADEUS, 1756-1791.

The Fowler, a favorite song by the celebrated
Mr. Mozart. Philadelphia, G. Willig
[c1795] 2p. Evans 47497

THE MUSICAL REPERTORY [REPOSITORY] Number 1...Boston,
William Norman [1796] 32p. Evans 30832

*Note: No complete copy is known. For a dis-
cussion of The Musical Repertory and its
relation to The Musical Repository, see
Sonneck-Upton, p. 279-282.*

Contents

| p. 1 | When first to Helen's lute. A song in the opera of the Children in the Wood [Samuel Arnold] |
| 2-4 | Sister, see, on yonder bough. A song in the opera of the Children in the Wood [Samuel Arnold] |

The Musical repertory (continued)

5	A favorite air in the pantomime of Oscar and Malvina [William Reeve]
6-7	A blessing on Brandy & Beer: a favorite song in the comic opera of the Magician No Conjurer. Composed by Mr. Mazzinghi.
8	The Rosary. A ballad in the comic opera of the Midnight Wanderers: composed by Mr. Shield.
9	Walters sweethearts. A comic song in the opera of the Children in the Wood [Samuel Arnold]
10-11	The Shipwreck'd Seamans Ghost. A song in the Pirates. Composed by Mr. Storace.
11	[The same arranged] For the German flute.
12-13	Think your tawny Moor is true. A song in the comic opera of the Mountaineers. Composed by Dr. Arnold.

The Musical repertory (continued)

14-15	I sold a guiltless Negro boy: a sentimental ballad. Composed by Mr. Moulds.
15	Moorish March. In the opera of the Mountaineers [Samuel Arnold]
16	Dear Wanderer. A song in the opera of the Midnight Wanderers [William Shield] [Advertisement inserted between p. 16 and 17]
17	When first I slipp'd my leading strings, a song in the comic opera of the Woodman. Composed by Mr. Shield.
18-19	Rise Columbia! An occasional song written by Mr. Thomas Paine of Boston. The air altered and adapted from the tune of Rule Brittannia.
20	Ah can I cease to love her. Composed by Mr. Storace.

The Musical repertory (continued)

21-23	An ode to sleep. Adapted to a favorite air in the opera, La Rencontre Luprette. Composed by Chevalier Gluck.
24-25	To me a smiling infant came. A favorite ballad.
25	Quick March in the pantomime of Oscar & Malvina [William Reeve]
26-27	Ye streams that round my prison creep! A favorite song in the musical romance of Lodoiska. Composed by S. Storace.
28-29	A pastoral. Written by Metastasio, translated & adapted to the original air. [Ah Delia, by Franz Kotzwara]
29-31	Lorade in the tower. A song in the opera of the Mountaineers, composed by Dr. Arnold.
32	Sterne's Maria. A pathetic song set to music by Mr. Moulds.

THE MUSICAL REPERTORY [REPOSITORY]: being a collection of
the most modern & favorite songs, airs, marches, &c.
Taken from the works of the most celebrated authors,
and adapted to the voice, bass, & key'd instruments.
Vol. 1. Boston, William Norman [1799] 4, 49-64,
81-96p. Evans 35981

Note: *Known chiefly through this fragment. For a
discussion of The Musical Repertory and its relation
to The Musical Repository, see Sonneck-Upton,
p. 279-282.*

Evans' entry is under William Norman, ed.

Contents

p. 49	Oh ever in my bosom live. A favorite duett in the grand pantomime balle of Oscar and Malvina [William Reeve
50-51	Tom Tackle. A much admired song composed by Mr. Dibdin in his entertainment of Castles in the Ai
52-53	O say bonny lass. A favorite Scotch song in the opera of Incle [sic, Inkle] and Yarico [Samuel Arnold]

The Musical repertory (continued)

54-55	Love soft illusion. A favorite song in the opera of the Castle of Andalusia, the composition of this song by Bertoni [Samuel Arnold]
56-57	Nancy or the sailor's journal. Composed by Mr. Dibdin.
58-59	A favorite song in the opera of the Travellers in Switzerland, composed by Mr. Shield
60-61	When nights were cold, an original song composed by Mr. B. Carr of Philadelphia, introduced in the opera of the Children in the Woods [composed by Benjamin Carr and interpolated in Samuel Arnold's opera Children in the Wood]
62-64	A favorite song in the opera of the Spanish Barber. Composed by Dr. Arnold.

The Musical repertory (continued)

81-83	The death of Anna. A favorite ballad. Sung by Mr. Incledon, written by John Bayley Esqr. Composed with an accompaniment for the harp or piano forte by Reginald Spofforth.
84-85	Mens fate deserves a tear. Composed by Mr. Hook.
86-87	Sweet little cottage, a favorite song. Composed by J. G. Graeff.
88-89	The gipsy. A ballad. Words by Peter Pindar. Composed by J. Fisin.
90-91	The girl of my heart. Sung by Mr. Dignum. The words by Carlisle. Composed by Mr. Hook.
92-93	Ellen of the dee. Sung by Mr. Dignum. The words by Mr. Rannie. Composed by John Ross, organist of St. Paul's, Aberdeen.

The Musical repertory (continued)

94-95	Hey dance to the fiddle & tabor.
	A dialogue in the Lock and Key.
	Sung by Mrs. and Mr. Hodgkinson.
	[William Shield]
96	The streamlet [From The Woodman,
	composed by William Shield]

NEW-JERSEY HARMONY; being the best selection of psalm
tunes ever yet published. Together with plain
and concise rules for learners. Philadelphia,
John M'Culloch, 1797. 80p.   Evans 32547

A NEW VERSION OF THE PSALMS OF DAVID, fitted to the
tunes used in churches. By N. Brady, D. D.
Chaplain in Ordinary, & N. Tate, Esq: Poet-Laureat
to Her Majesty. Boston, J. Allen for Benjamin
Elliot, 1720. 2, 272p.   Evans 2094

> Note: Evans' entry for this and succeeding
> editions of A New Version of the Psalms of
> David is Biblia. Old Testament. Psalms.

----------. Boston, Draper, 1754. 1-385, 61-84,
16 plates.   Evans 40680

----------. Boston, J. Draper for T. Leverett, 1754.
320, 84p., 8 plates.   Evans 40681

> Note: This copy is bound with the appendix dated
> 1760. See Evans 41174, p. 211.

----------. Boston, B. Edes and J. Gill for J. Winter,
1755. 376p., 16 plates.   Evans 7358

A New version of the Psalms of David (continued)

----------. Boston, Green and Russell for J. Winter,
1757. 276, 8, 60p., 16 plates.   Evans 7846

----------. Boston, D. & J. Kneeland for J. Wharton and
N. Bowes, 1762. 276, 84, xiv p.   Evans 9069

----------. Boston, D. and J. Kneeland for Wharton &
Bowes, 1763. 276, 84p., 16 plates.   Evans 9344
   Note: "No copy has been found with the imprint
      given by Evans, but there are several variants,
      such as this. The music at the end differs."
      --American Antiquarian Society.

----------. Boston, J. Kneeland & S. Adams for Thomas
Leverett, 1765. 276, 84, 18p.   Evans 9913
   Note: "Different printings of the music section
      at the end are found in the various copies."
      --American Antiquarian Society.

----------. Boston, W. M'Alpine and J. Fleeming, 1765.
246, 74, 8p., 8 plates.   Evans 9914

----------. Boston, William M'Alpine, 1767. 246,
74p., 22 plates.   Evans 10558

A New version of the Psalms of David (continued)

----------. Boston [Mein & Fleeming] for Barclay,
1770. 261, 1, 78, 8, 16p.   Evans 42063

----------. Boston, A. Ellison, 1773. 276, 84p.,
16 plates.   Evans 12677

----------. Boston, Nicholas Bowes, 1774. 416p.,
16 plates.   Evans 13149

NICOLAI, VALENTIN, d. 1799.

A Favorite sonata. By Niccolai [sic] [Philadelphia]
G. Willig [1796] 7p.   Evans 30904

O DEAR WHAT CAN THE MATTER BE. A favorite song or duett.

    Philadelphia, Carr [1793] 2p.   Evans 25936

AN ODE SET TO MUSIC, consecrated to the memory of the

    Rev. George Whitefield, A. M. who left this

    transitory life, in full assurance of one more

    glorious, September 30th, 1770, AEtatis 56.

    By one of his friends in Boston, New-England.

    [Boston, 1770] Broadside.   Evans 11794

PAISIELLO, GIOVANNI, 1773-1836.

> For tenderness form'd. Philadelphia, B. Carr
>
> > [c1794] 1p.   Evans 26720
> >
> > *Note: The British Museum Catalog states that*
> >
> > *this is an adaptation by Thomas Linley,*
> >
> > *Sr., of "Saper bramate" from Paisiello's*
> >
> > *opera Il barbiere di Siviglia.*
> >
> > *Evans' entry under Sir John Burgoyne,*
> >
> > *1722-1792.*
>
> How can I forget. Sung by Miss Broadhurst.
>
> > Philadelphia, Carr [1795?]   2p.   Evans 29502
> >
> > -----. New York, B. Carr [1796]   2p.   Evans 47873

PAR SA LEGERETE.   [Philadelphia, Filippo Trisobio,

> 1798?]   Broadside.   Evans 48561

PELISSIER, VICTOR.

> Washington and independence. A favorite patriotic
>
> > song. New York, G. Gilfert [1798?]   2p.
> >
> >   Evans 34959
> >
> > *Note: Evans' entry under title.*

PENNSYLVANIA. UNIVERSITY.

An Exercise, performed at the public commencement,
in the College of Philadelphia, July 17, 1790.
Containing an ode, set to music, sacred to the
memory of Dr. Franklin. (This exercise consists
of lines, partly original, and partly selected
or altered from former familiar compositions
in this College, as they were hastily thrown
together, for the occasion of the present
commencement; it is hoped that they will be
received with the usual indulgence of a
candid public). Philadelphia, William Young,
1790. 11p.   Evans 22798

Note: Evans' entry is under Philadelphia.

College of, now University of Pennsylvania.

PERCY, JOHN, 1749-1797.

The Captive. New York, Moller [1797] 2p.

Evans 48223

THE PHILADELPHIA POCKET COMPANION FOR THE GUITTAR [sic]
OR CLARINETTE. Being a collection of the most
favorite songs & selected from the European per-

The Philadelphia pocket companion (continued)

formances and publications of the last twelvemonth
and as its continuation will be annual it may be
considered as a yearly journal of the most esteemd
[sic] lyric compositions. Vol. I for 1794.
[Philadelphia] Carr [1794] 40p.   Evans 27517

Contents

The Philadelphia pocket companion (continued)

22-23	Poor Richard. By B. Carr.
24-27	The sea boys duett in the Mariners ["Appears in the score of Thomas Attwood's The Mariners, where it is ascribed to Martini." Sonneck-Upton, p. 371]
28	Ballad in Caernarvon castle [Thomas Attwood]
29	Ca ira
30-31	The Seamans home. Sung in the Midnight Wanderers [William Shield]
32-33	Air in the Pirates [Ever remember me, by Stephen Storace]
34-37	Canzonett with an accompaniment [Richard Suett; see Sonneck-Upton, p. 54, 526]
38-39	Divertimento
40	Minuetto

PHILE, PHILIP, c1734-1793.

The Favorite new federal song, adapted to the President's
March. Sung by Mr. Fox...for the voice,
piano forte, guittar [sic], and clarinett
[Philadelphia, B. Carr, 1798] 2p.   Evans 33896

The President's March. Aranged [sic] for two
performers on one piano forte by R.[aynor]
Taylor. Philadelphia, William Priest [1795]
2p.   Evans 29609

---------. [For piano, German flute, or violin]
New York, G. Gilfert [1796?] 1 leaf.

Evans 31044

Note: Evans' entry is under title.

---------. A new federal song. Philadelphia,
G. Willig [1798] 2p.   Evans 33902

Note: Evans' entry is under Joseph Hopkinson,
1770-1842. "Yankee doodle" (1-1/2 p.)
is appended.

PICCINNI, NICCOLO, 1728-1800.

> Overture La Buona Figliuola. Arranged for the
> piano forte. Philadelphia, G. Willig
> [1795] 2p.   Evans 31009

> La Schiava. Overture. Arranged for the piano-forte
> by Alexander Reinagle. Philadelphia,
> Thomas Dobson [1789] 2p.   Evans 22069

PILSBURY, AMOS, fl. 1799.

> The United States' sacred harmony. Containing
> the rudiments of vocal music, in a concise
> and comprehensive manner; and a large and
> valuable collection of psalm tunes and
> anthems. Selected from the most celebrated
> authors in the United States and Great-Britain.
> For the use of schools, singing societies, and
> churches. Also, --a large number of tunes never
> before published. Boston, Thomas & Andrews,
> 1799. 224p.   Evans 36119

PLAIN PSALMODY, or supplementary music. An original

composition, set in three and four parts,

consisting of seventy psalm and hymn tunes and

an anthem, adapted to the numerous metres now

extant. For the use of worshipping societies

and singing schools. Boston, Isaiah Thomas &

Ebenezer T. Andrews, 1800. 71, 1p.   Evans 38276

PLEYEL, IGNAZ JOSEPH, 1757-1831.

Come blushing rose. [New York] G. Willig [c1794]

Broadside.   Evans 47183

Henry's cottage maid. A favorite song. New York,

G. Gilfert [1796] 1 leaf.   Evans 31017

Pleyel's German hymn, with variations. New York,

Peter Erben [1800?] 4p.   Evans 49136

POOR, JOHN, 1752-1829.

>A Collection of psalms and hymns, with tunes affixed;
>for the use of the Young Ladies' Academy of
>Philadelphia. By John Poor, A. M. Principal.
>Philadelphia, John M'Culloch, 1794. 48p.
>
>>Evans 27533

POWNALL, MARY ANN WRIGHTEN, 1751-1796.

>Jemmy of the glen [words and music by Mrs. Pownall]
>Baltimore, J. Carr [1798] 2p.   Evans 34409

>Kisses sue'd for. A favorite song. The words by
>Shakespear [sic] and music by Mrs. Pownall.
>New York, G. Gilfert, 1795. 2p.   Evans 28933
>*Note: Evans' entry under title.*

>Six songs for the harpsichord or piano forte.
>Composed by Mrs. Pownall and J. Hewitt. To
>which are added and selected Rossetti's
>celebrated La Chasse and a duet for two
>voices. New York, Pownall and Hewitt [1794]
>19p.   Evans 27542
>
>Contents
>>p. 1-4   La Chasse, Rossette [sic, Rossetti]
>>Adapted by J. Hewitt.

Pownall, Mary Ann Wrighten (continued)

5-8	A La Chasse.
9-10	Jemmy of the glen. Words and music by Mrs. Pownall.
11	A rural life. Composed by J. Hewitt.
12	Advice to the ladies. Composed by J. Hewitt.
13-14	The straw bonnet. Composed by Mrs. Pownall.
15	Lavinia. Composed and sung by Mrs. Pownall.
16	The primrose girl. Sung by Mrs. Pownall [composed by James Hewitt]
17-19	Canzonet [by] Jackson

THE PSALMS, HYMNS, AND SPIRITUAL SONGS, OF THE OLD &
NEW-TESTAMENT: faithfully translated into English
meetre. For the use, edification and comfort of
the Saints in publick and private, especially in
New-England [The ninth edition] Boston, B. Green
and J. Allen, 1698. 420, 10, 10p.   Evans 817

The Psalms, Hymns, and Spiritual Songs (continued)

> *Note: This and succeeding editions of The Psalms,*
> *Hymns, and Spiritual Songs were entered by Evans*
> *under Biblia. Old Testament. Psalms.*

----------. The twelfth edition. Boston, B. Green
for Elliot and Boone, 1705. 505, 7p.   Evans 39420

----------. The fourteenth edition. Boston, John Allen
for Eleazer Phillips, 1709. 340p., 12 tunes.

Evans 1381

----------. The fifteenth edition. Boston, B. Green for
Phillips, 1711. 378, 4p.   Evans 39518

----------. The twentieth edition. Boston, T. Fleet
for D. Henchman, 1720. 378, 6p.   Evans 2095

----------. The twentieth [twenty-first?] edition. Boston,
J. Franklin for D. Henchman, 1722. 312p., 11 tunes.

Evans 2317

> *Note: For remarks concerning the discrepancy of*
> *edition number, see Evans, v. 1, p. 306.*

156

The Psalms, Hymns, and Spiritual Songs (continued)

----------. The twenty-second edition. Boston,
J. Phillips, 1729. 2, 309p., 12 tunes. Evans 3134

----------. The twenty-fifth edition. Boston, Daniel
Henchman and Thomas Hancock, 1742. 2, 346p.,
12 plates.   Evans 4892

The Psalms, hymns, & spiritual songs, of the Old and
New-Testament, faithfully translated into English
metre. Being the New-England psalm-book revised
and improved; by an endeavor after a yet nearer
approach to the inspired original, as well as to
the rules of poetry. With an addition of fifty
other hymns on the most important subjects of
Christianity; with their titles, placed in order,
from--The Fall of Angels and Men, to--Heaven after
the General Judgment [Edited by Thomas Prince]
Boston, D. Henchman and S. Kneeland, 1758.
2, vi, 360p., 15 plates.   Evans 8082

Note: "The AAS has two copies in original
bindings lacking the music. No copy located
contains the 32 pages called for by Evans."

THE PSALMS OF DAVID, imitated in the language of the
New-Testament, and applied to the Christian State
and worship. Philadelphia, Dunlap for Noel, 1760.
viii, 308, 28p., 12 leaves.   Evans 41175

----------. The Twenty-first edition. Boston, M'Alpine,
1766. 328, 8p., 16 plates.   Evans 41672

----------. The fortieth edition, corrected, and
accommodated to the use of the Church of Christ in
America. Newburyport, John Mycall, 1781. 325,
11, 16p.
Second title: A select number of plain tunes,
adapted to Congregational worship. By Andrew Law,
A. B. 16p.   Evans 17098

----------. The forty-fifth edition, corrected, and
accommodated to the use of the Church of Christ in
America. Boston, Norman & Bowen, 1785. 2, 224,
179, 4, 16p.
Second title: Hymns and spiritual songs, in three
books. I. Collected from the Scriptures. II. Composed
on divine subjects. III. Prepared for the Lord's
Supper. By I. Watts, D. D.

The Psalms of David (continued)

Third title: A select number of plain tunes
adapted to Congregational worship. By Andrew
Law, A. B. 16p.   Evans 18930

THE PSALMS OF DAVID, in metre. According to the version
approved by the Church of Scotland. Philadelphia,
Young and M'Culloch, 1787. 303, 1p.   Evans 20233
    Note: Only the last page contains musical notation.

THE PSALMS OF DAVID, with the Ten Commandments, creed,
Lord's Prayer, &c. in metre. Also, the catechism,
confession of faith, liturgy, &c. translated from
the Dutch. For the use of the Reformed Protestant
Dutch Church of the City of New-York. New York,
James Parker, 1767. 4, 479, 9, 143, 1p.
                                        Evans 10561

READ, DANIEL, 1757-1836.

The American singing-book; or a new and easy guide
to the art of psalmody. Designed for the use
of singing schools in America. Containing in
a plain and familiar manner, the rules of
psalmody, together with a number of psalm
tunes, &c. Composed by Daniel Read, Philo
Musico. New Haven, Read, 1785. 72, 1p.

Evans 19213

----------. The second edition, corrected. New
Haven [printed for Daniel Read] 1786.
72, 2p. Evans 44957

----------. To which is added, a supplement,
containing twenty-five approved psalm tunes,
from different authors. By Daniel Read,
Philo-Musico. The third edition. New Haven,
Daniel Read, 1787. 72, 3, 16p. Evans 20673

----------. The fourth edition. New Haven, Daniel
Read [1793] 72, 4, 16p. Evans 26056

Read, Daniel (continued)

The Columbian harmonist. No. 1. Containing, first.
A plain and concise introduction to psalmody
fitly calculated for the use of singing
schools. Second. A choice collection of
new psalm tunes of American composition.
By Daniel Read, author of the American
Singing Book. New Haven, R. Atwell [1793]
39, 1p.   Evans 26057

The Columbian harmonist. No. 1[-3] Containing
first. A plain and concise introduction
to psalmody fitly calculated for the use of
singing schools. Second. A choice collection
of new psalm tunes of American composition.
New Haven [T. & S. Green, 1795?] 111, 9p.
                                         Evans 29389

The Columbian harmonist, no. II. Containing first.
A plain and concise introduction to psalmody
fitly calculated for the use of singing
schools. Second. A choice collection of
sacred music for public and social worship.
New Haven [T. & S. Green, 1795] 39, 1p.
                                         Evans 29390

Read, Daniel (continued)

The Columbian harmonist. No. III. Containing a
collection of anthems and set-pieces of
music chiefly new. New Haven, Daniel Read
[1795] 39, 1p.   Evans 29391

REEVE, WILLIAM, 1757-1815.

When seated with Sal. A favorite sea song sung by
Mr. Harwood in the Purse or benevolent tar.
Philadelphia, Carr, 1795. 2p.   Evans 28503
    Note: Evans' entry under John C. Cross.

The Witch, a favorite new song. New York,
G. Gilfert [1797] 2p.   Evans 48239

REINAGLE, ALEXANDER, 1756-1809.

America, commerce & freedom. Sung by Mr. Darley, junr.
in the ballet pantomime of the Sailor's Landlady.
Philadelphia, Carr [1794] 2p.   Evans 27647
    *Note: Evans' entry under Susanna Haswell
    Rowson, 1761-1824.*

A Chorus, sung before Gen. Washington as he passed under
the triumphal arch raised on the bridge at Trenton
April 21st 1789. Set to music and dedicated...to
Mrs. Washington by A. Reinagle. Philadelphia,
Reinagle [1789] 6, 4p.   Evans 22093

Reinagle, Alexander (continued)

A Collection of favorite songs, arranged for the
voice and piano forte. Philadelphia, Reinagle
[1789?] 2, 22p.   Evans 45572

Contents

Reinagle, Alexander (continued)

13 [What med'cine can soften the bosom's keen smart] A favorite song in the Chaplet. Composed by Dr. Boyce.

14-16 The soldier tir'd. Compos'd by Dr. Arne.

17-18 [For tenderness form'd] A favorite song in the Heiress. Composed by Sigr. Paesiello.

19-20 In vain fond youth. Sung by Mrs. Stuart at Vauxhall.

21-22 Caro bene. Del Sigr. Sarti.

A Collection of favorite songs divided into two books containing most of the airs in the Poor Soldier, Rosina, &c. and the principal songs sung at Vaux Hall. The basses rendered easy and natural for the piano forte or harpsichord. Book I. Philadelphia, Reinagle and Aitken [1789] 20p.

Contents   Evans 22095

p. 2 Drink to me only

Reinagle, Alexander (continued)

3	Farewell ye green fields [Samuel Howard]
4	I've kissed and I've prattled [from] Rosina [William Shield]
5	When William at eve [from] Rosina [William Shield]
6-7	The twins of Latona [from] Poor Soldier [William Shield]
8	How happy the soldier [from The Poor Soldier by William Shield]
9	May I never be married [alternative title of The Kiss by James Hook]
10	Norah the theme of my song [from] Poor Soldier [William Shield]
11	Altho heavn's good pleasure. In the favorite opera of Amintas. Composed by Sigr. Giordani.
12	The spring with smiling face [from] Poor Soldier [William Shield]

Reinagle, Alexander (continued)

13	My friend and pitcher [from]
	Poor Soldier [William Shield]
14	How imperfect is expression
15	A rose tree [from] Poor Soldier
	[William Shield]
16	Out of my sight or I'll box your
	ears. Duetto [From the Poor
	Soldier by William Shield]
17	Johnny and Mary [William Shield]
18-19	Ye sluggards. Hunting song
	[James Hook]
20	Good morrow to your night cap
	[from] Poor Soldier [William
	Shield]

Note: Following p. 20, the University of Pennsylvania copy continues with six pages of music in manuscript form which are therefore unaccounted for in Evans and in Sonneck-Upton. The first composition, although not entirely legible, appears to be "The Wells," composed by "R[aynor] Taylor,"

Reinagle, Alexander (continued)

> *followed by what seems to be a one-page*
>
> *movement of a pianoforte sonata, and*
>
> *concluding with "Tune from the Night-*
>
> *ingale..." the remainder of the title*
>
> *being illegible. Although the composer*
>
> *of the last is not known for certain,*
>
> *it is probably either James Hook or*
>
> *Raynor Taylor. It is interesting to*
>
> *note that, "A cantata 'The nightingale'*
>
> *--Miss Huntley, bird accompaniments on*
>
> *the flageolet Mr. Shaw--[by Raynor]*
>
> *Taylor," was to be sung at a concert in*
>
> *Philadelphia, on April 21, 1796. No such*
>
> *composition by Raynor Taylor has been*
>
> *found."--Sonneck-Upton, p. 297. Could*
>
> *this "Tune from the nightingale" perhaps*
>
> *be of Taylor's composition?*

Federal march as performed in the grand procession
in Philadelphia, the 4th of July 1788.
Composed and adapted for the piano forte,
violin or German flute by Alex. Reinagle.
[Philadelphia, John M'Culloch, 1788]
Broadside.   Evans 21421

Reinagle, Alexander (continued)

Indian march, of the much admeired [sic] American

play: caled [sic] Columbus, arranged for the

Piano Forte. Philadelphia, Hupfeld [c1797]

Broadside. Evans 48240

A Selection of the most favorite Scots tunes with

variations for the piano forte or harpsichord.

Philadelphia, T. Dobson & W. Young, 1787.

28p. Evans 20674

Contents

Tantivy hark forward huzza. The favorite hunting

song sung by Mrs. Iliff at Vax [sic] Hall.

Philadelphia, Thomas Dobson [1789] 2p.

Evans 22097

Reinagle, Alexander (continued)

Twelve favorite pieces arranged for the piano forte
or harpsichord by A. Reinagle. Philadelphia,
Reinagle [1789?] 2, 24p.   Evans 45573

Contents

p. 1-2	La Chasse. Allegro. Del Sigr. [Carlo Antonio] Campioni.
3	Brown's march
4	Overture to the Deserter [Dibdin]
5-6	Pastorale [from the Deserter, by Dibdin]
7-8	A favorite movement for the piano forte by Vanhal
9-10	Overture. La Schiava [Piccinni]
11-12	Favorite rondo. By Garth.
13-14	Haydn's celebrated Andante for the piano forte
15	A favorite minuet. Composed by G. C. Schetkey.
16	Faederal march. As performed in the grand procession in Philadelphia the 4th. of July, 1788. Composed and adapted for the piano forte, violin or German flute by Alex. Reinagle.

Reinagle, Alexander (continued)

17-18   A favourite rondo. Composed by

F. Staes.

19-20   Marian. Overture. [Composed by]

Shield.

21-24   Overture de Blaise et Babet.

Adapted for the piano forte by

A. Reinagle.

The Volunteers. A musical entertainment as performed

at the New Theatre. Composed by Alex. Reinagle.

The words by Mrs. Rowson. Philadelphia, 1795.

4-20p.   Evans 29440

Note: Evans' entry under Susanna Haswell

Rowson, 1762-1824.

RELFE, JOHN, 1763-c1837.

Mary's dream, or Sandy's ghost. Philadelphia, Carr

[1793] 2p.   Evans 26067

ROGERSON, ROBERT, fl. c1789.

Anthem, sacred to the memory of His Excellency John

Hancock, Esq; late Governor and Commander in

Chief of the Commonwealth of Massachusetts.

By Dr. Robert Rogerson. Boston, Thomas &

Andrews, 1793. 7p.   Evans 26104

ROSLINE CASTLE, a favorite Scots song, the words of

    Rd. Hewitt. New York, Hewitt [1799?] 2 leaves.

                                          Evans 48878

ROWE, J.

    Singing of psalms by seven constituted sounds,

        opened and explained, on the occasion of

        differences in many congregations, with

        reference to the old and new way of singing

        psalms. Composed by a council of Divines and

        musicians, chosen for to mediate the matter,

        and make means to reconcile the differences.

        [Boston?] 1722. 2, 14p.   Evans 39775

      Note: Makes use of numbers rather than

          traditional musical notation on the staff.

SAMMLUNG GEISTLICHER LIEDER NEBST MELODIEN, von verschidenen

    Dichtern und Componisten. Gedrucht und herausgegeben

    von Conrad Dell. Lancaster, Pa., Johann Albrecht und

    Conrad Dell, 1798. 12, 109, 4p.   Evans 33625

SCHUBART, CHRISTIAN FRIEDRICH DANIEL, 1739-1791.

    Schubart's Klaglied: Ich habe viel gelitten.
        [Philadelphia] Cist for Willig [1799?]
        2p.   Evans 48961

SHAW, ROBERT, fl. 1794.

    The Gentleman's amusement. A selection of solos,
        duetts, rondos & romances from the works of
        Pleyel, Haydn, Mozart, Hoffmeister, Fischer,
        Shield, Dr. Arnold, Saliment: several airs,
        dances, marches, minuetts & Scotch reels. Sixty
        four select songs from the favorite operas &
        Dibdin's latest publications with some general
        remarks for playing the flute with taste and
        expression and a dictionary of musical terms.
        The whole selected, arranged, & adapted for one,
        two and three German flutes or violins by R. Shaw
        of the Theatre Charlestown & B. Carr. Forming the
        cheapest, and most compleat, collection ever
        offered to the public; the contents...from

Shaw, Robert (continued)

the best authors, and what, purchased in any
other manner would amount to more than three
times the price. Philadelphia, Carr [1794]
98p.   Evans 27694

Note: For bibliographical development,
see Sonneck-Upton, p. 157-158.

Contents

p. 3   The Presidents march [Philip Phile]

3   Two favourite strathpey reels
                 introduced by Mr. Francis in
                 the Caledonian frolick [Benjamin
                 Carr]

4   Patty Clover from the opera of
                 Marian [William Shield]

4-5   [I travers'd Judah's barren sand]
                 Sung by Miss Broadhurst in the
                 opera of Robin Hood [William Shield]

5   [Ere around the huge oak] Sung by
                 Mr. Darley in the Farmer [William
                 Shield]

Shaw, Robert (continued)

6	Ben Backstay. A favorite new song composed by Mr. Dibdin.
7-9	Air des deux Savoyards. Varie pour deux flutes par F. Devienne.
9	[I am a brisk & sprightly lad] Sung by Mrs. Marshall in the Spoil'd Child.
	Stour lodge
10	[The trump of fame] Sung by Mrs. Warrell in the opera of Robin Hood [William Shield]

Note: Pages 13-16 not reproduced on microprint.

11-13	Duetto. Hoffmeister.
14-15	No good without exception. Written and composed by Charles Dibdin for his new entertainment called Castles in the Air.
16	Henry's cottage maid. Pleyle [sic]

Shaw, Robert (continued)

16-17	[Tho I am now a very little lad] Sung by Mrs. Marshall in the Highland Reel [William Shield]
17	Grand march from the opera of the Prisoner. Mozart [a simplified arrangement by Attwood of "Non piu andrai" from the Marriage of Figaro]
18	Ah weladay my poor heart. Sung by Mrs. Martyr in the Follies of a Day [William Shield]
18-19	Scotch medley in the overture to the Highland Reel [William Shield]
20	[Go George I can't endure you] Sung by Mrs. Shaw in the opera of No Song No Supper [Stephen Storace]
21	The Je ne scai quoi. A favorite ballad sung by Mrs. Oldmixon in Robin Hood [William Shield]

Shaw, Robert (continued)

22-23 The lucky escape. Written and

composed by Dibdin.

24 [Across the downs this morning]

Sung by Mrs. Oldmixon in the

opera of No Song No Supper

[Stephen Storace]

General Washingtons march

24-25 [I left my country and my

friends] Sung by Miss Broad-

hurst, Mrs. Oldmixon & Mr.

Marshall in the Critic [known

as the Mock Italian Trio]

25 [The streamlet that flow'd round

her cot] Sung by Mr. Marshall

in the Woodman [William Shield]

Prayer of the Sicilian mariners

26 Duetto. Pleyel. [see p. 182]

Note: For pages 27-43, see Shaw's The Gentleman's

amusement, or companion for the German flute,

Evans no. 29498, p.182 of this Bibliography.

Shaw, Robert (continued)

44   A medley duetto adapted for two
          German flutes from the Federal
          Overture. Selected & composed
          by B. Carr [continued from
          Evans no. 29498, p. 185 of this
          Bibliography]

     Note: Pages 45-48 not reproduced on
        microprint.

45   Conclusion of Federal overture [Carr]

46-47   The Highland laddie. Introduced
          by Mrs. Warrell in the Highland
          reel [William Shield]

48   Poor black boy. From the Prize.
          Sung by Miss Broadhurst and by
          Mr. Carr [Stephen Storace]

48-49   Lullaby. From the opera of the
          Pirates [Stephen Storace]

49   [Ye chearful (sic) virgins] Sung by
          Mrs. Marshall in the comedy of
          She Wou'd & She Wou'd Not
          [Cibber?]

Shaw, Robert (continued)

The Village maid

50-51   A Medley duetto adapted from the

overture to the Children in the

Wood. Composed by Dr. Arnold.

52   [That petty fogging Grizzle] Sung

by Miss Solomons in the character

of Tom Thumb [J. Markordt]

[How sweet when the silver moon]

Sung by Mrs. Oldmixon in the Purse

or Benevolent Tar [William Reeve]

Note: Pages 53-56 not reproduced on microprint.

53   [Page missing and contents unknown]

54   [Say how can words a passion feign]

[From My Grandmother by Stephen

Storace]

Favorite country dance compos'd

by Dibdin

55   Within a mile of Edinbourgh.   Introduced

& sung by Miss Broadhurst.

Shaw, Robert (continued)

	in the musical farce called My
	Grandmother [Stephen Storace,
	adapted from James Hook]
56	Ever remember me. From the opera
	of The Pirates [Stephen Storace]
56-57	[How charming a camp is] Sung by
	Mrs. Bland in the opera of the
	Prisoner [Thomas Attwood]
57	[We kings who are in our senses]
	Sung by Mr. Bates in Tom Thumb
	the Great [J. Markordt]
58-59	Rondo by Haydn
59	Pastorale [Were I oblig'd to beg my
	bread] Sung by Mrs. Warrell at
	the New Theatre.
60	[Tears that exhale] Sung by Miss
	Solomons in the Prisoner [by]
	Attwood
60-61	[Oh dear delightful skill] Sung by
	Mrs. Oldmixon in the Prize or
	2.5.3.8. [Stephen Storace]

Shaw, Robert (continued)

61	Winsome Kate. Compos'd by Mr. Hook.
62-64	The Vetrans [sic] Written for the new entertainment called Great News or a Trip to the Antipodes [composed by] Charles Dibdin.
64	[When scorching suns] Sung by Mrs. Oldmixon in the Noble Peasent [sic] [William Shield]
65	[Young Carlos sued a beauteous maid] Sung by Miss Broadhurst in the Prisoner [Thomas Attwood]
	[I lock'd up all my treasure] Sung by Mr. Marhsall in the Quaker [Charles Dibdin]
66	Happy tawny Moor. A favorite duett from the Mountaineers. For two flutes [Samuel Arnold]
67	Neighbour sly [composed by] Dibdin From Oscar and Malvina [William Reeve]

180

Shaw, Robert (continued)

68-69   Amidst the illusions. Sung by Miss
       Broadhurst [William Shield]

  Note: Pages 69-72 not reproduced on
   microprint.

69   Dans votre lit. Sung by Mr.
       Marshall in Patrick in Prussia
       [William Shield]

70-71   Ronde. Chantee a la reine par
       Monseigneur le Dauphin...
       Musique de M. Martini.

72   The way worn travellers. For two
       flutes [From The Mountaineers
       by Samuel Arnold]

73   The jolly gay pedlar [sic] from
       Oscar and Malvina [William Reeve]
       Finale to Inkle & Yarico [Samuel
       Arnold]

74   Duetto by Mozart

75-77   Minuetto with eight variations for
       the flute and violoncello composed
       by Geo. Ed. Saliment

Shaw, Robert (continued)

Note: *Pages 78-98 not reproduced on microprint.*

78-79 Lovely Nan. Written and composed
     by Mr. Dibdin.

80-81 Sigh no more ladies. For three
     German flutes or violins.

81   The Caledonian hunt

     The Fife hunt

82   Loose were her tresses seen [Giuseppe
     Giordani]

     When nights were cold. Introduced in
     the Children in the Wood [Samuel
     Arnold's opera with Benjamin Carr's
     song interpolated]

83-86 The Battle of Prague. Selected and
     adapted for a flute or violin, or
     for one or two flutes or violins,
     by B. Carr [Franz Kotzwara]

87   Whilst happy in my native land. Sung by
     Mr. Darley in the Patriot [alternate
     title of The Farmer, by William
     Shield]

Shaw, Robert (continued)

	Welch [sic] air in the Cherokee [Storace]
88-89	Lucy or Selim's complaint. A favorite song composed by Mr. Hook.
90-91	A Duetto for two flutes composed by Willm. Pirson [sic, Pirsson]
92-93	The Tinker. A favorite comic song in Merry Sherwood [Reeve]
94-95	"Some general remarks on playing the flute with taste and expression"
96-97	"A Complete index to the Gentleman's Amusement"
98	"A Short dictionary of musical terms"

[The Gentleman's amusement, or companion for the German
    flute. No. 4-5] Philadelphia, Carr [1795]
27-42p.   Evans 29498

Contents--No. 4

p. 27	Duetto. Pleyel [concluded from p. 26 of Evans 27694; see page 175 of this Bibliography]

Shaw, Robert (continued)

28	[My native land] Sung by Mr. Carr in the opera of the Haunted Tower [Stephen Storace]
28-29	O dear what can the matter be
29	The gipsy's song introduc'd in the Maid of the Mill by Mrs. Oldmixon [Samuel Arnold]
	Astleys hornpipe
30-31	When seated with Sal. A favorite sea song sung by Mr. Harwood in the Purse or Benevolent Tar [William Reeve]
32	The waxen doll. Sung by Miss Solomon in the Children in the Wood [From Shield's The Woodman, frequently interpolated in Samuel Arnold's Children in the Wood]
32-33	The indigent peasant [James Hook]
33	Romance by Haydn
34	Fishers minuet with new variations [Johann Christian Fischer]

[continued on p. 35]

Shaw, Robert (continued)

Contents--No. 5

Shaw, Robert (continued)

41   [Now all in preparation] Sung by

            Mr. Francis in the Haunted

            Tower [Stephen Storace]

            Quick march from the Battle of

            Prague [Franz Kotzwara]

42-43   A medley duetto adapted for two

            German flutes from the Federal

            Overture. Selected & composed

            by B. Carr [continued in Evans

            no. 27694, p. 176 of this

            Bibliography]

The Gentleman's amusement, or companion for the

    German flute. Arranged and adapted by R. Shaw.

    No. 6 [-7] Philadelphia, Carr [1796]

    44-76p.   Evans 31181

        Note: This is reproduced by the American

        Antiquarian Society as 27694; see p. 176-180

        of this Bibliography.

The Gentleman's amusement. A selection of solos,

    duetts, overtures, arranged as duetts, rondos &

Shaw, Robert (continued)

romances from the works of Pleyel, Haydn,
Mozart, Hoffmeister, Fischer, Shield, Dr.
Arnold, Saliment, etc. Several airs, dances,
marches, minuetts & Scotch reels. Sixty four
select songs from the favorite operas &
Dibdins latest publications with some general
remarks for playing the flute with taste and
expression and a dictionary of musical terms.
The whole selected, arranged & adapted for
one, two, & three German flutes or violins
by R. Shaw of the Theatre Charlestown &
B. Carr. Forming the cheapest, and most
complete collection ever offered to the
public; the contents being selected from the
best authors, and what, purchased in any other
manner would amount to more than three times
the price. Philadelphia, B. Carr [1796]
77p.   Evans 31182

Note: This is reproduced by the American
Antiquarian Society as 27694; see p. 171
ff. of this Bibliography.

SHE LEFT ME AH! FOR GOLD. A favorite song. New York,

G. Gilfert [1796] Broadside.　　　Evans 31183

SHIELD, WILLIAM, 1748-1829.

Amidst the illusions. A favorite song sung by

Miss Broadhurst in the New York Old City

Concert. New York, G. Gilfert [1795]

3p.　　　　　　　　　Evans 29501

Amidst the illusions. From Hartford Bridge or the

Skirts of a Camp. Philadelphia, Carr [1796]

2p.　　　　　　　　　Evans 30969

Note: Evans' entry under William Pearce.

The Cheering rosary. Sung with great applause

in the new opera of the Midnight Wanderers.

Philadelphia, Carr [1793]　2p.　　Evans 25966

Note: Evans' entry under William Pearce.

Court me not to scenes of pleasure [From The Woodman]

Philadelphia, Carr [1795?]　2p.　　Evans 28591

Note: Evans' entry under Sir Henry Bate

Dudley, 1745-1824.

Shield, William (continued)

The Green Mountain farmer, a new patriotic song.
Written by Thomas Paine, A. M. Music &
accompaniments by the celebrated Shield.
Boston, Linley & Moore [1798] 2p.

Evans 34302

Note: Evans' entry under Paine, Thomas,
afterwards Robert Treat, Junior, 1773-1811.

The Heaving of the lead. A favorite sea song.
Philadelphia, Carr [1793] 2p.   Evans 25967

Note: Evans' entry under William Pearce.

Hey dance to the fiddle & tabor. A dialogue in
the Lock & Key sung by Mrs. & Mr. Hodgkinson.
New York, J. Hewitt [1797?] 2p. Evans 32261

Note: Evans' entry under Prince Hoare,
1755-1834.

How can I forget the fond hour. Sung by Miss
Broadhurst [Found in Shield's opera Marian, but
composed by Paisiello] Philadelphia, Carr
[1795?] 2p.   Evans 29502

Johnny and Mary. New York, J. Hewitt [1798?]
1 leaf.   Evans 34539

Shield, William (continued)

Marian. Overture. Arranged for the pianoforte by
Alexander Reinagle. Philadelphia, Thomas
Dobson [1789] 2p.   Evans 22142

My soul is thine sweet Norah. A favorite song.
Sung by Mr. Jonstone in Love in a Camp
or Patrick in Prusia [sic] Arranged for
the piano or harpsichord by A. Reinagle
[Philadelphia, Thomas Dobson, 1789] 2p.
                                       Evans 22096

O come away my soldier bonny. Sung by Mrs.
Warrell of the New Theatre with universal
applause, in the opera of the Rival Soldiers.
Philadelphia, G. Willig [1798] 2p.
                                       Evans 34262

    Note: Evans' entry under title.

Old Towler, a favorite hunting-song...sung by Mr.
Tyler at the New York Theatre. New York,
G. Gilfert [1796] 2p.   Evans 47915

What are the boasted joys of love. Cavatina.
Philadelphia, B. Carr, 1798. 2p. Evans 34541

Shield, William (continued)

When William at eve. New York, G. Gilfert

[1797] Broadside.   Evans 31873

Note: Evans' entry under Frances Moore

Brooke, 1724-1789.

SHUMWAY, NEHEMIAH, 1761-1843.

The American harmony. Containing, in a concise

manner, the rules of singing. Together with

a collection of psalm tunes, hymns, and anthems

from the most approved authors, ancient and

modern. By Nehemiah Shumway, A. B.

Philadelphia, John M'Culloch, 1793. 212p.

Evans 26162

Note: Pages 177-180 omitted in pagination.

SICARD, STEPHEN, fl. 1788.

The President of the United States' march. Philadelphia

John M'Culloch [1789?] Broadside.   Evans 45591

SMITH, THEODORE, fl. 1770-1810.

Three duetts, for two performers on one harpsichord or

piano forte. Philadelphia, J. C. Moller

[1793] 13p.   Evans 27712

SO DEARLY I LOVE JOHNNY O. A favorite new song sung by

Mrs. Franklin. New York, G. Gilfert [1796] 2p.

Evans 47920

SPOFFORD, REGINALD, 1770-1827.

Ellen, the Richmond primrose girl. Philadelphia,

B. Carr [1797?] 2p. Evans 48256

-----. Boston, von Hagen [1798?] 2p. Evans 48620

Hark the goddess Diana. A favorite duett. Sung by

Messrs. Hodgkinson & Williamson at the Ana-

creontic Society. New York, Hewitt [1797?]

3p. Evans 48257

STICKNEY, JOHN, 1744-1827.

The Gentleman and lady's musical companion.

Containing, a variety of excellent anthems,

tunes, hymns, &c.--collected from the best

authors; with a short explanation of the

rules of musick: the whole corrected and

rendered plain. Newburyport, Daniel Bayley,

1774. 9, 3, 212p. Evans 13642

Note: "None of the copies located by Evans

agrees with his entry."--American

Antiquarian Society.

Stickney, John (continued)

‑‑‑‑‑‑‑‑‑. Newburyport, Bayley for Boyle, 1774.

9, 3, 212p.   Evans 42707

‑‑‑‑‑‑‑‑‑. Newburyport, Daniel Bayley [1774?]

8, 212p.   Evans 42045

STONE, JOSEPH C., c1758-1837.

The Columbian harmony. Containing the rules of

psalmody: together with a collection of sacred

music. Designed for the use of worshipping

assemblies & singing societies. By Joseph

Stone and Abraham Wood [Boston, Isaiah

Thomas and Ebenezer T. Andrews, 1793]

viii, 112p.   Evans 26215

STORACE, STEPHEN, 1763-1796.

Ah can I cease to love her. Philadelphia, Carr,

1793. 1p.   Evans 26217

Captivity. A ballad supposed to be sung by Marie

Antoinette during her confinement in the Temple

[Philadelphia, Carr, 1793] 2p.   Evans 26218

Storace, Stephen (continued)

The capture. A favorite song in The Pirates.
Philadelphia, Carr [1793] 2p.   Evans 25306
Note: Evans' entry under James Cobb,
1756-1818.

Fal lal la. The favorite Welch air. Sung by
Mrs. Bland in the Cherokee. New York,
G. Gilfert [1797] 2p.   Evans 48259

The favorite ballad of the poor black boy.
In the new musical farce of The Prize.
Philadelphia, Carr [1794] 2p.   Evans 27126

Lullaby. A favorite ballad in the comic opera of
the Pirates. Philadelphia, Carr [1793]
2p.   Evans 25308
Note: Evans' entry under James Cobb,
1756-1818.

Lullaby, a favorite song in The Pirates. New York,
G. Gilfert [1795] Broadside.   Evans 47612

Storace, Stephen (continued)

The much admired ballad of the willow...sung by
Mrs. Warrel. Philadelphia, B. Carr, 1798.
2p.   Evans 34608

No more his fears alarming, an admired new song
composed by Stephen Storace & sung by
Sr. Storace in the opera of the Pirates
[Philadelphia] G. Willig [1795?] 2p.
                                    Evans 47613

The Sailor boy. A favorite sea song introduced
with great applause by Mr. Hodgkinson in
No Song No Supper [Philadelphia, B. Carr,
1793] 2p.   Evans 25613

A Sailor lov'd a lass. Composed by S. Storace
for the Cherokee. Philadelphia, B. Carr
[1796] 2p.   Evans 30203
        Note: Evans' entry under James Cobb,
        1756-1818.

The Shipwreck'd seamans ghost. A song. Philadelphia,
Carr, 1793. 2p.   Evans 26160

Storace, Stephen (continued)

Spirit of my sainted sire. Sung by Mr. Hodgkinson.

New York, B. Carr [c1795] 3p.   Evans 47614

Sweet little Barbara. A favorite duett in the Iron

Chest. Philadelphia, B. Carr [1799] 3p.

Evans 36375

Tho' you think by this to vex me, a favorite duett

sung by Mrs. Seymour & Mr. Jefferson in

the Siege of Belgrade. New York, Hewitt

[1797?] 2p.   Evans 48260

Whither my love. A favorite song in The Haunted

Tower. Philadelphia, Carr [1793] 2p.

Evans 25309

Note: Evans' entry under James Cobb,

1756-1818.

SWAN, TIMOTHY, 1758-1842.

The Federal harmony. In three parts, containing,

I. An introduction to the grounds of musick.

II. A large collection of celebrated psalm and

Swan, Timothy (continued)

hymn tunes from the most approved ancient and
modern authors; together with several new ones,
never before published: suited to all metres
usually sung in churches. III. Select anthems
&c. &c. Compiled for the use of schools and
singing societies. Boston, John Norman
[1788] 1-17, 1, 18-131p.   Evans 21485

----------. Boston, John Norman, 1790. 128p.

                                             Evans 22919

----------. Boston, John Norman, 1792. 130p.

                                             Evans 24831

----------. Boston, John Norman, 1793. 130p.

                                             Evans 46884

TANS'UR, WILLIAM, 1706-1783.

The American harmony: or, royal melody complete.
In two volumes. Vol. I. Containing I. A new
and correct introduction to the grounds of
musick, rudemental [sic] practical and technical.
II. A new and complete body of church musick,

Tans'ur, William (continued)

adapted to the most select portions of the
Book of Psalms, of either versions; with many
fuging chorus's, and Gloria Patris to the
whole. III. A new and select number of hymns,
anthems, and canons, suited to several
occasions; and many of them neuer [sic] before
printed; set by the greatest masters in the
world. The whole are composed in two, three,
four and five musical parts, according to the
nicest rules; consisting of solo's, fuges,
and chorus's correctly set in score for voices
or organ; and fitted for all teachers,
learners, and musical societies, &c. The
fifth edition, with additions. By William
Tans'ur, senior, musico-theorico. Newburyport,
Daniel Bayley, 1769. 5, 1, 11, 96; 4, 96p.
[Second title] The American harmony; or
universal psalmodist. Containing a choice
and valuable collection of Psalm and hymn-tunes;
canons and anthems; with words adapted to each
tune. The whole composed in a new and easy

Tans'ur, William (continued)

taste, for two, three and four voices; in
the most familiar keys and clifts:--
calculated to promote and improve this
most excellent part of social worship; and
render it both useful and delightful; in
quires [sic] as well as in congregations
in the country. By A. Williams, teacher
of psalmody in London. To which is
added a variety of favourite hymn tunes
and anthems; collected from the latest and
most celebrated authors; carefully set in
score, and neatly engraved. Newburyport,
Daniel Bayley, 1769. 2, 2, 96p.   Evans 11489

----------. The sixth edition, with additions...
Newburyport, Daniel Bayley, 1771. 5, 1,
12, 96; 4, 96p.   Evans 12240

----------. The seventh edition, with additions...
Newburyport, Daniel Bayley, 1771. 5, 1, 10,
1, 7-8, 1, 96; 4, 96p.   Evans 12241

Tans'ur, William (continued)

--------. The eighth edition, with additions...
 Newburyport, Daniel Bayley, 1773. 5, 1,
 10, 7-8, 96; 4, 96p.   Evans 13035

--------. The ninth edition, with additions...
 Newburyport, Daniel Bayley, 1774. 5, 1,
 10, 7-8, 96; 4, 96p.   Evans 13647

 Note: It is the eighth, not the ninth,
 edition which has been reproduced on
 microprint.

The Royal melody complete: or the New Harmony of
 Zion. Containing I. A new and correct
 introduction to the grounds of musick, rudimental, practical, and technical. II. A new
 and complete body of church-musick, adapted
 to the most select portions of the Book of
 Psalms, of either version; with many fuging
 chorus's, and Gloria Patri's to the whole.
 III. A new and select number of hymns, anthems,
 and canons, suited to several occasions; and
 many of them never before printed; set by the

Tans'ur, William (continued)

greatest masters in the world. The whole are
composed in two, three, four, and five musical
parts, according to the nicest rules: consisting of solo's, fuges, and chorus's,
correctly set in score for voices or organ:
and fitted for all teachers, learners, and
musical societies, &c. with a preface on
church-musick, shewing the beauty and
excellency thereof. The third edition, with
additions. By William Tans'ur, Senior,
Musico Theorico. Boston, W. M'Alpine for
Daniel Bayley and Williams, 1767. 13, 3,
14, 2, 96p.   Evans 10782

----------. The fourth edition. To which is added,
a variety of favourite psalm and hymn tunes,
and one new anthem, from Williams's Psalmody
[Boston] Daniel Bayley, 1768. Front., 2, 13,
3, 14p., 112 plates.   Evans 11085

Note: The following is a summary of the
Tans'ur-Bayley psalmbooks.

Tans'ur, William (continued)

> Third ed. [first American ed.] Royal Melody
> Complete, or New Harmony of Zion. Boston,
> 1767.   Evans 10782.

> Fourth ed. Royal Melody Complete, or New
> Harmony of Zion. Boston, 1768. Evans
> 11085.

> Fifth ed. American Harmony, or Royal
> Melody Complete [This and succeeding
> editions contained Aaron Williams'
> Universal Psalmodist designated as
> Vol. II in the seventh, eighth, and
> ninth editions] Newburyport, 1769.
> Evans 11489.

> Sixth ed. American Harmony, or Royal
> Melody Complete. Newburyport, 1771.
> Evans 12240.

> Seventh ed. American Harmony, or Royal
> Melody Complete. Newburyport, 1771.
> Evans 12241.

> Eighth ed. American Harmony, or Royal
> Melody Complete. Newburyport, 1773.
> Evans 13035.

Tans'ur, William (continued)

>*Ninth ed. American Harmony, or Royal*
>*Melody Complete. Newburyport, 1774.*
>*Evans 13647.*

TAYLOR, RAYNOR, 1747-1829.

Amyntor, a pastoral song. Philadelphia, B. Carr
[c1795] 2p.   Evans 47617

Citizen soldiers, a new patriotic song. Words by
Amyntor, music by Mr. R. Taylor [Philadelphia,
1795?] Broadside.   Evans 47618

An easy and familiar lesson for two performers on
one piano forte. Philadelphia, B. Carr,
179- . 2p.   Evans 45796
>*Note: Probably published 1795-1797. See*
>*Sonneck-Upton, p. 226.*

Independent and free. From the American Tar or
the Press Gang Defeated. Sung by Mr.
Rowson at the New Theatre, Philadelphia.
[Philadelphia] B. Carr [1796] 2p. Evans 47929

Taylor, Raynor (continued)

The Kentucky volunteer. A new song written by a

lady of Philadelphia. Philadelphia, Carr

[1794] 3p. Evans 27186

The Lass of the cott. Philadelphia, Carr [1795]

2p. Evans 29607

The Merry piping lad. A ballad in the Scots taste.

Philadelphia, Carr [1795] 2p. Evans 29608

Nancy of the vale, a pastoral ballad. Philadelphia,

B. Carr [1795] 2p. Evans 47619

Nobody. Philadelphia, B. Carr [1798?] 2p.

Evans 48621

Rustic festivity. A new song. Philadelphia,

Carr [1795] 2p. Evans 29610

Silvan the shepherd swain. Composed by R. Taylor,

the words from the celebrated romance of The

Knights of the Swan, written by Madame Genlis.

Philadelphia, B. Carr [1798] 2p. Evans 33786

Note: *Evans' entry under Stephanie Felicite*

Brulart Ducrest de St. Aubin Genlis,

Comtesse de Sylvan.

Taylor, Raynor (continued)

Silvan, the shepherd swain. Composed by R. Taylor,

the words from the celebrated romance of the

Knights of the Swan, written by Madame de

Genlis. Philadelphia, B. Carr [1798]

2p.   Evans 48622

Sonata for the piano forte, with an accompaniment

for a violin. Philadelphia, B. Carr

[1797] 2, 6p.   Evans 32911

Viva la liberte. A new song. Philadelphia,

Carr [1795] 2p.   Evans 29611

The Wand'ring village maid. Philadelphia, Carr

[1795] 2p.   Evans 29612

The Wounded sailor. Philadelphia, Carr [1794]

2p.   Evans 27784

THEN I FLY TO MEET MY LOVE, a favorite song. New York,

G. Gilfert [1795] 6-7p.   Evans 47622

THESPIAN CHAPLE. Inscribed to the memory of Mr. John P.

Morton, late of the new Theatre, Philadelphia.

Thespian Chaple (continued)

> The words by Mr. Derrick [Philadelphia] G. Willig
> [1798] Broadside.   Evans 33627
>> *Note: Evans' entry under _____ Derrick.*

THOMAS, ISAIAH, 1749-1831.

> A Specimen of Isaiah Thomas's printing types.
>> Being as large and complete an assortment
>> as is to be met with in any one printing-
>> office in America. Chiefly manufactured by
>> the great artist, William Caslon, Esq; of
>> London. Worcester, Isaiah Thomas, 1785.
>> 42p., 50 leaves.   Evans 19272

THREE SWEET HEARTS I BOAST, a favorite song. New York,
> G. Gilfert [1797] 2p.   Evans 48268

TRISOBIO, FILIPPO, -1798.

> La marmotte, avec accompagnement de harpe, ou
>> forte piano. Philadelphia, Trisobio
>> [1797?] 2p.   Evans 48276

TRUXTON'S VICTORY. A naval patriotic song. Sung by
Mr. Hodgkinson. Written by Mrs. [Susanna]
Rowson, of Boston [Boston, Thomas & Andrews,
1799] 2p.   Evans 36248

Note: Evans' entry under Susanna Roswell
Rowson, 1761-1824.

TUFTS, JOHN, 1689-1752.

An Introduction to the singing of psalm tunes, in
a plain & easy method. With a collection
of tunes in three parts. The fifth edition.
Boston, Gerrish, 1726. 2, 9, 1p., 12 plates.
                                            Evans 39856

---------. The seventh edition. Boston, Gerrish,
1728. 2, 9, 1p., 12 plates.   Evans 39898

---------. The eighth edition. Boston, Gerrish,
1731. 2, 9, 1, 24p.   Evans 3482

---------. The ninth edition. Printed from copper-
plates, neatly engraven. Boston, Gerrish, 1736.
2, 8, 2p., 6 plates.   Evans 40104

Tufts, John (continued)

----------. The tenth edition. Boston, Gerrish,

1738. 2, 7, 3p., 12 plates. Evans 4315

----------. The eleventh edition. Boston, Gerrish,

1744. 1, 7, 3p., 12 plates. Evans 5502

TUNES IN THREE PARTS, for the several metres of Dr.

Watts's version of the psalms; some of which tunes

are new. Philadelphia, Anthony Armbruster,

1763. 43, 1p. Evans 9526

----------. This collection of tunes is made from the

works of eminent masters; consisting of six tunes

for short metre; eight for common metre; seven for

long metre; and a tune for each special metre.

To which are added the gamut, with directions to

learners of music. The second adition [sic]

Philadelphia, Anthony Armbruster, 1764.

viii, 43, 1p. Evans 9858

TWENTY-FOUR FASHIONABLE COUNTRY DANCES FOR THE YEAR 1799.

With their proper figures as performed at court, &

Bath, and all public assemblys. Boston, W. Norman

[1799] 14p. Evans 36460

URANIAN SOCIETY, PHILADELPHIA.

Introductory lessons, practised by the Uranian

Society, held at Philadelphia for the

promoting the knowledge of vocal music.

Jan. 1, 1785. Philadelphia, 1785.

20p.   Evans 19194

Note: Evans' entry under Philadelphia.

Pennsylvania. Uranian Society.

THE VILLAGE HARMONY, or youth's assistant to sacred

musick. Containing, a concise introduction to

the grounds of musick, with such a collection of

the most approved psalm tunes, anthems, and

other pieces, in three and four parts, as are

most suitable for divine worship. Designed for

the use of schools and singing societies...the

second edition, with large additions. Exeter,

H. Ranlet, 1796. 187, 1p.   Evans 31494

Note: "The only copy known is defective."--

American Antiquarian Society.

---------. Designed principally for the use of schools

and singing societies...Fourth edition, corrected

The Village harmony (continued)

and improved. Exeter, Henry Ranlet, 1798.

2, 201, 1p.   Evans 34930

---------. Fifth edition, corrected and improved...

Exeter, Henry Ranlet, 1800. ix, 12-205, 1p.

Evans 38938

WALTER, THOMAS, 1696-1725.

The Grounds and rules of musick explained; or, an

introduction to the art of singing by note.

Fitted to the meanest capacities. By Thomas

Walter, M. A. Recommended by several

ministers. Boston, J. Franklin for S.

Gerrish, 1721. iv, 24, 32p.   Evans 2303

---------. Second edition, enlarged, corrected, and

beautified. Boston, Thomas Johnston, 1723.

iv, 25, 32p.   Evans 2490

---------. The third edition. Boston, S. Gerrish,

1740. 40, 24p.   Evans 4622

Walter, Thomas (continued)

----------. [The fourth edition] Boston, Samuel

Gerrish, 1746. 2, iii, 1, 25p., 16

leaves music. Evans 5878

----------. [The fifth edition] Boston, Benjamin

Mecom for Thomas Johnston [1760] 2, iv,

25p., 23 plates. Evans 8760

----------. [The sixth edition] Boston, Johnston,

1764. 1, 25p., 24 plates. Evans 41504

WASHINGTON'S MARCH. As performed at the New Theatre,

Philadelphia [Philadelphia] G. Willig [1795?]

2p. Evans 29834

----------. Washington's march [and] Washington's march

at the Battle of Trenton. Philadelphia, G. Willig

[1796] Broadside. Evans 31555

----------. The New President's march [and] Washington's

march [Philadelphia] B. Carr [1796] Broadside.

Evans 31554

Washington's March (continued)

--------. The New President's march. New York,

    J. Hewitt [1799?] 1 leaf.   Evans 35638

WATTS, ISAAC, 1674-1748.

    Appendix, containing a number of hymns, taken

        chiefly from Dr. Watts's scriptural collection.

        Boston, Leverett, 1760. 84, 1p., 16 plates.

                            Evans 41174

      Note: This is also bound with "A New

        version of the Psalms of David...1754."

        See Evans 40681, p. 142 of this

        Bibliography.

WEBBE, SAMUEL, 1740-1816.

    The Mansion of peace, composed by Mr. Webbe.

        New York, Hewitt [1797?] 2p.   Evans 48317

    --------. Sung by Mr. Chambers at the opening of

        the New Theatre. The words by a Lady,

        composed by Mr. Webbe. Philadelphia,

        G. Willig [1797?] 2p.   Evans 48318

WHEN RURAL LADS AND LASSES GAY, a favourite song.

New York, G. Gilfert [c1795] 2p.   Evans 47680

WHEN THE MIND IS IN TUNE. Sung by Miss Broadhurst.

New York, B. Carr, [1797?] 2p.   Evans 33214

WILLSON, JOSEPH.

Javotte or the maid of the Alps. Written by John
Gretton Esqr, composed by Joseph Willson,
organist of Trinity Church. New York,
J. and M. Paff [1804] 2p.   Evans 35569

Note: Evans' entry under John Gretton.

Wolfe redated Evans' 1799 to 1804.

WOOD, ABRAHAM, 1752-1804.

Divine songs, extracted from Mr. J. Hart's Hymns,
and set to musick in three and four parts.
Suitable to be sung in churches immediately
before or after divine worship. Boston,
Isaiah Thomas, 1789. 32p.   Evans 21877

Note: Evans' entry under Joseph Hart,

1712-1768.

213

Wood, Abraham (continued)

A Funeral elegy on the death of General George

Washington. Adapted to the 22d of February,

by Abraham Wood. Boston, Thomas & Andrews,

1800 [Words by Dr. Watts] 8p.   Evans 39131

A Hymn on peace. Worcester, Abraham Wood [1784]

16p.   Evans 18890

Note: Evans' entry under "An anthem

on peace."

THE WOOD ROBIN. Boston, von Hagen [1800?] Broadside.

Evans 49196

WOODRUFF, MERIT N., 1780-1799.

Devotional harmony: a posthumous work of Merit N.

Woodruff, late of Watertown, (Connecticut)

deceased. Published by his relatives and

friends, under the inspection of Asahel Benham.

A short narrative of the life and death of

the author, may be found in the introduction.

n.p. [1800?] 60p.   Evans 39140

WRIGHT, THOMAS, 1763-1829.

A Smile from the youth that I love. Written by
the author of the marvellous pleasant love
story, and set to music by Thomas Wright.
Philadelphia, G. Willig [1798?] 2p.

Evans 34552

Note: Evans' entry under title.

YANKEE DOODLE. An original American air, arranged
with variations for the pianoforte. Philadelphia,
Carr [1796?] 4p.

Evans 31676

YANKEE DOODLE, sung with great applause at the
theatre by Mr. Hodgkinson. New York, Hewitt
[1798] 4p.

Evans 48535

Note: Pages 3-4 lacking from microprint.

YARRIMORE. An Indian ballad. Philadelphia, Carr
[1794] 2p.

Evans 28143

YOUNG, JOHN.

Young's vocal and instrumental musical miscellany;

being a collection of the most approved songs,

duets, catches and glees, adapted for the

voice, piano-forte, violin and German flute

[No. 1-8] Philadelphia, John Young and

Carey [1793] 63p.   Evans 26522

Contents

No. 1

p. 3   The reconsaliation [sic] The words

            by a gentleman of Philadelphia.

            Music by I. Gehot.

4   [Across the downs this morning]

            Sung by Mrs. Hodgkinson in No

            Sung [sic] No Supper [Stephen

            Storace]

5   Batchelors hall. By Dibdin.

6-7   [Send him to me] Sung by Mrs.

            Myrter in The Farmer [William

            Shield]

7   Bonny Lem of Aberdeen as a country

            dance

Young, John (continued)

8-9	The bleak wind wistles [sic] o'er the main [From The Highland Reel, by William Shield]
10	From night till morn. A favorite duett [Probably composed by William Shield]

No. 2

11-13	Still the lark finds repose. A favourite rondo. Sung by Miss Phillips [From The Spanish Rivals, by Thomas Linley, the Elder]
14-15	Such pure delight. Taken from the Highland Reel [William Shield]
16-17	[From aloft the sailor looks around] A favourite song in No Song No Supper [by] Storace
17	Crymbo oble, or the Welch [sic] question
18	Lafayette. A new song.

Young, John (continued)

19   The lamplighter. Written and composed by Mr. Dibdin.

20   The poor mariner

No. 3

21   Bonny Charley. A favorite new Scotch song [James Hook]

22-23   Go with you all the world over. The much admired dialogue duett in the Surrender of Calais [Samuel Arnold]

24-25   The village spire. A celebrated song by Giordani.

25   [Sweet transports, gentle wishes go] Sung by Miss Harper [From Rosina, composed by William Shield]

26   A smile from the girl of my heart [From The Woodman, composed by William Shield]

27   Tom Bowling or the Sailor's epitaph by Dibdin

Young, John (continued)

<u>No. 4</u>

28	Henrys cottage maid [Ignaz Pleyel]
29-30	A favourite French song [J'ai perdu mon Euridice from Orphee et Euridice, by Gluck]
30	Dibdin's fancy
31-32	The Sailor's allegory
32-33	Paddy Bull's expedition [From A Picture of Paris, composed either by William Reeve or William Shield
33-34	Heaving the lead. A favourite new song [From the Hartford Bridge, composed by William Shield]
35	No more I'll court the town bred fai [From The Farmer, composed by William Shield]

<u>No. 5</u>

36	Chelmer's banks. Sung by Miss Hunt Composed by R. Taylor.

Young, John (continued)

37   The Walls of my prison [Isabella

        Theaker More]

38   Hark the lark at heav'n's gate

        sings

39-40   Jack the guinea pig. A favorite

        song composed by R. Taylor.

40   Hark the lark at heav'n's gate

        sings. For the flute.

41   The shepherds evening. A new song

        composed by R. Taylor.

42   The Tartan plaidy

No. 6

43   [When the men a courting came] Sung

        by Miss Broadhurst in the opera

        of Robin Hood [William Shield]

44-45   The trump of fame. Sung by Mrs.

        Warrell in the opera of Robin

        Hood [William Shield]

45   Drink to me only with thine eyes

46   What shepherd or nymph

Young, John (continued)

47   The request. An admired new song
composed by G.[erard] Vogler.

48-49   The flowing cann. As sung by Mr.
Hodgkinson in No Song No Supper
[From The Oddities by Charles
Dibdin and sung by Mr. Hodgkinson
in Stephen Storace's No Song
No Supper]

No. 7

50   Young Lubin was a shepherd boy
[From Carnival of Venice by
Thomas Linley, the Elder]

51-52   When first this humble roof I knew
[From The Lord of the Manor by
William Jackson of Exeter]

52   Lullaby. A favorite ballad in the
opera of The Pirates [Stephen
Storace]

53-54   The lucky escape. Written and
composed by Dibdin.

55-56   The patriot. A new song sung by Mr.
Robins, the words by Mrs. Hatton

Young, John (continued)

> 56   The streamlet. A favorite new
>   song in the opera of The Woodman
>   [William Shield]

No. 8

> 57   [When a little merry he] A favorite
>   song sung by Mrs. Marshall in the
>   new musical drama called The
>   Purse [William Reeve]

> 58   The gipsy's song introduc'd in The
>   Maid of the Mill by Mrs. Oldmixon
>   [Samuel Arnold]

> 59   Poor black boy. Sung by Miss
>   Broadhurst in The Prize [Stephen
>   Storace]

> 60-61   The jolly ringers. Composed by Dibdin.

> 62   The village holyday. A favorite new
>   air.

> 63   Sweet Nan of Hampton Green. An
>   admired song composed by Mr. Hook.

YOUNG JEMMY IS A PLEASING YOUTH. A favorite song. Boston,
P. A. von Hagen, jr [1799] 2p.   Evans 36747

YOUNG WILLY FOR ME. Sung with great applause by Mrs.

    Seymour at the ladies concert. New York, Hewitt

    [1797] 2p.   Evans 33252

      Note: Evans' entry under Mrs. _____ Wrighten.

PART TWO

MUSIC CURRENTLY NOT REPRODUCED IN

EARLY AMERICAN IMPRINTS, 1639-1800

For a variety of reasons, the items cited in the
following pages are not currently available in microtext form in the American Antiquarian Society's
Early American Imprints, 1639-1800. Some of the
items have not yet been located, some were never
published, others bibliographical "ghosts" of other
similar editions, and still others withheld by the
owning library. At such time in the future when any
of these items are issued on microprint by the American
Antiquarian Society, this section of the Bibliography
will become immediately more useful. At present,
however, it helps provide a much more complete picture
of early America's music publishing activities than if
such items had been eliminated entirely.

Every attempt has been made to include only those
items containing actual printed musical notation.
Inasmuch as none of these items was available for

inspection, however, it is possible that some of the items contained herein would have been eliminated had visual inspection been possible.

The valuable remarks and explanations prepared by the American Antiquarian Society, identified in the following pages by "AAS," have been included in italics beneath each citation; they originally appeared on the target cards for the appropriate citation in the Early American Imprints microprint edition.

ADGATE, ANDREW, c1750-1793.

> The Mechanics lecture: showing the usefulness of
> mechanic arts, and who was the first mechanic;
> and giving a short history of taylors, masons,
> carpenters, ship carpenters, joiners, cabinet-
> makers, blacksmiths, white smiths, bakers,
> barbers, weavers, fullers, hatters, tanners,
> shoemakers, coblers, dyers, carvers, coopers,
> coach-makers, saddlers, sail makers, and

Adgate, Andrew (continued)

printers. Reverently dedicated to those
respectable supporters of liberty and
property, the mechanics of Philadelphia,
by their faithful servant, and fellow-
laborer, Absalom Aimwell [pseudonym for
Andrew Adgate], esquire. By these we
support our families, and enrich our
country. To which is affixed, The
Mechanics' song, composed and set to
music by a Native of the United States.
Philadelphia, John M'Culloch, 1789.

Evans 21627

AAS: *Entry from an adv.*

AMERICAN ACADEMY OF COMPLIMENTS, or the complete
American secretary. With a collection of the
newest songs. Wilmington, Delaware, Peter
Brynberg, 1797.   Evans 31717
AAS: *Imprint assumed by Evans from adv.*

THE AMERICAN COCK ROBIN: or, a choice collection of
English songs, both old and new, being such as
are generally esteemed, and agreeable to the

The American Cock Robin (continued)

North-American taste. New York, John Holt,

1764.   Evans 9569

AAS: From an adv.

THE AMERICAN HARMONY, being a collection of the most

approved church music and anthems from the

different authors published in America;

together with a variety of pieces either

entirely new or never before published.

Philadelphia, John M'Culloch, 1793.   Evans 25096

AAS: The Evans entry came from advs.,

apparently of 26162 [See p. 190 of

this Bibliography]

THE AMERICAN MOCK-BIRD. A collection of the most

familiar songs now in vogue. New York, 1760.

                                         Evans 8528

AAS: Unique copy formerly owned by Dr.

John P. Failing of Albany.

---------. THE NEW AMERICAN MOCK-BIRD. A collection

of the best songs on different subjects. New York,

The New American mock-bird (continued)

> Hugh Gaine, 1761.   Evans 8940
>
> > *AAS: See Ford, Gaine, I, 107.*

THE AMERICAN SONGSTER, being a collection of the

> most celebrated ancient and modern songs.
>
> Portsmouth, John Melcher, 1790.   Evans 22311
>
> > *AAS: Entry from an adv.*

THE APOLLO; being a collection of such English songs

> as are most eminent for poetical merit. To which
>
> is added, a table of first lines, with the author's
>
> names annexed. Philadelphia, William Spotswood,
>
> 1789.   Evans 21660
>
> > *AAS: "American Edition. Just published."*
> >
> > *Federal Gazette, Apr. 9, 1789.*

ARNE, THOMAS AUGUSTINE, 1710-1778.

> Columbia and liberty. A new patriotic song.
>
> > Written by Mr. [James] Davenport. The music
> >
> > by Dr. Arne. Boston, Lindley & Moore, 1798.
> >
> > > Evans 33602
> >
> > > *AAS: The only recorded copy is not now*
> > >
> > > *to be found [Evans' entry under James*
> > >
> > > *Davenport, fl. 1798]*

ARNOLD, SAMUEL, 1740-1802.

Dear Walter [alternative title of Dorothy Dump]
A song from "The Children in the wood."
New York, G. Gilfert, 1795. 1p.   Evans 29118
AAS: Not available for reproduction.

In the dead of the night [alternative title of
Cupid Benighted] From the late new opera
of Zorinski. New York, Carr [1796]
Evans 30829
AAS: Imprint assumed by Evans from adv.
"This day published" in N. Y. Daily
Advertiser, Feb. 8, 1796.

THE BALTIMORE SONGSTER. Baltimore, J. Keatinge,
1794.   Evans 26607
AAS: Imprint assumed by Evans from
adv. for "new publications" in the
Baltimore Telegraph, Mar. 26, 1795.

THE BALTIMORE SONGSTER; or festive companion. A choice
and approved collection of songs, interspersed
with many originals, and the patriotic song of

The Baltimore songster (continued)

Hail Columbia! Second edition. Baltimore,

Henry S. Keatinge, 1798.   Evans 33367

AAS: *Imprint assumed by Evans from adv.*

"New publications" in the Telegraph,

Aug. 15, 1798.

BAPTISMAL HYMNS. Some of which are newly selected.

Boston, Edes and Son, 1791.   Evans 23149

AAS: *"This day published...and to be sold*

at Edes," Boston Gazette, Sept. 5,

1791.

BAYLEY, DANIEL, 1725?-1799.

A Collection of anthems and hymn tunes. Newbury-

port, Daniel Bayley [1784] 8p.   Evans 18341

AAS: *See Music Library Assoc., Notes,*

XI, 38.

A New and complete introduction to the grounds and

rules of music, in two books. Book I. Con-

taining the grounds and rules of music, or an

Bayley, Daniel (continued)

introduction to the art of singing by note,
taken from Thomas Walter, A. M. Book II.
Containing a new and correct introduction
to the grounds of music, rudimental and
practical, from William Tans'ur's Royal
Melody: the whole being a collection of a
variety of the choicest tunes from the
most approved masters. [The third edition]
Boston, Mascoll Williams, 1764.   Evans 9600
*AAS: No copy with this var. of imprint
    located.*

BELCHER, SUPPLY, 1751-1836.

Mr. Belcher's celebrated Ordination anthem, which
was performed in Hallowell and Augusta.
Together with a number of other fuguing
pieces never before published. Boston,
Isaiah Thomas and Ebenezer T. Andrews
[1797]   Evans 31791
*AAS: Entry from Edes' adv. "Just
    received, and to be sold by the printer*

Belcher, Supply (continued)

> *hereof," Kennebeck Intelligencer,*
>
> *Dec. 19, 1797.*

BELKNAP, DANIEL, 1771-1815.

> The Harmonist's companion. Boston, Thomas &
>
> Andrews, 1794. 31p.   Evans 28255
>
> > *AAS: A ghost of 31792, q.v. [See p. 36-37*
> >
> > *of this Bibliography]*

BENHAM, ASAHEL, 1757-1805.

> Federal harmony; containing, in a familiar manner,
>
> the rudiments of psalmody; together with a
>
> collection of church music (most of which
>
> are entirely new.) The third edition.
>
> Middletown, Moses H. Woodward [1793] Evans 25159
>
> *AAS: Imprint assumed by Evans from adv.*
>
> > *"Benham's Singing Books for Sale at this*
> >
> > *Office" in Middlesex Gazette, Jan. 26,*
> >
> > *1793.*

Benham, Asahel (continued)

    ---------. The fifth edition. Middletown,

        Moses H. Woodward [1795] 58p.   Evans 28261

        AAS: The unique copy located by Evans is

         not to be found.

BILLINGS, WILLIAM, 1746-1800.

    An Anthem for Thanksgiving, entitled, Universal

        praise. Boston, Thomas and Andrews,

        1793.   Evans 25196

        AAS: Adv. in Salem Gazette, Jan. 27, 1797.

    The Bird and the lark. The author supposes the

        airs to be original. Boston, William

        Billings, 1790.   Evans 22362

        AAS: "Just published, two pieces, entitled

         the Bird and the Lark," Independent

         Chronicle, May 20, 1790.

    Easter anthem, with an addition, entirely new

        inserted in the middle. Boston, Thomas &

        Andrews, 1795.   Evans 28301

        AAS: "To be sold by the author," Ind.[ependent]

         Chron.[icle], Nov. 26, 1795.

Billings, William (continued)

The Republican harmony, containing the rudiments of
music, in a concise manner; together with a
collection of sacred music, both ancient and
modern. Some of the latter original.
Designed for the use of singing schools and
worshipping societies. Troy, Gardner and
Billings, 1795. Evans 28300
AAS: Imprint assumed by Evans from adv., "Just
published," in The Recorder, July 14, 1795.

The Singing master's assistant, or key to practical
music. Being an abridgement from the New-
England Psalm-singer; together with several
other tunes, never before published...The
second edition. Boston, Draper and Folsom,
1779. 32, 104p. Evans 16206
AAS: There was a copy in the Lowell Mason Coll.

----------. Boston, Draper and Folsom, 1780.
32, 104p. Evans 16716
AAS: The recorded copies on examination turn
out to be defective copies of other editions.

BROADDUS, ANDREW, 1770-1848.

A Selection of hymns and spiritual songs from the
best authors. By Andrew Broaddus, V. D. M.
Richmond, Va., Samuel Pleasants, Jun., 1798.

Evans 33460

AAS: "Lately published, and for sale at
Samuel Pleasants," Va. Argus, Nov. 20, 1798.

CALLCOTT, JOHN WALL, 1766-1821.

Werter to Charlotte, a favorite ballad. Philadelphia, Carr, 1798.   Evans 33483

AAS: Entry from advs.

CARR, BENJAMIN, 1768-1831.

In vain the verdure of spring. The music composed
by Benjamin Carr. Philadelphia, G. Willig
[1796]   Evans 31129

AAS: Entry from advs. [Evans' entry under
Susanna (Haswell) Rowson, 1762-1824.]

The Musical journal. [Baltimore, 1800] 2 vol.

Evans 38022

AAS: Reproduced as 37106 and 37107 [See
pp. 46-52 of this Bibliography]

Poor Richard. Philadelphia, Carr, 1793. Evans 25265
AAS: Entry from adv. "published...printed singly."

Carr, Benjamin (continued)

Why huntress why. Sung by Mr. Tyler in the opera
of The Archers at the New York Theatre and by
Mr. John Darley at the request of several
subscribers. Philadelphia, B. Carr, 1796.

Evans 30370

AAS: No separate printing located.

CHARMS OF MELODY; a choice collection of the most
approved songs, catches, duets, &c. Philadelphia,
Mathew Carey, 1794. Evans 26760

AAS: From "books printed by Mathew Carey,"

adv. in Independent Gazetteer, Jan. 25,

1794.

A CHOICE COLLECTION OF HYMNS AND SPIRITUAL SONGS.
Richmond, Va., John Dixon, 1794. Evans 26767

AAS: Imprint assumed by Evans from advs.

A CHOICE COLLECTION OF HYMNS FROM VARIOUS AUTHORS.
New York, S. and J. Loudon, 1787. Evans 20271

AAS: "Just published," N. Y. Packet,

Mar. 13, 1787.

CLEAVELAND, BENJAMIN, 1733-1811.

Hymns on different spiritual subjects. Norwich
[John Trumbull] 1786. Evans 19562
AAS: No copy of this first ed. has been located.

----------. (Adapted to Baptist worship.)
[The second edition] Norwich, John Trumbull,
1788. Evans 21002
*AAS: "This day published," Norwich Packet,
June 12, 1788.*

Hymns, on different subjects. In two parts. Part I.
Containing XXVI hymns, on various subjects,
suitable for Christian worship...Fourth
edition. Part II. Containing XXXII hymns.
By Anna Beeman, of Warren in Connecticut,
and XXIV hymns by Amos Wells. To which is
added a number of hymns by different authors.
Particularly adapted to the Baptist worship.
Norwich, John Trumbull, 1793. 121p.

Evans 25304

*AAS: J. H. Trumbull's description of a
defective copy in his own library.*

COLE, JOHN, 1774-1855.

Episcopalian harmony. Baltimore, 1800.   Evans 49049

   AAS: Minick 570; no copy known.

Sacred harmony, containing a variety of plain and

   simple airs, adapted to all the metres in Dr.

   Watts' Psalms, improved by Mr. Barlow; and a

   choice collection of the most approved hymn

   tunes, adapted to all the metres in the

   Methodist Pocket hymn book, together with a

   concise introduction to the art of singing.

   Baltimore, J. Carr, 1799.   Evans 35319

   AAS: "Just published," Federal Gazette,

   Mar. 1, 1799.

A COLLECTION OF CHURCH MUSIC. No. 1. Philadelphia,

   Young and M'Culloch, 1786.   Evans 19563

   AAS: Entry from an adv.

A COLLECTION OF CONTRA DANCES, containing a hundred and

   forty fashionable figures. Hanover, Dunham and

   True, 1796.   Evans 30236

   AAS: Title taken by Evans from adv. "Just

   published and for sale at this office," in

   the Eagle, March 7, 1796.

A COMPLEAT TUTOR FOR THE FIFE, comprehending the

> first rudiments of music and of that
>
> instrument in an easy, familiar manner. To
>
> which is annexed besides the fife duty, and
>
> the usual collection of lessons, airs on
>
> marches, in the English edition, a variety of
>
> new favourite ones never before printed.
>
> Philadelphia [Hall and Sellers] 1776.

Evans 14686

> *AAS: Adv. in Pa. Gazette, June 19, 1776.*

DAVY, JOHN, 1763-1824.

> Crazy Jane. A favorite song. Boston, von Hagen
>
> for G. Gilfert [1800] Broadside.

Evans 37269

> *AAS: No copy of this printing could be*
>
> *located.*

DAWSON, W.

> The Youth's entertaining amusement, or a plain
>
> guide of psalmody; being a collection of the

Dawson, W. (continued)

most usual and necessary tunes sung in the
English Protestant congregations in Philadelphia, &c. In two parts, viz. treble and
bass; with all proper and necessary rules
adapted to the meanest capacities. By
W. Dawson, writing master and accomptant,
at the hand and pen, in Third-street.
Philadelphia, B. Franklin and D. Hall,
1754.   Evans 7181
*AAS: "Just published," Pa. Gazette,
July 11, 1754.*

DIBDIN, CHARLES, 1745-1814.

Ben Backstay. A favorite new song. Philadelphia,
H. & P. Rice, 1794.   Evans 26877
*AAS: Not found printed separately from The
Gentleman's Amusement [see p. 173]*

The Favorite song of Nancy or the sailors journal.
As sung by Mr. Williamson, at the Hay-Market
Theatre, Boston, with universal applause.

Dibdin, Charles (continued)

Boston, Thomas & Andrews [1798] 3p. Evans 34166

AAS: A dup. of 32040, q.v. [See p. 57 of

this Bibliography]

Jack at the windlass. The most popular song in Mr.

Dibdin's last new entertainment. Philadelphia,

Carr, 1793. 2p. Evans 25392

AAS: The only copy reported could not be

filmed. See Sonneck-Upton, p. 213.

Songs in the Deserter. Philadelphia, Mathew

Carey, 1794. Evans 26882

AAS: Entry from Sabin, apparently from

an adv.

The Veterans. Philadelphia, Carr [1796] Evans 30345

AAS: Entry from an adv. No separate printing

found.

DUPORT, PIERRE LANDRIN, c1755-c1840.

United States country dances. With figures also

accompaniments for the piano forte. Composed

in America by Mr. P. Landrin Duport, professor

of dancing from Paris & original composer of

Duport, Pierre Landrin (continued)

cadriels [sic] New York, Duport, 1800.

Evans 37336

Contents

Duport, Pierre Landrin (continued)

>AAS: *Copyright, but apparently not printed.*

ELLEN'S FATE DESERVES A TEAR. Song. New York,

G. Gilfert, 1798.   Evans 33668

>AAS: *No copy of a separate printing has*
>
>*been found.*

FISCHER, JOHANN CHRISTIAN, 1733-1800.

Fishers minuet. With new variations. Philadelphia,

Carr [1795] 2p.   Evans 28673

>AAS: *No separate printing located. See*
>
>*Sonneck-Upton, p. 142.*

[FREEDOM TRIUMPHANT, a new song] [New York, Carr, 1793]

Evans 25508

>AAS: *A ghost; see Sonneck-Upton, p. 148.*

THE GAMUT OR SCALE OF MUSIC, containing all the necessary

rules for young beginners. Hartford, Nathaniel

Patten, 1788.   Evans 21103

>AAS: *"Just published and now selling,"*
>
>*Conn. Courant, Feb. 11, 1788.*

THE GAMUT, OR SCALE OF MUSIC for teaching the
rudiments of psalmody. Norwich, John D.
Trumbull, 1793. Evans 25525

> *AAS: Imprint assumed by Evans from adv.*
> *"To be sold at this office," Norwich*
> *Packet, Jan. 17, 1793.*

THE GAMUT, OR SCALE OF MUSIC, adapted to the use of
beginners in psalmody. Albany, Charles R. and
George Webster, 1795. Evans 28724

> *AAS: Imprint assumed by Evans from adv.*
> *"For sale at this office," in Albany*
> *Gazette, Apr. 20, 1795.*

----------. Norwich, John Trumbull, 1795. Evans 28725

> *AAS: Imprint assumed by Evans from adv.*
> *"To be sold at this office" in Norwich*
> *Packet, Jan. 8, 1795.*

----------. Windsor, Vt., Alden Spooner, 1796.

Evans 30470

> *AAS: Imprint assumed by Evans from adv.*
> *"Just from the press," in Spooner's*
> *Vt. Journal, Nov. 4, 1796.*

The Gamut, or scale of music (continued)

----------. Greenfield, Mass., Thomas Dickman, 1798.

Evans 33778

> *AAS: Imprint assumed by Evans from adv.*
>
> *"For sale at this office" in Greenfield*
>
> *Gazette, Feb. 18, 1798.*

----------. Lansingburgh, Gardiner Tracy, 1799.

Evans 35532

> *AAS: Imprint assumed by Evans from adv.*
>
> *"For sale at this office," Lansingburgh*
>
> *Gazette, Jan. 15, 1799.*

THE GAMUT; or scale of music. For the use of schools.
Troy, Luther Pratt, 1797.   Evans 32173

> *AAS: Imprint assumed by Evans from adv.*
>
> *"To be sold at this office," Farmers'*
>
> *Oracle, Mar. 14, 1797.*

GODDARD, JOSIAH.

> A New and beautiful collection of select hymns and
> spiritual songs: selected from all authors that
> are entertaining, spiritual and divine...
> [Walpole, N.H., David Carlisle, 1799?] 396,
> 10p.   Evans 35554

> > *AAS: Apparently a ghost arising from the*
> >
> > *Mass. copyright of 33802, q.v.*

GRAM, HANS, fl. 1793.

Resurrection, an anthem for Easter. Charlestown,

1794. 8p.　　　　　　　　Evans 47067

AAS: *An analytic of 47066　[See p. 79 of*

this Bibliography]

GRIFFITHS, JOHN, fl. 1787-1797.

A Collection of the newest cotillions, and country

dances. To which is added, instances of ill

manners, to be carefully avoided by youth of

both sexes. Greenfield, Mass., Thomas Dickman,

1794.　　　　　　　　　　　Evans 28774

AAS: *Imprint assumed by Evans from adv.*

"For sale at this office," Greenfield

Gazette, Nov. 26, 1795.

A Collection of the newest cotillions, and country

dances. Principally compiled by J. Griffiths,

dancing-master. To which is added, rules for

conversation, and instances of ill manners to be

avoided by youth. Hartford, Elisha Babcock

for John Babcock, 1797.　　　　Evans 32213

AAS: *Imprint assumed by Evans from Babcock advs.*

HAGEN, PETER ALBRECHT VON, SR., 1750-1803.

Funeral dirge on the death of General Washington, as

sung at the Stone Chapel. The music

Hagen, Peter Albrecht von, Sr. (continued)

　　　composed by P. A. von Hagen, organist of

　　　said church. Boston, von Hagen for G.

　　　Gilfert [1800] Broadside.　　　　Evans 37481

　　　AAS: Also entered as 37009, q.v.

　　　[See p. 81 of this Bibliography]

Songs in the musical drama of The Adopted Child.

　　　Boston, Benjamin Edes, 1798.　　　Evans 33423

　　　AAS: "This day published," Boston Gazette,

　　　Apr. 9, 1798. Apparently not the same as

　　　33422 which was adv. ibid. Aug. 27.

　　　Note: "The Adopted Child, or The Baron of

　　　Milford Castle" originally composed by

　　　Thomas Attwood (1795), with music "entirely

　　　new and composed by P. A. von Hagen," pre-

　　　sumably the elder. See Sonneck-Upton,

　　　p. 6. Evans' entry is under Samuel Birch,

　　　1757-1841 [the author of the words]

HAIL PATRIOTS ALL. A new patriotic song. Boston,

　　　von Hagen, 1798.　　　　　　　Evans 33832

　　　　AAS: From von Hagen's adv. for another ed.

　　　　[See Sonneck-Upton, p. 175]

HANDEL, GEORGE FRIEDRICH, 1685-1759.

An anthem for Christmas. New Haven, Greens for

Read, 1794.   Evans 27087

AAS: *Imprint assumed by Evans from adv.*

"Just published, and to be sold by Daniel...

Never before published in America" in Conn.

Journal, Feb. 13, 1794.

Te Deum laudamus. Philadelphia, M'Culloch,

1788.   Evans 21130

AAS: *"Just published," Federal Gazette,*

Apr. 8, 1788.

HART, JOSEPH, 1712-1768.

Hymns, &c. Composed on various subjects...Middletown,

Woodward and Green, 1787.   Evans 20405

AAS: *From an adv. in Middlesex Gazette,*

Oct. 8, 1787.

----------. The supplement, and appendix. The tenth

edition. Philadelphia, William Young, 1787.

Evans 20406

AAS: *Entry from an adv.*

HEWITT, JAMES, 1770-1827.

Collin's ode on the passions, to be spoken by

Mr. Hodgkinson. With music representative of

each passion, as performed at the Anacreontic

Hewitt, James (continued)

Society, composed by J. Hewitt. New

York, 1795.   Evans 28444

AAS: Imprint assumed by Evans from an adv.

The Lass of Lucerne Lake. Sung in the opera of

the Patriot. New York, G. Gilfert

[1795] 2p.   Evans 28949

AAS: Imprint assumed by Evans from adv.

O had it been my happy lot. Boston, von Hagen,

1798. [From Flash in the pan]   Evans 34263

AAS: Imprint assumed by Evans from von

Hagen's adv.

When the old heathen gods in debate first assembled.

Boston, von Hagen, 1798. [From Flash in

the pan]   Evans 34114

AAS: Apparently a ghost of 34115 arising

from von Hagen's adv. [See p. 85 of this

Bibliography]

Note: Evans' entry under William Milns,

1761-1801.

HOLDEN, OLIVER, 1765-1831.

Sacred dirges, hymns, and anthems, commemorative of
the death of General George Washington, the
guardian of his country, and the friend of man...
an original composition by a citizen of Massachusetts. Boston, Isaiah Thomas and Ebenezer
Andrews [1800] 24, 4p.   Evans 38445

*AAS: Also entered as 37635, q.v. [See p.
88 of this Bibliography]*

HOOK, JAMES, 1746-1827.

Lash'd to the helm. New York, B. Carr [1797]
2p.   Evans 48151

AAS: Not located, 1968.

Lillies and roses. Boston, von Hagen [1799]
2p.   Evans 48884

AAS: Not located, 1968.

May day morn, a favorite sonnett. [New York]
Hewitt [1798?] 2p.   Evans 48152

AAS: Not located, 1968.

Now's the time to sing and play. New York, Hewitt
[1797?] 2p.   Evans 48153

AAS: No copy located.

Hook, James (continued)

Rondo. n.p., n.d. 11p.   Evans 49089

     AAS: Copy not located.

'Twas pretty Poll and honest Jack. Song.

     Philadelphia, G. Willig, 1795.   Evans 29664

     AAS: Impring [sic] assumed by Evans from

       advs.

'Twas with in a mile of Edinburgh Town. A song,

     sung by Miss Broadhurst. New York, Carr, 1796.

                              Evans 30371

     AAS: Imprint assumed by Evans from adv.

HOPKINSON, FRANCIS, 1737-1791.

The battle of the kegs. Philadelphia, 1779.

                              Evans 16305

     AAS: Adv. Pa. Evening Post, Jan. 15, 1779.

HUMMING BIRD, or collection of fashionable songs.

     Philadelphia, Henry Taylor, 1791.   Evans 23456

       AAS: Adv. in sale of Taylor's estate

       as "half finished."

HYMNS AND SPIRITUAL SONGS. In three books. I. Collected

     from the scriptures. II. Composed on divine subjects.

     III. Prepared for the Lord's supper. By I. Watts, D. D.

Hymns and spiritual songs (continued)

Boston, Kneeland and Davis, 1773.   Evans 13068

   AAS: Entry from an adv.

---------. Philadelphia, Robert Campbell, 1790.

                                           Evans 23042

   AAS: Entry from an unlocated adv.

JACKSON, WILLIAM, OF EXETER, 1730-1803.

   When first this humble roof I knew. A favourite

       song [New York, Carr, 1796] 1 leaf. Evans 30140

   AAS: This unique copy is mislaid.

   Note: Evans' entry under Sir John Burgoyne,

       1722-1792.

JENKS, STEPHEN, 1772-1856.

   Laus Deo. The New-England harmonist. Danbury,

       Conn., Douglas and Nichols [1799] 24p.

                                           Evans 35667

   AAS: This is the first part of 37707, q.v.

   [See p. 106-107 of this Bibliography]

JOCELIN, SIMEON, 1746-1823.

   The Chorister's companion. New Haven, Greens for

       Jocelyn, 1792. 120p.   Evans 24433

   AAS: A ghost arising from the old NL catalogue.

Jocelin, Simeon (continued)

    ----------. (2d Part). New Haven, Greens for

        Jocelyn, 1790. 8, 72p.   Evans 22588

        AAS: Adv. Conn. Journal, Sept. 8, 1790.

JOHNSTON, THOMAS.

    [Rules for singing, with a collection of about

        fifty tunes, for psalms and hymns, engraved

        on copper] Boston, Thomas Johnston, 1755.

        32p.   Evans 7442

        AAS: One of any of the several printings made

        to be bound at the end of psalmbooks, q.v.

THE JOVIAL SONSTER. Philadelphia, H. Kammerer,

    1793.   Evans 25675

        AAS: Imprint assumed by Evans from

        Kammerer advs.

JUHAN, ALEXANDER, 1765-1845.

    A Set of six songs, with an accompaniment for the

        pianoforte or harpsichord. Charlestown,

        Young, 1794.   Evans 27176

        AAS: See Sonneck-Upton, pp. 376-377.

KIMBALL, JACOB, 1761-1826.

    The Rural harmony...[Second edition] Boston, Isaiah

Kimball, Jacob (continued)

Thomas & Ebenezer T. Andrews, 1796.   Evans 30662

AAS: Such a 2nd ed. was adv., but no copy
has been identified.

KOTZWARA, FRANZ, 1730 (?)-1791.

The Battle of Prague. Philadelphia, Reinagle
[179?] 7p.   Evans 45773

AAS: No copy located.

When Delia on the plain appears. Composed by Kotzwara,
author of the Battle of Prague. New York,
George Gilfert, 1798. 1 leaf.   Evans 33970

AAS: The present location of the one reported
copy is unknown.

LADIES PATRIOTIC SONG. Boston, von Hagen [1799?]
2p.   Evans 33973

AAS: The one recorded copy could not be
located for reproduction.

A LARGE COLLECTION OF COTILLIONS AND COUNTRY DANCES.
Rutland, Vt., Josiah Fay, 1797.   Evans 32352

AAS: Imprint assumed by Evans from an adv.
in Rutland Herald, Aug. 21, 1797.

LAUS DEO! THE WORCESTER COLLECTION OF SACRED HARMONY.
In three parts. Containing, I. An introduction to
the grounds of musick: or, rules for learners.
II. A large number of celebrated psalm and hymn
tunes, from the most approved ancient and modern
authors; together with several new ones, never
before published: the whole suited to all metres,
usually sung in churches. III. Select anthems,
fughes, and favourites [sic] pieces of musick,
with an additional number of psalm and hymn tunes...
Boston, Isaiah Thomas & Ebenezer T. Andrews, 1800.
143, 1p.   Evans 37636

> *AAS: Also entered as 37786, q.v. [See p. 116*
> *of this Bibliography]*

----------. Part III. Worcester, Thomas, 1787.

Evans 20452

> *AAS: This is pp. 113-198 of 19752, q.v.*
> *[See p. 114-115 of this Bibliography]*

LAW, ANDREW, 1748-1821.

A Collection of hymn tunes from the most modern and
approved authors. By Andrew Law, A. M.
Cheshire, Conn., William Law [1786] 2, 36p.

Evans 19753

> *AAS: This is the first part of 17571, q.v.*
> *[See p. 117 of this Bibliography]*

Law, Andrew (continued)

--------. Cheshire, Conn., William Law,

1792.   Evans 24463

AAS: *Imprint assumed by Evans from*

copyright record.

A Collection of the best and most approved tunes and

anthems, for the promotion of psalmody. [New

Haven, Thomas and Samuel Green, 1779]

Evans 16317

AAS: *Entry apparently from an adv. in the Conn.*

Gazette for 16318.

--------. New Haven, 1781.   Evans 17201

AAS: *Assumed by Evans from the copyright.*

A Collection of the best and most approved tunes and

anthems, known to exist. Cheshire, Conn.,

William Law, 1782.   Evans 17572

AAS: *Entry apparently from an adv. for 16317*

[See second preceding item above]

The Musical magazine, being the third part of the

Art of Singing: containing a variety of

favorite pieces--a periodical publication.

By Andrew Law, A. M....Number third.

Law, Andrew (continued)

Cheshire, Conn., William Law, 1794.

16p.   Evans 27206

AAS: Evans entry was from the copyright

notice.

The Musical magazine. Containing a number of

favorite pieces European and American...

Number fifth. Philadelphia, 1799.

Evans 35719

AAS: Entry from the copyright

notice.

The Musical primer... [New Haven, Thomas and

Samuel Green, 1780]   Evans 16816

AAS: Assumed by Evans from later Conn.

eds.

The Rudiments of music, or a short and easy treatise

on the rules of psalmody. To which are

annexed, a number of plain tunes and chants.

By Andrew Law, A. M....Cheshire, Conn.,

William Law, 1792.   Evans 24465

Law, Andrew (continued)

> *AAS: Entry from the copyright notice of*
> *Aug. 28, apparently corrected by that*
> *of Sept. 18 for item reproduced as*
> *24466 [See p. 119 of this Bibliography]*

----------. Cheshire, Conn., William Law,
   1794. 2, 16p.   Evans 27207
   AAS: No such ed. has been located.

Select harmony: containing, in a plain and
   concise manner, the rules for singing,
   together with a complete collection of
   psalm tunes, hymns and anthems. An
   original work, by A. Law. Baltimore,
   1786. 8, 100p.   Evans 19754
   AAS: Origin of this entry unknown.

----------. Cheshire, Conn., William Law,
   1792.   Evans 24467
   AAS: Evans assumed the imprint from the
   copyright; copies described as this ed.
   have no imprint.

Law, Andrew (continued)

A Select number of plain tunes adapted to congregational worship. Boston, John

Hodgson, 1772.   Evans 12427

AAS: This music is commonly bound at the
back of psalm books, but no copy located
has this imprint.

----------. By Andrew Law, A. M. [Cheshire,
Conn., William Law, 1794] 16p.   Evans 27208

AAS: No such ed. located.

LINLEY, THOMAS, 1733-1795.

Still the lark repose. New York, George Gilfert,
1798.   Evans 34002

AAS: Imprint assumed by Evans from advs.
"Just published" by George Gilfert.

Note: From Linley's The Spanish Rivals.

LITTLE, WILLIAM, fl. 1798.

The Easy instructor; or, a new method of teaching
sacred harmony, containing the rudiments of
music on an improved plan wherein the naming

Little, William (continued)

and timing the notes are familiarized to the
weakest capacity. Likewise, an essay on
Composition with directions to enable any
person with a tolerable voice to take the
air of any piece of music at sight and
perform it by word without singing it by
note. Also the transposition of Mi,
rendering all the keys in music as easy
as the natural key whereby the errors in
composition and the press may be known.
Together with a choice collection
of psalm tunes and anthems from the most
celebrated authors in Europe with a number
composed in Europe & America entirely new,
suited to all the metres sung in the different
churches in the United States. Published for
the use of singing societies in general, but
more particularly for those who have not the
advantage of an instructor. n.p., [1798]

Evans 34004

Little, William (continued)

> *AAS: Date assumed by Evans from copyright*
> *notice. Apparently not published until*
> *1802. See Musical Quarterly, Jan. 1937,*
> *pp. 89-97.*

> *Note: See Sonneck-Upton, p. 117.*

LITTLE ROBIN RED BREAST; a collection of pretty
songs, for children, entirely new. Worcester,
Mass., Isaiah Thomas, 1799.   Evans 35735

> *AAS: Evans assumed the imprint from an*
> *adv. in 35482; apparently a remainder*
> *of 20461.*

LYON, JAMES, 1735-1794.

Friendship: anthem. Philadelphia, M'Culloch,
1788.   Evans 21578

> *AAS: "Lately published," Federal Gazette,*
> *Apr. 8, 1788.*

> *Note: See Sonneck-Upton, p. 149-150.*

Lyon, James (continued)

Urania: or, a choice collection of psalm tunes,

anthems and hymns, from the most approved

authors, with some entirely new. In two,

three and four parts. The whole peculiarly

adapted to the use of churches, and private

families. To which are prefix'd the

plainest and most necessary rules of

psalmody. By James Lyon, A. M. A new

[second] edition. [Philadelphia, W. and

T. Bradford, 1767] 2, 2, xxii,198p.

Evans 10666

AAS: Adv. in Pa. Journal, Nov. 19,

1767. The copy described and located

by Evans was 8908. [See p. 125 of this

Bibliography]

MISS ASHMORE'S CHOICE COLLECTION OF SONGS, such as are
sung at the theatres and public gardens in London
and Dublin. To which are prefix'd the songs of
the Padlock, Lionel and Clarissa, and many other
opera songs, never before published. Containing
in the whole, near three hundred: in which are
many originals, and a variety of other songs,
by different composers, which upon comparing,
will be justly allowed (by every person) to be
the best of the kind yet published, and may well
be termed "The beauties of all the songs
selected." New York, William Bailey, 1774.

Evans 13124

‒‒‒‒‒‒‒‒‒. The New song book being Miss Ashmore's
favorite collection of songs, as sung in the
theatres and public gardens in London and Dublin.
To which are prefix'd the songs of the Padlock,
Lionel and Clarissa, and many other opera songs,
never before published. Containing in the whole,
near three hundred: in which are many originals, and
a variety of other songs, by different composers,
which upon comparing, will be justly allowed (by

Miss Ashmore's choice collection of songs (continued)

every person) to be the best of the kind yet

published, and may well be termed "The beauties

of all the songs selected." Boston, William

McAlpine, 1771.   Evans 11969

    AAS: Adv. Boston Evening Post, Nov. 25,

      1771.

    Note: Evans' entry under Miss ____ Ashmore.

THE MOCKING-BIRD: a collection of songs, a number of

which are set to music. Philadelphia, M'Culloch,

1793.   Evans 25830

    AAS: Imprint assumed by Evans from adv.

    "Has also for sale" in National Gazette,

    Mar. 30, 1793.

A NEW AND SELECT COLLECTION OF THE BEST ENGLISH, SCOTS

AND IRISH SONGS, catches, duets, and cantatas, in

the true spirit and taste of the three different

nations--Being an attempt to improve upon others

in the true spirit of social mirth and good fellow-

ship--With a collection of the various sentiments

and hob-nobs in vogue. New York, James Rivington,

1780.   Evans 16874

A New and select collection (continued)

> *AAS: "This day published," Royal Gazette,*
>
> *June 17, 1780.*

NEW INSTRUCTIONS FOR THE GERMAN FLUTE. Containing the easiest and most modern methods for learners to play; to which are added a favourite collection of minuets, marches, songs, tunes, duets, etc. Also, the method of double tongueing, and a compleat scale and description of a new invented German flute, with the additional keys, such as played on by two eminent masters, Florio and Tacet. New York, James Rivington, 1778.

Evans 15925

> *AAS: Adv. Rivington's Royal Gazette,*
>
> *Aug. 1778.*

A NEW SONG, TO THE TUNE OF HEARTS OF OAK. Come join hand in hand, brave Americans all...The Liberty song. In freedom we're born...[with music] [Boston, Mein and Fleeming, 1768] Broadside.

Evans 10881

A New song, to the tune of Hearts of Oak (continued)

> *AAS: Adv. Boston Chronicle, Sept. 5,*
>
> *1768.*
>
> *Note: See Sonneck-Upton, p. 227-228.*
>
> *Evans' entry under John Dickinson,*
>
> *1732-1808.*

A NEW VERSION OF THE PSALMS OF DAVID, fitted to the
tunes used in churches. By N. Brady...and
N. Tate, ...Boston, D. & J. Kneeland for T.
Leverett, 1762. 276, 84, xiv p.   Evans 9068

> *AAS: No copy with this variety of imprint*
>
> *located; there are several varieties not*
>
> *listed by Evans. For the text see 9069*
>
> *[See p. 143 of this Bibliography]*
>
> *Note: Evans' entry is Biblia. Old Testament.*
>
> *Psalms.*

----------. By N. Brady, D. D. Late Chaplain in
Ordinary, and N. Tate, Esq. late poet-laureat,
to the King of England. Boston, D. & J. Kneeland
for Thomas Leverett, 1763. 344p.   Evans 9345

> *AAS: The pagination given by Evans would*
>
> *indicate a distinct edition, but a census*

A New version of the psalms of David (continued)

> *of copies with this imprint shows only*
>
> *proprietary issues of 9344 [See p. 143*
>
> *of this Bibliography]*
>
> Note: *Evans' entry is Biblia. Old Testa-*
>
> *ment. Psalms.*

----------. Boston, Kneeland & Davis for Nicholas
Bowes, 1773.   Evans 12673

> AAS: *No copy of this imprint variant*
>
> *could be located.*
>
> Note: *Evans' entry under Biblia. Old*
>
> *Testament. Psalms.*

NICHOLS, THOMAS, fl. 1791.

> Hymns and divine songs. Providence, Wheeler,
> 1791. 200p.   Evans 23632
>
> AAS: *The origin of this entry is unknown.*

THE NIGHTINGALE, or Songster's companion. Consisting of
an elegant and polite selection of the most
approved ancient and modern songs. Philadelphia,
W. Woodhouse, 1791.   Evans 23634

The Nightingale (continued)

>*AAS: Evans' entry is from an adv. in*
>
>*23440: "Books published by W. Woodhouse."*

OLNEY HYMNS, in three books. Book I. On select

texts of scripture. Book II. On occasional

subjects. Book III. On the progress and

changes of the scriptural life. New York,

1787.   Evans 20588

>*AAS: Apparently a ghost of a later ed.*
>
>*Note: Evans' entry under John Newton,*
>
>*1725-1807.*

PAISIELLO, GIOVANNI, 1740-1816.

Recitativo e rondo. Philadelphia, Trisobio

[1797] 8p.   Evans 48212

>*AAS: Not located, 1968.*

THE PATRIOTIC SONGSTER FOR JULY 4TH, 1798. (Addressed to

the volunteers of Baltimore.) Containing all the late

patriotic songs that have been published. Baltimore,

S. Sower for Thomas, Andrews, and Butler, 1798.

                                               Evans 34314

>*AAS: Imprint assumed by Evans from adv.*

THE PHILADELPHIA POCKET COMPANION FOR THE GERMAN FLUTE

OR VIOLIN, being a collection of the most

favourite songs, etc.--Selected from the European

The Philadelphia pocket companion (continued)

> publications of the last twelve months.
>
> Philadelphia, Carr [1794]   Evans 27516
>
> > *AAS: "This day is published," Dunlap's*
> >
> > *Daily Amer. Adv., Apr. 28, 1794.*

PHILE, PHILIP, c1734-1793.

> New federal song [Hail Columbia]; written to
> the tune of the "President's March" by
> J. Hopkinson, esq. and sung by Mr. Fox,
> at the New Theatre with great applause,
> ornamented with a very elegant portrait
> of the President. Philadelphia, Carr,
> 1798.   Evans 33897
>
> > *AAS: No copy of this ed. located.*

> The Truly federal song Hail Columbia, (Death or
> liberty) to the tune of the President's
> March, adapted for the voice, piano forte,
> violin, guitar, clarinet, hautboy, German
> flute, or any other instrument. Boston,
> von Hagen, 1798.   Evans 33898

Phile, Philip (continued)

> *AAS: No copy located.*
>
> *Note: Evans has entered this and the*
> *preceding item under Joseph Hopkinson,*
> *1770-1843.*

THE PLEASING SONGSTER; or festive companion: containing a...collection of songs...calculated
for the entertainment of the social mind...
Philadelphia, 1795.   Evans 29328

> *AAS: Entry apparently from an adv.*

PLEYEL, IGNAZ JOSEPH, 1757-1831.

Twelve duets for 2 clarinets. Adapted from
Pleyel by Mr. Priest of the New Theatre,
Philadelphia. New York, James Harrison,
1794.   Evans 27528

> *AAS: Imprint assumed by Evans from*
> *Harrison's advs. "for sale."*

A POCKET BOOK FOR THE GERMAN FLUTE, containing necessary
directions and remarks on that instrument, with an
agreeable variety of celebrated airs, duets and

A Pocket book for the German flute (continued)

songs, collected from the favourite operas,
entertainments, etc. composed by the most
admired authors, in two parts. New York,
James Rivington, 1778.   Evans 16014

AAS: *Adv. Rivington's Royal Gazette,
July 1778.*

A POCKET BOOK FOR THE GUITAR, with directions
whereby every lady and gentleman may become
their own tunes. New York, James Rivington,
1778.   Evans 16015

AAS: *Adv. in Rivington's Royal Gazette,
July 1778.*

A POCKET BOOK FOR THE VIOLIN. Embellished with curious
remarks and excellent examples by the late
celebrated Signor Geminiani, etc. To which are
added a pleasing variety of songs, duets and
airs, judiciously selected from the most favorite
operas, entertainments, etc. New York, James
Rivington, 1778.   Evans 16016

AAS: *Adv. in Rivington's Royal Gazette,
July 1778.*

A PRESENT TO CHILDREN. Consisting of several new

divine hymns and moral songs. Norwich,

Trumbull, 1791.   Evans 23715

AAS: "Just published, at this office,"

Norwich Packet, June 6, 1791.

THE PSALMS OF DAVID, imitated in the language of the

New-Testament: and applied to the Christian state

and worship. By I. Watts, D. D. The twenty-fifth

edition. With hymns and spiritual songs. Boston,

John Perkins, 1767. 304, 312, 22p.   Evans 10560

AAS: No copy located with this imprint variant.

Note: Evans' entry is Biblia. Old Testament. Psalms.

READ, DANIEL, 1757-1836.

The American Singing-Book, or a new and easy guide

to the art of psalmody. Designed for the

use of singing schools in America. The

second edition. New Haven, Daniel Read

[1788]   Evans 21416

AAS: Entry from an adv. in the Conn. Journal,

Jan. 2, 1788, but perhaps for the remainder

of 19213 [see p. 159 of this Bibliography]

Read, Daniel (continued)

--------. Containing in a plain and familiar
manner, the rules of psalmody, together
with a number of psalm tunes, &c. To which
is added a Supplement, containing twenty-
five approved psalm tunes, from different
authors. By Daniel Read, philomusico.
The fifth edition. New Haven [T. and S.
Green] 1795.   Evans 29388
AAS: No copy of a 5th ed. located.
Evans constructed his entry from advs.
which give no clue as to ed., date,
or imprint.

An Introduction to psalmody; or, the child's
instructor in vocal music. Containing a
series of familiar dialogues, under the
following heads, viz. Psalmody in general,
stave, musical letters and cliffs, an
exercise for the bass, an exercise for the
tenor or treble, an exercise for the counter,
tones, semitones, flats, sharps and natural,

Read, Daniel (continued)

solfaing, transposition, &c. the several

notes and rests, and their proportion,

the several moods of time, several other

characters used in music, key notes, &c.

pitching tunes &c. graces. (Illustrated

with copper-plates). New Haven [T. and

S. Green] 1790.   Evans 22829

AAS: "Just published," Conn. Journal,

Mar. 17, 1790 [See following item]

----------. New Haven [T. and S. Green] 1795.

Evans 29392

AAS: Apparently a ghost of 22829, Evans'

entry being from advs. which gave no

clue as to imprint [See preceding item]

REEVE, WILLIAM, 1757-1815.

The Desponding Negro. By Collins. Philadelphia,

Carr, 1793 [From The Evening Brush]

Evans 25313

AAS: See Sonneck-Upton (1945), p. 106.

Note: Evans' entry under William Collins,

1721-1759.

Reeve, William (continued)

Our country is our ship. A new patriotic

song. Boston, von Hagen, 1798.   Evans 34287

AAS: Imprint assumed by Evans from

von Hagen's adv.

When seated with Sal. A favorite sea song sung

by Mr. Harwood in the musical drama of

The Purse, or benevolent tar, Philadelphia,

R. Shaw, 1795.   Evans 28504

AAS: Imprint assumed by Evans from

Shaw's advs.

REINAGLE, ALEXANDER, 1756-1809.

A Collection of favorite songs; divided into two

books. Each containing most of the airs in

the Poor Soldier, Rosina, &c. and the

principal songs sung at Vauxhall. The basses

rendered easy and natural for the piano forte

or harpsichord. Philadelphia, Rice, Poyntell,

Dobson, and Young, 1788.   Evans 21420

AAS: The only copy recorded cannot be

located.

Reinagle, Alexander (continued)

[The Music of the historical play of Columbus.

Composed and adapted for the piano forte,

flute or violin. Philadelphia, 1799]

Evans 36194

AAS: See Sonneck-Upton, p. 80.

RUSS, D.

The Urian harmony. Philadelphia, M'Culloch,

1791. 76p. Evans 23749

AAS: Adv. in Carlisle Gazette,

Aug. 3, 1791.

SALIMENT, GEORGE EDWARD.

Minuetto with eight variations for the flute and

violoncello. New York, Carr [1796]

Evans 31154

AAS: No separate printing known.

SELBY, WILLIAM, 1738-1798.

Apollo and the muses musical compositions.

By William Selby, organist of the Stone

Selby, William (continued)

Chapel, in Boston, Massachusetts.

Boston, William Selby, 1790.   Evans 22881

AAS: Publication proposed in Columbian

Centinel, June 16, 1790.

Two anthems, for three and four voices.

Composed in an easy and familiar stile

[sic], adapted for the use of singing

societies. By William Selby, professor

of music in Boston, New England.

Boston [1790?]   Evans 22882

AAS: Sonneck-Upton, p. 28. Not now to

be located.

Note: "Presumably from Apollo and the muse's

musical compositions..."--Sonneck-Upton,

p. 28 [See preceding item]

A SELECTION OF SACRED HARMONY: containing an explanation

of the gamut and other characters used in music:

and a collection of the most celebrated church

tunes now in use. Philadelphia, John M'Culloch,

1788.   Evans 21453

A Selection of sacred harmony (continued)

> *AAS: "Just published," Federal Gazette,*
>
> *Mar. 15, 1788.*

SHAW, ROBERT, fl. 1794.

> The Gentleman's amusement, or companion for the
> German flute. Arranged and adapted by
> R. Shaw. No. 6[-7] Philadelphia, Carr
> [1796] 44-76p. Evans 31181
> *AAS: A part of 27694 [see p. 171 ff.*
>
> *of this Bibliography]*

> The Gentleman's amusement. A selection of solos,
> duetts, overtures, arranged as duetts,
> rondos & romances from the works of
> Pleyel, Haydn, Mozart, Hoffmeister,
> Fischer, Shield, Dr. Arnold, Saliment, etc.
> Several airs, dances, marches, minuetts &
> Scotch reels. Sixty four select songs from
> the favorite operas & Dibdins latest
> publications with some general remarks for

Shaw, Robert (continued)

playing the flute with taste and expression and a
dictionary of musical terms. The whole selected,
arranged & adapted for one, two & three German
flutes or violins by R. Shaw of the Theatre Charlestown and B. Carr. Forming the cheapest, and most
complete collection ever offered to the public; the
contents being selected from the best authors, and
what, purchased in any other manner would amount to
more than three times the price. Philadelphia,
Carr [1796] 77p.   Evans 31182

   AAS: This is reproduced as 27694, q.v.

   [See p. 171 ff. of this Bibliography]

SHIELD, WILLIAM, 1748-1829.

   Fame, let thy trumpet sound. A song. Philadelphia,
   Town, 1779.   Evans 16523

   AAS: Hildeburn 3877, from an adv.

   The Morning is up. A favorite hunting song.
   New York, Hewitt, 1798.   Evans 34540

   AAS: No copy of a separate printing located.

SICARD, STEPHEN, fl. 1788.

The New Constitution march, and federal minuet.
Composed by Mr. Sicard, adapted to the
pianoforte, violin and German flute, &c.
Philadelphia, 1788.   Evans 21462
AAS: Adv. in Philadelphia newspapers,
Oct. 1788.

SMITH, JOSHUA, d. 1795.

Divine hymns, or spiritual songs for the use of
religious assemblies and private
Christians. The third edition corrected.
With an addition of thirty-two hymns.
Exeter, N. H., Henry Ranlet, 1791. Evans 23768
AAS: Adv. in Exeter, N. H. Gazette,
Oct. 14, 1791.

Divine hymns or spiritual songs for the use of
religious assemblies and private Christians.
By Joshua Smith and others. Corrected and
enlarged. Portsmouth, John Melcher, 1791.

Evans 23769

AAS: "Just published, by the printer hereof,"
N. H. Gazette, Oct. 16, 1791.

Smith, Joshua (continued)

 ---------. ...second Norwich edition. Norwich,

  Hubbard, 1795.   Evans 29529

  AAS: "Just published, and ready for sale by the

  printers hereof," Weekly Register, Feb. 10, 1795.

 ---------. Portsmouth, Melcher, 1795. Evans 29530

  AAS: Imprint assumed by Evans from adv. "Also

  lately published, and for sale," N. H. Gazette,

  Sept. 29, 1795.

 ---------. The sixth edition...Poughkeepsie,

  Nathan Douglas, 1796.   Evans 31206

  AAS: Imprint assumed by Evans from advs.

 ---------. ...Seventh Exeter edition. Exeter,

  Ranlet, 1797.   Evans 32848

  AAS: "Just published, and for sale at this

  office," N. H. Spy, Feb. 25, 1797.

A SONG BOOK. Containing upwards of forty of the most

 modern and elegant songs now in vogue. Amherst,

 N. H., Samuel Preston, 1798.   Evans 34571

  AAS: Title and imprint assumed by Evans from

  adv. "Just published, by Samuel Preston," in

  Village Messenger, Jan. 20, 1798.

[SONGS FOR THE AMUSEMENT OF CHILDREN] Middletown,

    M. H. Woodward, 1790.   Evans 22894

        AAS: Title constructed by Evans from adv.

           for "Song books just published" in

           Middlesex Gazette, 1790, passim.

THE SONGSTER'S MAGAZINE, containing a choice collection

    of the most approved songs in the English language.

    Philadelphia, 1795.   Evans 29542

        AAS: Imprint assumed by Evans from advs.

STICKNEY, JOHN, 1744-1827.

    The Gentleman and ladies musical companion;

        containing a variety of excellent anthems,

        psalm tunes &c. Collected from the best

        authors; with a short explanation of the rules

        of music. The whole corrected and rendered

        plain...A new edition. Newburyport, Daniel

        Bayley, 1783.   Evans 18197

        AAS: Adv. Salem Gazette, Dec. 4, 1783.

          There is a fragment of what is apparently a

          copy of this ed. in private hands.

STORACE, STEPHEN, 1763-1796.

    The Favorite songs from the last new comic opera,

        called the Pirates. Philadelphia, Carr

        [1793] 16p.   Evans 25307

282

Contents   [From *Sonneck-Upton*, p. 401)

AAS: The only copy recorded was in the

collection of Harry F. Bruning of

San Francisco.

SWAN, TIMOTHY, 1758-1842.

The Federal harmony, in three parts. Part I.

An introduction to the art of singing.

Part II. A large collection of psalm tunes.

Part III. Select anthems, &c. Compiled

for the use of schools and singing societies...

Boston, John Norman, 1785.   Evans 19268

AAS: No 1785 ed. has been found.

---------. The Federal harmony: containing I.

An introduction to the grounds of music.

II. A valuable collection of sacred music

Swan, Timothy (continued)

consisting of Psalm tunes, anthems, fuges, chorusses, and other favorite pieces of music; selected from the most approved European and American authors: together with a number of Psalm tunes never before published in America: the eighth edition. Compiled for the use of schools and singing societies. Boston, William Norman, 1794. 100p.

Evans 27762

AAS: Imprint assumed by Evans from adv.

THE SYREN; or, musical bouquet. Being a new selection of favourite songs sung at the various places of amusement in Great-Britain, Ireland and America. New York, Berry and Rogers, 1792.   Evans 24839

AAS: Adv., "Just published" in 24146.

Note: 24146 is Jacques Pierre Brissot de Warville's [1754-1793] New Travels in the United States of America. Performed in 1788...Translated from the French. New York, T. & J. Swords for Berry and Rogers, 1792.

TANS'UR, WILLIAM, 1706-1783.

The Royal melody complete, or the new harmony
of Zion. Boston, W. McAlpine & Daniel
Bayley, 1761?   Evans 9021

*AAS: Evans entry from an adv., but Boston
News-Letter, June 11, 1761, says "Lately imported*

TAYLOR, RAYNOR, 1747-1829.

An Anthem, for public or private worship.
Composed by Raynor Taylor, professor of
music, Philadelphia, late organist of
Annapolis. Philadelphia, Carr, 1794.
6p.   Evans 27783

*AAS: Adv. Baltimore Gazette, Dec. 26,
1793.*

Divertimenti, or familiar lessons for the piano-
forte, to which is prefixed a ground for
the improvement of young practitioners.
Philadelphia, Carr, 1797.   Evans 32910

*AAS: Adv. in Philadelphia newspapers
in May 1797.*

Taylor, Raynor (continued)

Rustic festivity. A new song. Philadelphia,

    B. Carr [1798]   Evans 34633

    AAS: Adv. as "republished" in Feb., 1798.

      Perhaps identical with 29610 [See p. 203

      of this Bibliography]

Summer, a pastorale song. Philadelphia,

    B. Carr, 1798.   Evans 34634

    AAS: Adv. as "republished," Feb. 1798.

THREE NEW MARCHES. Philadelphia, G. Willig [1798?]

    2p.   Evans 34660

Contents

        Buonaparte's march, called the Pyrenees

          [C. Kalkbrenner?]

        Buonaparte's march, called the Mantuane

          [C. Kalkbrenner?]

        Prussian march

    AAS: No copy located.

    Note: Sonneck-Upton, p. 250, indicates copies

      at the Library of Congress and in the private

      collection of Lester S. Levy, Baltimore.

TUFTS, JOHN, 1689-1752.

A Collection of thirty-eight psalm tunes in
    three parts, treble, medius, and base
    [sic] In the easy method of singing by
    letters instead of notes contrived by
    Rev. Mr. Tufts. Printed from copper
    plate. Boston, 1723.   Evans 2488
    AAS: See Music Lib. Assoc., Notes,
        XI, 47.

Introduction to the singing of psalm-tunes,
    with a collection of tunes, in three parts.
    Boston, B. Green?, 1715.   Evans 1785
    AAS: See Music Lib. Assoc., Notes,
        XI, 46.

A Very plain and easy introduction to the art of
    singing psalm tunes; with the cantus or trebles
    of twenty-eight psalm tunes, contrived in such
    a manner, as that the learner may attain the
    skill of singing them, with the greatest ease
    and speed imaginable. Boston, J. F.[ranklin]

Tufts, John (continued)

for S. Gerrish, 1721. 4, 12p. Evans 2297

AAS: Brinley 5885; bought by Forest.

See Music Lib. Assoc., Notes, XI, 46-47.

URANIAN SOCIETY, PHILADELPHIA.

Introductory lessons...for promoting the knowledge

of vocal music. Philadelphia, Aitken, 1786.

Evans 19920

AAS: Entry from an adv., perhaps for 19194

[See p. 208 of this Bibliography]

THE VENDUE, on six month's credit. A new song.

By the author of Simon Sad. Poughkeepsie,

Nicholas Power, 1796. Evans 31484

AAS: "Just published, and for sale by N.

Power, and the Posts," Poughkeepsie

Journal, Oct. 26, 1796.

VICTOR, H. B.

The Compleat instructor for the violin, flute, guitar,

and harpsichord. Containing the easiest and

best method for learners to obtain a proficiency;

with some useful directions, lessons, graces,

etc....To which is added, a favourite collection

of airs, marches, minuets, etc. now in vogue...

Also, a dictionary explaining such Greek,

Latin, Italian and French words, as

Victor, H. B. (continued)

> generally occur in music. Philadelphia,
>
> J. Norman, 1778. Evans 16152
>
> *AAS: "Just published," Pa. Ledger,*
>
> *Apr. 4, 1778.*

THE VILLAGE HARMONY, or youth's assistant to sacred

> musick. Containing a concise introduction to
> the grounds of musick, with such a collection of
> the most approved psalm tunes, anthems, and other
> pieces, in three and four parts, as are most
> suitable for divine worship. Designed for the
> use of schools and singing societies. Exeter,

H. Ranlet, 1795. 150p. Evans 29793

> *AAS: Offered C. W. Unger, List 980,*
>
> *Item 49.*
>
> *Note: Seventeen editions were printed before*
>
> *the year 1820.--Evans, v. 10, p. 237.*

---------. The third edition. Exeter, H. Ranlet,

1797. Evans 33123

> *AAS: Assumed by Evans from the sequence*
>
> *of editions.*

THE VILLAGE HOLIDAY. Song. New York, G. Gilfert,

   1795.   Evans 29794

       AAS: See Sonneck-Upton, p. 443.

THE VOCAL CHARMER. Philadelphia, Spotswood, 1793.

                                    Evans 26410

       AAS: A ghost of 22400 resulting from Evans'
       misreading of the adv. in Dunlap's Am.
       Daily Advertiser, Jan. 19, 1793.

       Note: 22400 is The Chairmen: being a select
       collection of English, Scotch and American
       songs, including the modern; with a
       selection of favourite toasts and senti-
       ments. Philadelphia, Spotswood, 1790.
       This item contained no printed music.
       Sonneck-Upton, p. 445, remarks that "The
       vocal charmer" probably contained no music,
       but that no copy has been located.

THE VOCAL MUSE; or ladies songster: containing a

   collection of elegant songs, selected from British

   and American authors [Philadelphia] T. Dobson,

The Vocal muse (continued)

W. Young, and H. Kammerer, 1792.   Evans 24978

    AAS: Entry from adv. "just published" in

      Dunlap's Am. Daily Adv., Oct. 5,

      1792.

THE VOCAL REMEMBRANCER: being a choice selection of
the most admired songs, including the modern.
Philadelphia, Spotswood, 1793.   Evans 26411

    AAS: Imprint assumed by Evans from Spotswood's

      advs. for "new books."

    Note: Sonneck-Upton, p. 445-446, notes that

      the 1790 ed. of this title contained poetry

      only but not music. Therefore, if this

      1793 ed. was ever published, it is unlikely

      that it included musical notation.

[THE VOLUNTEER SONGSTER, or vocal remembrances: for 1799.
Containing the newest and most approved songs
now extant...Baltimore, Thomas Dobbin? 1799]

                    Evans 36662

    AAS: Imprint assumed by Minick from adv.

    "For sale" in Telegraphe, Jan. 29, 1799.

WATTS, ISAAC, 1674-1748.

Divine and moral songs for the use of children.

Bennington, Vt., Haswell and Russell, 1790.

Evans 23040

AAS: "Just published," Vt. Gazette,

Apr. 5, 1790.

Divine songs for children. A new and compleat

edition. Charlestown, John W. Allen, 1787.

Evans 20857

AAS: From a bookseller's adv. for the

London ed.

THE WAVES WERE HUSH'D, THE SKY SERENE. Song. New

York, G. Gilfert, 1798.   Evans 34967

AAS: Title and imprint assumed by Evans

from Gilfert's adv.

WRIGHT, THOMAS, 1763-1829.

Peter Pindar's new gypsy song. Philadelphia,

B. Carr, 1793.   Evans 26495

AAS: Adv. in Dec. newspapers.

YANKEE DOODLE. A new federal song...Philadelphia,

1798. Evans 35063

AAS: Evans' entry from an adv., possibly

for 33902 [See p. 150 of this

Bibliography]

PART THREE

BIOGRAPHICAL SKETCHES

These short biographies do not pretend to
represent a complete account of the life and
activities of the composers, musicians, editors,
and compilers concerned. But they do place the
musicians in a historical context, provide some
basic facts of their lives, and lend some idea of
the types of music with which they are associated.
Biographies of J. C. Bach, Mozart, Handel,
Boccherini, Gluck, and the like abound in numerous
basic sources of musical biography, and it seemed
unnecessary to include them here. In such instances,
references are made to Grove's *Dictionary of
Music and Musicians* or to *Baker's Biographical
Dictionary of Musicians* when *Grove* lacked a
biography, both readily accessible in even the
smaller libraries. Similarly, referrals to
standard reference works are made for persons whose
works and activities were essentially non-musical,

e.g. Colley Cibber, Timothy Dwight, etc. In a very few cases, a particular composer has so completely slipped into the ranks of obscurity that any meaningful biographical sketch proved virtually impossible.

ABRAMS, HARRIET.

Born, ?, 1760.

Died, ?, ?

Soprano, composer, and pupil of Thomas Augustine Arne. She made her first public appearance at the Drury Lane Theatre in Arne's "May Day," October 28, 1775. She and her sister, Theodosia, appeared as vocalists in many London concerts before retiring to private life. Harriet was the composer of several songs, notably "Crazy Jane" and "The Orphan's Prayer." Both sisters lived to an advanced age, Theodosia dying in her 70s sometime after 1834.

ADGATE, ANDREW.

Born, Philadelphia, c1750.

Died, Philadelphia, September 30, 1793.

Church organist and choral conductor. In 1784, Adgate helped organize an Institution for the Encouragement of Church Music, and the following year founded in Philadelphia a "Free School for Spreading the Knowledge of Vocal Music." This latter organization was later restructured as the Uranian Academy (1787), the purpose being to encourage musical study as a necessary part of a general education. On May 4, 1786, he presented a "Grand Concert of Sacred Music," performing works by Handel and Billings with a 230-voice choir and a 50-piece orchestra. Adgate's principal compilations include Select Psalms and Hymns (1787), Rudiments of Music (1788), and Selection of Sacred Harmony (first ed., 1788). He died of yellow fever in Philadelphia in 1793.

AITKEN, JOHN.

Born, Dalkeith, Scotland, probably in 1745. Died, Philadelphia, September 8, 1831. Composer, music engraver and publisher, and metalsmith. Aitken arrived in Philadelphia

sometime prior to 1785, and was the first to
engrave music in America from pre-cast metal
punches (1787). As skillful engravers
arrived from Europe, however, he was forced
to retire, and after 1811 appears to have
returned to metalsmithing. He died in
Philadelphia in 1831 at the age of 86.

ARNE, MICHAEL.

Born, London, 1741.

Died, London, January 14, 1786.

The son of Thomas Augustine Arne, Michael
received his musical education from his
father, and developed skill both as a
composer and harpsichordist. His best work
is generally considered Cymon (1767), based
on David Garrick's dramatic romance of the
same title. Shortly afterward, he abandoned
his musical activities and engaged in chemical
research, attempting the discovery of the
philosopher's stone. This endeavor proved
financially unprofitable, and he returned to
composing the music for several dramatic
works, some adaptations of the works of

Shakespeare. Of the great quantities of music he wrote for the stage, very little has survived to this day.

ARNE, THOMAS AUGUSTINE.

Born, London, March 12, 1710.

Died, London, March 5, 1778.

His father's wishes to the contrary, Arne was forced to develop his early musical interests in secret. His sister was an accomplished vocalist, and he supervised the production of numerous works for her. In 1738, he was commissioned to write the music for John Milton's Comus. Two years later saw the production of his masque, Alfred; the finale of this work is known through the patriotic air, Rule Britannia. Arne is credited with having introduced the female voice into the oratorio chorus, an innovation found in his production of Judith (1773). His works include several masques and operas, incidental songs, much of it based on the verses of Shakespeare, and many glees, catches, and other shorter vocal forms.

ARNOLD, SAMUEL.

Born, London, August 10, 1740.

Died, London, October 22, 1802.

English composer and editor of the works of
Handel. Educated at the Chapel Royal,
Arnold in 1765 composed for Covent Garden
his <u>Maid of the Mill</u>, the first of a long
series of compilations from the works of
other composers combined with sufficient
originality to win for him the distinction
of an operatic composer. In 1777, he
became music director of the Theatre Royal
in Haymarket, and in 1783 was made composer
to the court of George III. Between 1765
and his death in 1802, Arnold composed
the music for nearly 100 musical productions,
including operas, farces, pantomimes,
and oratorios, and also published numerous
sonatas and symphonies. His chief fame,
however, rests on his edition of the works
of Handel, the earliest attempt to publish
an edition of the collected works of a
single composer.

ATTWOOD, THOMAS.

> Born, London, November 23, 1765.
>
> Died, Chelsea, March 24, 1838.
>
> English organist and composer.
>
> *See Baker, p. 55-56.*

ATWELL, THOMAS H.

> Little-known American composer and compiler
> of sacred music. Flourished c1794.

BABCOCK, SAMUEL.

> Flourished, c1795.
>
> Babcock is known chiefly through his collection
> of church music, The Middlesex Harmony
> (1795, with second ed. in 1803). From the
> prefaces to these two editions, we learn
> that he was a resident of Watertown, Mass.
> and that, regarding his views on the proper
> function of sacred music, he belonged to the
> anti-Billings faction of composers, preferring
> simple chordal compositional techniques to
> the imitative fuguing tunes which he felt
> "make a jargon of the words." His four
> anthems, the first three appearing in the first

edition of <u>The Middlesex Harmony</u> and the last in the second edition, are entitled, "Comfort ye, my people," "Lord, thou hast been our dwelling place," "O come, let us sing unto the Lord," and "Remember now thy Creator."

BACH, JOHANN CHRISTIAN.

Born, Leipzig, September 5, 1735.

Died, London, January 1, 1782.

Youngest son of Johann Sebastian Bach and Anna Magdalena Bach. *See Grove, v. 1, p. 329-331.*

BARNARD, JOHN.

Born, Boston, November 6, 1681.

Died, Marblehead, Mass., January 24, 1770.

Congregational clergyman. Graduated from Harvard College in 1700 and entered the ministry in 1707 as chaplain to a Massachusetts army regiment. After travelling to London, he returned to New England in 1710, and in 1714 was nominated, along with Edward Holyoke, as candidate for the church at Marblehead. Unable to decide upon the proper candidate,

the congregation split and Barnard became
minister of the original church. In 1737,
he was largely responsible for the appointment
of Edward Holyoke to the presidency of
Harvard College. John Barnard published
more than twenty sermons, three volumes
of religious dogma (1725), and A New
Version of the Psalms of David (1752).
In 1770, Barnard died in Marblehead at
the age of 89.

BARTHELEMON, FRANCOIS HIPPOLITE.

Born, Bourdeaux, France, 1741.

Died, London, 1808.

Violinist and composer. After residing some
time in Paris, he went to England in 1765,
where he produced a serious opera, Pelopida,
for the king's theatre. It was there that
he met David Garrick, and Barthelemon set one
of Garrick's poems, The Country Girl, to
music. The success of this short song was so
great that Garrick encouraged him to set to
music the operatic farce, A Peep Behind the

Curtain; this work received 108 performances in a single year. His works also include a setting of General Burgoyne's Maid of the Oaks (Drury Lane, 1774). Later, Barthelemon and his family moved to Dublin, but soon returned to London where he died in 1808. A noted violinist, he was particularly admired for his interpretations of the works of Corelli.

BAYLEY, DANIEL.

Born, West Newbury, Mass. (?), 1725 (?).

Died, ?, February 22, 1799.

Organist and publisher of music. Living across from St. Paul's Church in West Newbury, Bayley established a printing and engraving business around 1770. He also taught music and was organist in the church over which Bishop Edward Bass had been rector since 1752. Daniel Bayley's organ is said to have been the first pipe organ introduced into the United States, and had been imported by Thomas Brattle of Boston. Bayley's first

book was A New and Complete Introduction to
the Grounds of Music (1764), the second
part taken from William Tans'ur's Royal
Melody, published ten years earlier in
London. Other works include Essex Harmony
(several editions issued up to 1785), The
Psalm Singer's Assistant (1767), and The
New Harmony of Zion, or Complete Melody
(1788).

BEISSEL, JOHANN CONRAD.

Born, Eberbach, Germany, April 1690.

Died, Ephrata, Pennsylvania, July 6, 1768.

Hymn writer and founder of the Solitary
Brethren of the Community of Seventh Day
Baptists at Ephrata. In the autumn of
1720, Beissel left Germany for religious
reasons and arrived in Boston. He soon
settled in Germantown, Pennsylvania, and
in 1732 was joined by some of the Solitary
Brethren (unmarried men) and Sisters (women
devoted to virginity) who, upon joining the
community, were sworn to chastity. In the

year 1747, the hymnal of the Ephrata Cloister,
Turtel Taube, appeared with both words and
music largely by Beissel. Although not a
trained musician, he supposedly composed
over 1,000 hymns, evolved a unique system of
harmony, and developed a distinctive musical
notation. His hymn tunes became highly
influential in the development of American
hymnology. The decline of the Ephrata Cloister
began with Beissel's death in 1768, but its customs
continued well into the nineteenth century.

BELCHER, SUPPLY.

Born, Stoughton, Massachusetts, March 29, 1751.
Died, Farmington, Maine, June 9, 1836.
Little is known of Belcher's life, other than that
he was a member of the famous Stoughton Musical
Society until 1785, when me moved to Hallowell,
Maine, and six years later to Farmington, where he
became one of that town's leading citizens. He was a
justice of the peace as late as 1815, and was an important
public official, often representing Farmington

in the Massachusetts legislature (Maine did
not gain statehood until 1820). Belcher
was also credited with having taught the
first school in Farmington. Even though
he was a respected choir leader and for many
years music director in the Farmington
Church, he was more successful as a
violinist and composer, and earned the
title of "The Handel of Maine." In 1794,
Isaiah Thomas and Ebenezer T. Andrews of
Boston published his The Harmony of Maine,
an original collection of psalm and hymn
tunes and a discussion of the rudiments
of music.

BENHAM, ASAHEL.

Born, Framingham, Massachusetts, February 9, 1771.
Died, Pawtucket, Rhode Island, October 31, 1815.
After a rudimentary education, Belknap settled
on a farm in Framingham, where he became a
mechanic and farmer. His interests in music,
however, led him to begin teaching singing at
the age of 18. Upon invitation, he spent some
time teaching in Whitesboro, New York. He

returned to Framingham, remaining until 1812,
when he moved to Pawtucket. He died there
of yellow fever in 1815. Belknap's first
musical publication was called The Harmonist's
Companion (1797), which contained a small
collection of sacred airs, an Easter anthem,
and a Masonic Ode. In 1800, his Evangelical
Harmony was issued from the press of Thomas
and Andrews in Boston. His last and most
elaborate work was The Village Compilation
of Sacred Music, published in 1806, a rather
large volume of 152 pages containing much music
previously not published.

BENHAM, ASAHEL.

Born, New Hartford, Connecticut, 1757.

Died, ?, 1805.

Teacher and compiler of music. Most of Benham's
teaching was carried on in the New England and
Middle Atlantic states, and as was common for
the period, he traveled from town to town,
finding positions available where he could.
This was particularly so due to his slight

education, even for the time. Benham's

works include his Federal Harmony,

published in 1790, and containing "the

rudiments of psalmody with a collection

of sacred music." Other editions

appeared subsequently until 1796.

Benham's Federal Harmony should not be

confused with another work of the same

title generally attributed to Timothy

Swan. Devotional Harmony, a posthumous

work by the late Merit N. Woodruff of

Watertown, Conn., was published (1800)

under the supervision of Asahel Benham.

BENJAMIN, JONATHAN.

Flourished, c1799.

American psalmodist about which very little

has been discovered. His chief publication

is Harmonia Coelestis, published in 1799,

containing for the most part anthems of

European origin, "correctly figured for the

organ and harpsichord."

BILLINGS, WILLIAM.

Born, Boston, October 7, 1746.

Died, Boston, September 26, 1800.

Often credited as America's first professional composer, William Billings actually spent the early years of his life as a tanner. Soon, however, he devoted more and more of this time to hymnology. A self-educated musician, he studied the comparatively few books on music theory then available in English, and developed a simple chordal style for the composition of his hymn tunes and anthems. In 1770, he published The New England Psalm Singer, which contained many traditional hymns as well as some of his own "fuguing pieces," these latter crude imitations of canonic writing. Billings' other publications include The Singing Master's Assistant (1778), The Psalm Singer's Amusement (1781), and The Continental Harmony (1794). In addition to being a composer, he was a choir singer and singing teacher, and his influence on choral technique was far-reaching.

Musical instruments were not used in church singing
at this time, and in order to establish the
proper pitch of a hymn, Billings was the first
to make use of the pitch-pipe in congregational
singing. In order that this pitch could be
maintained throughout the composition, he also
introduced the "viol" or violoncello as an
adjunct to choral singing.

BILLINGTON, THOMAS.

Born, Exeter, c1754.

Died, Tunis, 1832.

English pianist, harpist, singing-master,
and composer. See Grove, v. 1, p. 709.

BOCCHERINI, LUIGI.

Born, Lucca, February 19, 1743.

Died, Madrid, May 28, 1805.

Italian composer and cellist.

See Grove, v. 1, p. 778-779.

BOYCE, WILLIAM.

Born, London (?), c1710.

Died, London, February 7, 1779.

English organist, composer, and musical editor.

See Grove, v. 1, p. 860-865.

BROADDUS, ANDREW.

Biographical information not available.

BROWN, WILLIAM.

Flourished, 1783-1787.

Flute player and composer who settled in America sometime during the middle years of the eighteenth century. He is known to have been in Baltimore in 1784, where he gave a flute concert on January 30. He then moved to Philadelphia, where he performed in many benefit concerts. In 1785, together with Alexander Reinagle, Alexander Juhan, and Henri Capron, Brown helped establish a series of subscription concerts in New York and Philadelphia. He composed 3 Rondos for the Pianoforte or Harpsichord, dedicated to Francis Hopkinson. It is likely that he was of German origin, and possible that he may be identical with a Wilhelm Braun of Kassel.

BROWNSON, OLIVER.

Virtually nothing is known about Brownson's

life or musical activities, other than that
he was apparently a singing master in
Litchfield, Connecticut, and that he was
the compiler of two collections of sacred
music. In 1783, his Select Harmony was
published in New Haven and contained several
tunes seemingly of his own composition as
well as others by such figures as Edson,
Billings, and Timothy Swan. Another edition
appeared eight years later (1791). His second
publication is A New Collection of Sacred
Harmony, printed in Simsbury, Connecticut,
in 1797, and sold at Brownson's own home.

BULL, AMOS.

Born, Connecticut (?), 1744 (?)

Died, ?, ?

Little is known of Bull's life or musical
activities. He apparently was born in
Connecticut and compiled at least one
collection of sacred music. The Responsary
was printed in 1795 by Isaiah Thomas of
Worcester and sold in Hartford, Connecticut,

by Bull himself. By the year 1805, he had
moved to Hartford, where he was engaged as
a school teacher and offered, in addition
to music instruction, "Reading, writing,
and arithmetick."

CALLCOTT, JOHN WALL.

Born, London [Kensington] November 20, 1766.

Died, Bristol, May 15, 1821.

English organist and composer. *See Grove,*

v. 2, p. 22-23.

CAPRON, HENRI.

Flourished late 18th century.

Prominent early American cellist and composer
of French origin. Capron was a pupil of
the French violoncellist and composer Pierre
Gavinies (1728-1800) in Paris, and later
became part manager with Alexander Reinagle,
William Brown, and Alexander Juhan, of a series
of subscription concerts in New York and
Philadelphia. He lived in New York from 1788 to
1792, where he performed in the Old American
Company orchestra. He settled permanently in
Philadelphia and was later the principal of a

French boarding school. He was the composer
of numerous songs, and his New Contredance
achieved wide popularity.

CARR, BENJAMIN.

Born, London, September 12, 1768.

Died, Philadelphia, May 24, 1831.

Benjamin Carr received his early musical
training from two of England's most
respected musicians, the organist-composer
Samuel Arnold and the son of the founder of
the Wesleyan Methodist Church, Charles
Wesley. In 1793, Carr emigrated to America,
and established in Philadelphia what was
probably this country's first music store,
the Musical Repository. Through his Musical
Journal and Musical Miscellany, works of many
contemporary American composers became more
readily accessible in anthologies and
collections. A New York branch was sold to
James Hewitt a few years later. In 1820,
Carr and Raynor Taylor founded the Musical
Fund Society, designed to advance the cause of

chamber music in America, as well as provide
funds through benefit concerts for needy
musicians. As a composer, Carr's most
significant contribution is The Archers,
an opera based on the legend of William Tell,
and first produced in New York by the Old
American Company on April 18, 1796. His list
of compositions includes many songs and piano
pieces, in addition to psalms, motets, and
masses. Generally considered one of the
foremost musical figures of the late eighteenth
and early nineteenth centuries, the Musical Fund
Society erected a monument to Benjamin Carr
in St. Peter's Churchyard, Philadelphia, on
his death in 1831.

CHERUBINI, MARIA LUIGI.

Born, Florence, September 14, 1760.

Died, Paris, March 15, 1842.

Italian composer of the French school.

See Grove, v. 2, p. 198-201.

CIBBER, COLLEY.

Born, London, November 6, 1671.

Died, ?, December 12, 1757.

English actor and dramatist. *See DNB*,

v. 4, p. 352-359; see Grove, v. 2, p. 294.

CLEAVELAND, BENJAMIN.

Biographical information not available.

COLE, JOHN.

Born, Tewksbury, England, 1744.

Died, Baltimore, August 17, 1855.

Composer, music publisher, and conductor.

Cole arrived with his family in America in

1785, settling in Baltimore. His early

musical instruction was received from

Andrew Law, Ishmail Spicer, and Thomas

Atwell. For a long time he was organist and

choir director of St. Paul's Episcopal

Church in Baltimore. As early as 1804, he

engaged in printing and ten years later

became active as a bookseller. In 1821 he

opened his music store on Baltimore Street,

soon to become the major music publisher in

Baltimore during the late 1820s and 1830s.

Cole published exclusively psalm books, and

compiled numerous sacred collections.

COSTELOW, THOMAS.

Unidentified English composer of songs and
short pieces for pianoforte and harpsichord.
Active from about 1792.

CRAMER, JOHANN BAPTIST.

Born, Mannheim, February 24, 1771.

Died, London, April 16, 1858.

It was his father Wilhelm Cramer, an eminent
violinist, who introduced Johann Baptist
to music, and later teachers included the
viola da gamba player and composer Karl
Friedrich Abel and the celebrated pianist-
composer Muzio Clementi. While on a concert
tour in Europe, Cramer was privileged to
meet Beethoven and Haydn in Vienna. Both these
masters, along with Bach, Handel, and
Scarlatti, helped shape Cramer's keyboard
style. He wrote 105 sonatas, a piano quintet,
piano quartet, and many short rondos,
variations, and salon-type fantasias. Perhaps
his most significant contribution is the piano
method <u>Grosse praktische Pianoforte Schule</u> (1815),

the last part of which, ''84 Studien,'' is
still important in piano pedagogy. After
returning from his European tour in 1845,
Cramer retired and died in London at the
age of 87.

DAVY, JOHN.

Born, Upton Helions near Exeter, December 23,
1763.

Died, London, February 22, 1824.

English composer. *See Grove, v. 2,*
p. 615-616.

DAWSON, W.

Little-known theatre manager; flourished
c1732.

DEARBORN, BENJAMIN.

Born, Portsmouth, New Hampshire, 1754.

Died, Boston, February 22, 1838.

An inventor and amateur musician, Dearborn was
apprenticed to a printer, but did not continue
in that business. About 1785, he established
a girls school in Portsmouth, later to be
relocated in Boston. His chief invention was
the spring balance, or spring scale, to

measure weight by the elasticity of a steel

spring. His only wholly musical publication

is <u>The Vocal Instructor</u>, published in Boston

in 1797.

DE CLEVE, V.

Little-known English composer, active from

about 1790.

DEVIENNE, FRANCOIS.

Born, Joinville, Haute-Marne, France,

January 31, 1759.

Died, Charenton, September 5, 1803.

French composer, flautist, and bassoonist.

At the age of ten, Devienne joined a regimental

band in Paris as a flautist, and in 1788

entered the orchestra of the Theatre de

Monsieur as a bassoonist. Although he wrote

twelve operas, several symphonies, and numerous

short romances, his chamber music for woodwinds

was the most popular during his own lifetime.

Much of this chamber music, highly virtuosic

in style, was reprinted by British publishers,

and his flute compositions in particular were

extremely popular around the turn of the
century. His <u>La Bataille de Jemmapes</u> was
originally composed for an instrumental
ensemble of twenty members, and is here
presented as an arrangement for solo piano.

DEVONSHIRE, GEORGIANA SPENCER CAVENDISH, DUCHESS OF.

Born, ?, June 9, 1757.

Died, Piccadilly (Devonshire House), March 30,
1806.

Daughter of first Earl Spencer, wife of fifth
Duke of Devonshire. Although her light verse
was often dominated by sentiment, she was a
respected friend of Fox, Sheridan, Selwyn,
and Dr. Johnson. Her modest musical talents
produced the melodies of a number of short
songs, the most popular of which, "Sweet is
the vale," ran through numerous editions as
late as 1838.

DIBDIN, CHARLES.

Born, Southampton, baptized March 4, 1745.

Died, London, July 25, 1814.

British musician, composer, dramatist, actor,
and song-writer. The son of a parish clerk at

Southampton, Dibdin was naturally expected to enter the clergy. At the age of eleven, he was sent to Winchester Cathedral, where he remained with the choir until 1759. However, he was vitally interested in music, and made his debut in 1762 at the Richmond summer theatre, the next year being engaged at Birmingham. Upon his return to London, he was engaged as a singer at Covent Garden Theatre, where his "Shepherd's artifice" was first performed on May 21, 1764. He achieved wide public recognition when, in 1765, he sang a role in Arnold's opera, The Maid of the Mill. Three years later, he transferred his services to Drury Lane, where many of his most popular sea songs were composed: "'Twas in the good ship Rover," "I sailed from the Downs in the Nancy," "Tom Bowling," the last written on the death of his eldest brother, Captain Thomas Dibdin. His last opera, The Round Robin, was composed in 1811 for performance in the Haymarket Theatre. In 1813, Dibdin was attacked by paralysis, and died the following year in London.

DIGNUM, CHARLES.

>Born, London [Rotherhithe] 1765.

>Died, London, March 29, 1827.

>English tenor and composer of Irish descent.

>*See Grove, v. 2, p. 707.*

DUBOIS, WILLIAM.

>Flourished, 1795-1800.

>French clarinettist, composer, and opera singer. Arrived in America around 1795 and was active as a clarinettist in Philadelphia during the late 1790s. Sonneck-Upton (p. 504) states that Dubois opened a music store in New York sometime after 1800. However, there were at least two William Dubois active during this period, and Wolfe (v. 1, p. 255) feels that it was probably a relative of William Dubois the clarinettist who actually was engaged in selling music in New York.

DUPORT, PIERRE LANDRIN.

>Born, Paris, 1762 or 1763.

>Died, Washington, April 11, 1841.

>French dancing master, music teacher, and

composer. Settled in America in 1790,
arriving at either New York or Perth
Amboy, settling first in Philadelphia.
Taught music and produced ballets in
New York, Baltimore, Boston, and Norfolk
before moving to Washington, where he
died in 1841.

DUSSEK, JAN LADISLAV.

Born, Caslav, Bohemia, February 12, 1760.
Died, Saint-Germain-en-Laye, France,
March 20, 1812.
Bohemian composer and pianist. *See
Grove, v. 2, p. 825-829.*

DWIGHT, TIMOTHY.

Born, Northampton, Massachusetts, May 14, 1752.
Died, New Haven, Connecticut, January 11, 1817.
Congregational divine, author, and president
of Yale College from 1795 to 1817. *See DAB,
v. 3, p. 573-577.*

FISCHER, JOHANN CHRISTIAN.

Born, Freiburg, 1733.
Died, London, April 29, 1800.
German composer and oboist. *See Grove,
v. 3, p. 144.*

FISIN, JAMES.

Born, ?, 1755.

Died, ?, September 8, 1847.

English composer. *See Grove, v. 3,*

p. 147.

FLAGG, JOSIAH.

Born, Woburn, Massachusetts, May 28, 1737.

Died, ?, c1795.

Josiah Flagg, born the son of Gershom and
Martha Flagg, had the distinction of
introducing the anthem to the New England
colonies. His first composition appeared
in 1764 under the title, A Collection of
the best psalm tunes in 2, 3 and 4 parts...,
with Paul Revere responsible for the engraving.
This first endeavor was such a success
that, two years later, he published Sixteen
anthems, collected from Tans'ur, Williams,
Knapp, Ashworth & Stephenson... Flagg
organized and drilled Boston's first military
band, perhaps the first in the country, with its
concert given in Boston's Concert Hall, June 29,

1769. Upon leaving Boston, he moved to
Providence, where he served as lieutenant
colonel during the Revolution. From this
point, little is known of Flagg's life,
but on January 31, 1795, a benefit concert
was offered in Boston for a "Widow Flagg,"
and it is from this that Flagg's date of
death has been fixed.

FRENCH, JACOB.

Born, Stoughton, Massachusetts, July 15, 1754.
Died, Northampton, Massachusetts (?), ?
French's first music book was entitled The
New American Melody, published in 1789, and
sold by him in Medway, Massachusetts. Four
years later, The Psalmodist's Companion was
printed in Worcester by Isaiah Thomas (1793),
wherein he states that he has been a teacher of
music for several years. French's most popular
anthem, "The Heavenly vision," did not appear
in any of his publications. However, Isaiah
Thomas acquired the copyright to this work and
published it in his Worcester Collection of
1791, although the composer was not identified.

French's last work was issued in Northampton,
and it is likely that he may have died there.
His younger brother, Edward (1761-1845), was
a talented vocalist and composed at least
one example of sacred music, "New Bethlehem."

FRITH, EDWARD.

Unidentified composer, presumably British.
His "Contented cottager" was issued in London
by E. Riley about 1800.

GALLI, SIGNORA _____.

Biographical information not available.

GARNET, HORATIO.

Little-known American composer, flourished
c1789.

GARTH, JOHN.

Born, Durham, 1722.
Died, London (?), 1810.
English composer. *See Grove, v. 3, p. 570.*

GAULINE, JOHN BAPTISTE.

Born, ?, 1759.
Died, ?, 1824.
Little-known American composer, a native of
Marseilles, France, settling in America and
taking up citizenship in Maryland.

GAVEAUX, PIERRE.

Born, Beziers, August 1761.

Died, Paris, February 5, 1825.

French tenor and composer. *See Grove,*

v. 3, p. 581-582.

GEHOT, JOHN.

Born, Liege (?), c1750.

Died, Philadelphia (?), ?

Walloon composer and violinist. *See*

Grove, v. 3, p. 587-588.

GILMAN, JOHN WARD.

Born, ?, 1741.

Died, ?, 1823.

Music engraver residing in Exeter, New
Hampshire, during the last decade of the
eighteenth century and presumably until his
death in 1823. From data gained in the New
Hampshire census of 1790, it appears that
the Gilman family consisted of Mr. and Mrs.
Gilman, three sons, and three daughters. At
the age of 27, he engraved the music to Daniel
Bayley's A New and Complete Introduction to the
Grounds and Rules of Musick (1768).

GIORDANI, GIUSEPPE.

>Born, Naples, c1744.
>
>Died, Fermo, January 4, 1798.
>
>Italian composer. *See Grove, v. 3,*
>*p. 647.*

GLUCK, CHRISTOPH WILLIBALD VON.

>Born, Erasbach, Upper Palatinate, July 2, 1714.
>
>Died, Vienna, November 15, 1787.
>
>German composer of Bohemian stock.
>
>*See Grove, v. 3, p. 674-684.*

GODDARD, JOSIAH.

>Biographical information not available.

GRAEFF, JOHN GEORGE.

>Born, Mentz, now Mainz, Germany, c1762.
>
>Died, ?, ?
>
>Violinist, flautist, and composer. Although
>originally intended for the church, his strong
>predilection for music led Graeff to receive
>music instruction from Charles Frederic Abel,
>and later from Haydn. Leaving Mainz at an
>early age, he subsequently lived in Basel,
>Berne, and Lausanne, meeting with great success
>during his five years' residence in Switzerland.

At Lausanne, he met the celebrated Monsieur
Bonnet de la Reve. Leaving Switzerland,
Graeff resided in Paris for about a year,
again receiving favorable critical acclaim.
Little is known of him after his taking
residence in Paris.

GRAM, HANS.

Born, Denmark, ?

Died, ?, ?

Neither the date of birth nor death of Hans
Gram are known, and it is even uncertain
where he died. He was, however, born in
Denmark and educated in Stockholm, and was for
many years organist of Boston's Brattle Street
Church. Notable musicians including Jacob Kimball,
Oliver Holden, and Samuel Holyoke received
musical instruction from Gram. In 1793, his
Sacred Lines for Thanksgiving Day was published
at the request of Jacob Kimball and Isaac Lane.
Gram was one of the compilers of The Massa-
chusetts Compiler (Oliver Holden and Samuel
Holyoke being the others), reputed to have

contained the first article on harmony
published in this country. Written by
Gram himself, the article was based
largley on the writings of Rousseau and
D'Alembert. His secular music is
represented by a "Hunting Song" which
appeared in the Massachusetts Magazine
of 1789, and an "Ode to the President,"
written by "a lady" and to which Gram
set the music.

GRAUN, CARL HEINRICH.

Born, Wahrenbrück, near Dresden, May 7, 1704.

Died, Berlin, August 8, 1759.

German composer and tenor. *See Grove,*
v. 3, p. 762-763.

GRIFFITHS, JOHN.

Flourished, 1787-1797.

Composer and dancing master. Although little
is known of his personal life and activities,
he may be traced in Providence, Rhode Island,
Boston, New York, and Charleston, South
Carolina.

GRISWOLD, ELIJAH.

> Little-known compiler of sacred music;
> flourished c1800.

H., S. M.

> Unidentified composer, possibly English.

HAGEN, PETER ALBRECHT VON, SR.

> Born, Holland, 1750.
>
> Died, Boston, 1803.
>
> Dutch musician active in America. Arriving
> from Holland, Hagen Sr. settled in 1774 in
> Charleston as a music teacher. From 1789
> to 1796, he lived in New York, giving
> concerts with his wife and son. In 1796,
> the family moved to Boston. He is the
> composer of a Federal Overture (1797), not
> to be confused with Benjamin Carr's Federal
> Overture, a Funeral Dirge on the death of
> George Washington (1800), and much theatre
> music.

HAGEN, PETER ALBRECHT VON, JR.

> Born, Charleston, South Carolina, 1781.
>
> Died, Boston, 1837.
>
> Music teacher, publisher, and composer, son of

the preceding. First mentioned on New York
concert programs in 1789 as a pianist "eight
years of age." Late in 1796, the Hagen
family moved from New York to Boston, where
he continued his career as concert piano
virtuoso. He wrote numerous songs and also
composed an <u>Overture.</u>

HAIGH, THOMAS.

Born, London, 1769.

Died, London, April 1808.

English violinist, pianist and composer.

See Grove, v. 4, p. 17.

HANDEL, GEORGE FRIEDRICH.

Born, Halle, Germany, February 23, 1685.

Died, London, April 14, 1759.

English composer. *See Grove, v. 4, p. 37-60.*

HARINGTON, HENRY.

Born, Kelston, Somerset, September 29, 1727.

Died, Bath, January 15, 1816.

English physician and composer of glees and
catches. In 1745, Harington entered Queen's
College with an intention to enter the clergy.

Under the influence of his uncle, however, he became interested in music. In 1748 he abandoned his intention of taking religious orders and began the study of medicine; he received his M. A. and M. D. degrees from Oxford. Harington was really only an amateur musician, and in addition to some vocal glees, he composed a religious dirge entitled The Death of Christ (Eloi! Eloi!), published in 1800.

HARRISON, RALPH.

Born, Chinley, Derbyshire, England, September 10, 1748.

Died, Manchester, November 10, 1810.

Nonconformist divine and Presbyterian minister. In 1763, Harrison entered the Warrington Academy, where John Aikin, D. D. (1713-1780) was tutor of divinity. Later, in 1771, he became minister at Cross Street Chapel, Manchester. After a protracted illness, he died in 1810. His chief musical publication is Sacred Harmony (1786), published in two volumes and containing psalm tunes of his own composition.

HART, JOSEPH.

Born, London, 1712.

Died, London, May 24, 1768.

English independent minister and hymn writer.

In 1757, Hart achieved his spiritual con-

version, and from that time until his death

eleven years later, he preached at Jewin

Street Chapel in London. He was buried in

Bunhill Fields, and it is said that several

thousand persons listened to his moving funeral

sermon. His two chief publications include

The Unreasonableness of Religion (1741),

arguing that religion is diametrically

opposed to logical reasoning, and Hymns, &c.,

Composed on Various Subjects (1759), con-

taining tunes "of an ultra-Calvinistic tone."

(DNB, v. 9, p. 62). The preface of this

hymnal was later (1862) reprinted under the

title, The Experience of Joseph Hart.

HAWKINS, JOHN.

Born, London, March 30, 1719.

Died, London, May 21, 1789.

English musical historian, antiquarian, and

attorney. *See Grove, v. 4, p. 142-144.*

HAYDN, FRANZ JOSEPH.

Born, Rohrau, Austria, March 31, 1732.

Died, Vienna, May 31, 1809.

Austrian composer. *See Grove, v. 4,*

p. 145-205.

HEWITT, JAMES.

Born, Dartmoor, England, June 4, 1770.

Died, Boston, August 1, 1827.

Composer, violinist, music publisher,

and conductor. Hewitt came to America

in 1792, landing in New York where he

became very active in the musical life

of that city. In 1798, the New York

branch of Benjamin Carr's Musical

Repository was sold to Hewitt, who then

issued a large number of musical publications,

including most of his own compositions.

He managed a series of subscription concerts

in New York and was active as performer in

and conductor of the Old American Company.

In 1820 he moved to Boston, where he was later

engaged in Southern theatrical ventures,
and where he died in 1827. Clearly, Hewitt
was one of the most important figures in the
early musical life of Boston and New York,
and many of his works are represented in
numerous libraries throughout this country.

HODGKINSON, JOHN.

Born, England, 1767.

Died, Washington, 1805.

English actor and singer. Hodgkinson's real
name was Meadowcroft, and in 1792 he and his
wife went to America. They appeared in New
York, Philadelphia, and Boston with the Old
American Company for about ten years. In
1797, he managed Boston's Haymarket Theatre.
Hodgkinson was noted especially for his
effectiveness as an actor in the many ballad
operas in which he appeared. During the
years 1795-1799, he was president of the
Columbian Anacreontic Society, of which he
was the founder.

HOFFMEISTER, FRANZ ANTON.

Born, Rottenburg, Württemberg, May 12, 1754.

Died, Vienna, February 9, 1812.

German composer and publisher. *See*

Grove, v. 4, p. 315-316.

HOLDEN, OLIVER.

Born, Shirley, Massachusetts, September 18,

1765.

Died, Charlestown, Massachusetts, September

4, 1844.

About 1787, Oliver Holden settled in Charles-

town, Massachusetts, which had been razed

by the British during the Revolution. Being

a carpenter by trade, he assisted in the town's

reconstruction. Holden was a justice of the

peace and also represented Charlestown,

later annexed to Boston, in the State House

of Representatives in 1818, 1825, 1826, and

continually from 1828 to 1833. A composer of

psalm and hymn tunes, no less than 21 tunes

have been attributed to Holden. His most

popular hymn is "Coronation," published in

the first volume of his <u>Union Harmony</u> (1793).

He also compiled several hymn books, among
them The American Harmony (1792), The
Massachusetts Compiler (1795), perhaps
his most ambitious work, and The Worcester
Collection (1797-1803).

HOLYOKE, SAMUEL.

Born, Boxford, Massachusetts, October 15,
1762.

Died, East Concord, New Hampshire, February 7,
1820.

His father was a clergyman, and it was only
natural that Holyoke should have been drawn
to sacred music. His most famous hymn tune,
"Arnheim," was written at the age of 16.
Four years after his graduation from Harvard
College in 1789, Holyoke had established
himself as a respected music teacher in
Massachusetts. The Groton Academy, designed
to provide instruction in the theory and
performance of sacred music, was founded
under Holyoke's leadership. From 1800 on,
most of his life was spent in Salem, where

he conducted singing schools and academies.
In the preface to Holyoke's first publication,
Harmonia Americana (1791), we learn of his
preference for the slower, more deliberate
hymn tune and of his distaste for the brilliant
and more intricate fuging tunes of William
Billings. The Massachusetts Compiler, a
joint effort by Holyoke, Hans Gram, and
Oliver Holden, appeared in 1795. After a
short illness, Holyoke died in 1820 of a
lung complication.

HOOK, JAMES.

Born, Norwich, June 3, 1746.

Died, Boulogne, France, 1827.

English organist and composer. Hook's early
musical instruction was received from Garland,
organist at the Norwich Cathedral, and it is
likely that he was tutored by Charles Burney
during the latter's residence in Norfolk.
Upon his father's death in 1757, when James
was only eleven, Hook supported his mother
and himself by teaching guitar, spinet,

harpsichord, violin, and German flute, and
even advertised that he could copy and
transpose music as well as tune and compose
for any keyboard instrument. From 1769 until
1773, he was organist and composer of
Marylebone Gardens, and from 1774 until
1820 at Vauxhall Gardens. He is credited
with over 2,000 compositions, consisting
chiefly of short songs, glees, catches,
keyboard concertos, piano sonatas, and an
oratorio entitled The Ascension (1776).
Hook wrote a piano method, Guida di Musica
(1796), and his two most popular songs are
probably Within a Mile of Edinboro' Town
and Sweet Lass of Richmond Hill.

HOPKINSON, FRANCIS.

Born, Philadelphia, October 2, 1737.

Died, Philadelphia, May 9, 1791.

One of the signers of the Declaration of
Independence, jurist, first Secretary of
the Navy, musician, and composer. Graduated
from the College of Philadelphia, now the

University of Pennsylvania, afterward
embarking on the study of law. During
the Revolution, he was a successful
satirist, both in the fields of politics
and social foibles. When Washington
became President, Hopkinson received a
commission as United States district
judge for Pennsylvania. He was an
accomplished organist and harpsichordist,
and gave thought to the improvement of
the harpsichord and other instruments.
Having composed numerous short songs and
keyboard pieces, Hopkinson himself claimed
to be America's first native composer.
Sonneck-Upton (p. 512) confirms this
assertion, and gives credit to James Lyon
and William Billings for being the second
and third, respectivley. Hopkinson was
born in Philadelphia, spent his entire
life there, and died there in 1791.

HOWARD, SAMUEL.

Born, ?, 1710.

Died, London, July 13, 1782.

English organist and composer. *See*

Grove, v. 4, p. 388.

HOWE, SOLOMON.

Born, North Brookfield, Massachusetts,
September 14, 1750.

Died, New Salem, Massachusetts, November 18,
1835.

In 1777, at the age of 27, Solomon Howe
graduated from Dartmouth College, whereupon
he began a somewhat eccentric series of
"careers." He was first a preacher, then
a teacher, next a printer, then a farmer.
During much of this time he lived in
Greenwich, in western Massachusetts, and
it was here that his three music books were
compiled. He died in New Salem in 1835 at
the age of 85. His first book was The
Worshipper's Assistant, printed from music
type for the author in 1799. His other works
published after 1800 include The Farmers'
Evening Entertainment (1804), and Divine
Hymns on the Sufferings of Christ (1805),
intended for the use of religious assemblies.

HUNTINGTON, JONATHAN.

Born, Windham, Connecticut, November 17, 1771.

Died, St. Louis, July 29, 1838.

Huntington was a singer by occupation, and studied voice while living with his uncle in Norwich. He had ten children, and from about 1797 to 1804, he was living in Windham. In 1806, he moved to Troy, New York, two years later settling in Northampton. From 1814 to 1829, he lived in Boston, where he taught vocal music, as he was to do later in St. Louis. It was there that he made his home until his death in 1838. Huntington's chief musical compilations include The Apollo Harmony (1807) and Classical Sacred Music, the latter composed of European sources and printed in Boston in 1812.

J., H.

Unidentified composer, possibly English.

JACKSON, GEORGE K.

Born, Oxford, England, 1745.

Died, Boston, November 18, 1822.

Organist, composer, music publisher, and
teacher. Came to America in 1796, where
he was active principally in New York,
Philadelphia, and Boston. Composer of
numerous short songs, piano pieces, and
sacred psalms and chants.

JACKSON, WILLIAM, OF EXETER.

Born, Exeter, May 29, 1730.

Died, Exeter, July 5, 1803.

English composer. *See Grove, v. 4,*
p. 565-566.

JENKS, STEPHEN.

Born, New Canaan, Connecticut, 1772.

Died, Thompson, Ohio, June 5, 1856.

Jenks was vitally interested in music from
an early age, and tried to encourage its
dissemination by both composing and teaching.
While living for a time at Ridgefield,
Connecticut, he published his first book,
The New England Harmony (1800). This was
soon reissued under the title, The New
England Harmonist, a second edition appearing

in 1803. Jenks later moved to New Salem,
New York, where The Delights of Harmony
was issued in 1805, followed two years later
by The Hartford Collection of Sacred Harmony,
in which Jenks was assisted by Elijah
Griswold and John C. Frisbie. Jenks' last
work, Laus Deo, the Harmony of Zion, or the
Union Compiler, was published in 1818.

In 1829, Jenks and his family moved to
Thompson, Ohio, where he was employed as a
drum- and tambourine-maker until his death
in June, 1856.

JOCELIN, SIMEON.

Born, Branford, Connecticut, October 22, 1746.
Died, New Haven, Connecticut, June 5, 1823.
Simeon Jocelin, often spelled Jocelyn, was
not a composer, but rather an engraver,
publisher, and compiler of tune books.
As early as 1782, he had established himself
in business, and soon afterward had formed a
partnership with Amos Doolittle. The Chorister's
Companion was his first and chief publication,
with later editions containing additional

psalm tunes, hymns, and anthems. He died

in New Haven in 1823 at the age of 77.

JOHNSTON, THOMAS.

Little-known organist, son of Thomas Johnston

(c1708-1767). *See DAB, v. 5, p. 152.*

JUHAN, ALEXANDER.

Violinist and composer. Arrived in

Philadelphia in December 1783 from

Halifax, settling first in Boston in

1768. He is mentioned as violinist in

many of Philadelphia's concert programs.

Juhan resided in Charleston, South Carolina,

for a year or two (1791), finally returning

to Philadelphia. His compositions include

works for solo violin, numerous short songs,

and a set of six sonatas for piano-forte.

KALKBRENNER, CHRISTIAN.

Born, Minden, Westphalia, September 22, 1755.

Died, Paris, August 10, 1806.

German composer, father of Friedrich Wilhelm

Michael Kalkbrenner. *See Grove, v. 4,*

p. 691-692.

KELLY, MICHAEL.

Born, Dublin, about 1764.

Died, Margate, Kent, England, October 9, 1826.

Irish actor, composer, and vocalist. Kelly
began his musical studies under Michael Arne
and Rauzzini, the former offering instruction
in the piano and the latter in voice. In 1779,
Kelly had the unexpected opportunity to
appear on the Dublin stage during the illness
of a performer, and his performance in
Piccinni's opera, La Buona Figliuola,
was highly successful. Soon, he sailed to
Italy, where he gave a concert at Leghorn
with the assistance of Stephen Storace and
his family. Later, in Vienna, Gluck coached
him for a role in his Iphigenia in Tauride,
and Mozart trained him for the role of
Basilio in the first performance of Le
Nozze di Figaro. Kelly left Vienna with
the Storaces in 1787, arriving in London,
where he first appeared at Drury Lane.
In 1797, he began his long series of musical

settings of plays, one of the most notable
based on Sheridan's Pizarro. His last
appearance at Drury Lane was in No Song
No Supper, composed by Stephen Storace,
June 17, 1808. Kelly died of the gout
at Margrave, and was buried in St. Paul's
churchyard, Covent Garden.

KIMBALL, JACOB, JR.

Born, Topsfield, Massachusetts, February 22,
1761.

Died, Topsfield, Massachusetts, February 6,
1826.

At the age of 14, Kimball was drummer in a
regiment of the Massachusetts Militia in
1775, and soon entered Harvard University,
from which he graduated in 1780. Although
he studied law and was admitted to the bar
in Stratford, Massachusetts, he soon found
his real interest in music and entered
teaching as a profession. Unsuccessful in
managing his funds, he died destitute in
Topsfield at the age of 65. Kimball compiled two music books, the earlier one entitled,

The Rural Harmony (1793), an original work
widely used in singing schools and assemblies.
The Essex Collection, also apparently an
original composition, was printed in 1800,
and contained 42 tunes and two anthems.
Kimball's Essex Harmony should not be confused
with another work of the same title issued in
various editions from 1770 to 1785 under the
editorship of Daniel Bayley. Although there
is some question about Kimball's connection
with it, The Village Harmony has been
attributed to him; many editions were issued
during the twenty years following 1795,
although the compiler was not named.

KOTZWARA, FRANZ.

Born, Prague, 1730 (?)

Died, London, September 2, 1791.

Bohemian composer. *See Grove, v. 4,*
p. 794-795.

KRUMPHOLTZ, JOHANN BAPTIST.

Born, Zlonice, Bohemia, 1745.

Died, Paris, February 19, 1790.

Bohemian composer and harpist. *See*

Grove, v. 4, p. 859-860.

LANE, ISAAC.

Flourished, 1797.

Lane's residence was established in Bedford,
Massachusetts, around 1791, as we learn from
the list of subscribers to Samuel Holyoke's
Harmonia Americana (1791). He also was one
of the signers of the endorsement printed
in Hans Gram's Sacred Lines for Thanksgiving
(1793). As a teacher of vocal music, Lane
proposed the opening of a "School for Sacred
Music," in advertisement appearing in the
New Hampshire Gazette (Portsmouth),
September 22, 1795. The school opened a few
days later, although with fewer pupils than
had been anticipated. His chief publication
is An Anthem: suitable to be performed at an
Ordination (1797), based on a portion of
Psalm 32, "Where shall we go to seek and find
a habitation for our God?" Regrettably,
nothing is heard from Isaac Lane after 1797.

350

LANGDON, CHAUNCY.

Born, Farmington, Connecticut, November 8,
1763.

Died, Castleton, Vermont, July 23, 1830.

Langdon pursued a largely classical education
and graduated from Yale in the class of 1787.
It was during his undergraduate days at Yale
that he compiled The Beauties of Psalmody,
an engraved pamphlet containing sacred tunes
by Swan, Billings, Brownson, and other
composers of New England. Afterwards, he
studied law in Hebron and Litchfield,
Connecticut, and soon settled in Castleton,
Vermont, where he was a State Representative
from 1813-1814, 1817, and 1819-1820, and a
Congressman from Vermont, 1815-1817. He
received a Bachelor's Degree from Middlebury
College in 1803, and was trustee of that
college from 1811 until his death in 1830
at Castleton.

LAW, ANDREW.

Born, Milford, Connecticut, March 1748.

Died, Cheshire Connecticut, July 13, 1821.

Composer, compiler, and teacher of sacred
music. At the age of five, he and his
family moved to Cheshire, where he remained
for most of his life. After graduating from
Rhode Island College (now Brown University)
in 1775, Law studied theology and was ordained
in Hartford in 1787. In 1767, when only 19,
he compiled a Select Number of Plain Tunes
Adapted to Congregational Worship, and by
1790 had issued no less than six books of
hymns and tunes. In 1802, he patented a
fourshaped notation, employing differently
shaped notes without lines and spaces of the
traditional staff. This new development was
not entirely accepted, however, and only a
few of his books were published employing it.
Law's chief published works appearing before
1800 include The Musical Primer (1780), the
first book published in fourshaped notation,
A Collection of the Best and Most Approved
Tunes and Anthems (1779), The Art of Singing
(1792), and The Musical Magazine (1792-1793).

LEE, CHAUNCY.

>Born, Salisbury, Connecticut, November 9, 1763.
>Died, Hartwick, New York, November 5, 1842.
>Shortly after graduating from Yale College in
>1784, Lee began the study of law, and upon
>being admitted to the bar in 1787, opened
>an office in Salisbury. He later resolved,
>however, to enter the ministry (1789).
>He preached in Stockbridge, Massachusetts,
>Salisbury, Connecticut, Sunderland, Vermont,
>Burlington, Vermont, and Lansingburg, New
>York. In 1799, he returned to Salisbury,
>and the next year became pastor of the
>Congregational Church of Colebrook. The
>degree Doctor of Divinity was conferred on
>him by Columbia College in 1823. He died
>in Hartwick, New York, in 1842 at the age
>of 79. He had considerable musical abilities
>which were displayed both as a composer and
>as a performer.

LEE, THOMAS.

>Little-known compiler of sacred music;
>flourished c1790.

LESUEUR, JEAN FRANCOIS.

> Born, Drucat-Pleissiel, near Abbeville, France,
>
> February 15, 1760.
>
> Died, Paris, October 6, 1837.
>
> French composer of religious and dramatic
>
> works. Lesueur's early musical training was
>
> received as a chorister at Amiens, and in
>
> 1781 he was appointed chapelmaster at the
>
> cathedral in Dijon. Five years later (1786),
>
> he was chapelmaster at Notre Dame in Paris.
>
> He anticipated the religious works of Berlioz,
>
> Gounod, and even Verdi through the use of
>
> a large orchestra to accompany his masses,
>
> and also in the successful blending of the
>
> sacred and secular styles. In 1818, he
>
> became music director of the Paris Conser-
>
> vatoire, with his pupils including Berlioz,
>
> Gounod, and Ernest Guiraud (1837-1892).
>
> Lesueur's compositions include 33 masses
>
> and several oratorios and motets.

LINLEY, FRANCIS.

> Born, Doncaster, England (?), 1774.
>
> Died, Doncaster, England, September 15, 1800.

Organist and composer, blind from birth.

About 1790, Linley was organist at St.

James Chapel, Pentonville, London, and in

1796 came to America, remaining for three

years, and returned only to die in 1800

at the age of 26. He was a composer of

numerous compilations for flute and piano,

songs, and organ pieces, including many

preludes, voluntaries, fugues, and psalms.

LINLEY, THOMAS.

Born, Badminton, England, January 17, 1733.

Died, London, November 19, 1795.

English ballad-opera composer. Linley studied

organ with Thomas Chilcot at Bath and in

London with the singing-teacher, Pietro

Domenico Paradisi. After studying singing

for a number of years in Bath, Linley went to

London in 1774 as a joint director of the

Drury Lane Theatre. He and his son Thomas

(1756-1778), a violinist and friend of Mozart,

composed music for The Duenna (1775), with

words by Richard Brinsley Sheridan. One year

later, Linley purchased an interest in the
Drury Lane Theatre, filling the post as
music director until 1791. He was the
composer of many stage works, in addition
to songs, cantatas, elegies, and madrigals.

LITTLE, THOMAS.

Little-known composer and compiler of
Southern folk hymns; flourished c1790.
With William Smith, introduced fourshaped
notation in the _Easy Instructor_ (Philadelphia, 1801), used in many early tunebooks,
particularly in the South.

LYON, JAMES.

Born, Newark, New Jersey, July 1, 1735.
Died, Machias, Maine, October 12, 1794.
Psalmodist, compiler of hymn tunes, and
Presbyterian minister. Lyon attended the
college of New Jersey (now Princeton
University), and in 1760 began work on a
collection of hymn tunes, to be published
the next year under the title _Urania_.
He was ordained in 1764 and in 1765 settled

in Halifax, Nova Scotia. Finally, in 1771,
he moved to Boston, and the next year found
him in Machias, Maine, as a preacher for the
newly-founded town. After serving in the
Revolution, Lyon operated a salt distillery
on Salt Island near Machiasport in an
attempt to provide an income. His health,
however, began to fail, and he died in 1794.
Lyon's chief fame rests with Urania, which
in 1767 went into a second edition. Perhaps
his best single composition is Hymn to
Friendship. Although he did not possess
extraordinary technical skill, this piece
attests to his innate musicality.

MANN, ELIAS.

Born, Weymouth, Massachusetts, 1750.
Died, Northampton, Massachusetts, May 12, 1825.
Though born in Weymouth, much of Mann's
life was spent in Northampton. It was here
that he moved around 1796, and here that he
taught singing, directed the Congregational
Church choir on Sundays, and published most

of his works. He was one of fifteen who met in Boston in June 1807 to help organize the Massachusetts Musical Society, from which was to come the Handel and Haydn Society (1815). Mann's earliest publication was The Northampton Collection of Sacred Harmony (1797), followed by a second edition in 1802. The Massachusetts Collection of Sacred Harmony appeared in 1807. A copy of this work was presented to Oliver Holden by Elias Mann, and it is this copy which is now located in the Library of Congress. Mann died in Northampton in 1825, and was buried there with his wife and five of his children.

MARKORDT, J.

Little-known English composer, active since c1780.

MARTINI IL TEDESCO.

Born, Freistadt, Upper Palatinate, September 1, 1741.

Died, Paris, February 10, 1816.

German organist, composer, and conductor.

Real name: Johann Paul Aegidius Schwartzendorf.

See Grove, v. 5, p. 597-598.

MAZZINGHI, JOSEPH.

Born, London, December 25, 1765.

Died, Downside, England, January 15, 1844.

As a result of his organ studies with Johann
Christian Bach, Joseph Mazzinghi was appointed
organist of the Portugueze Chapel at the
age of ten. Later teachers included
Bertolini, Antonio Sacchini (1730-1786),
and Pasquale Anfossi (1727-1797), all
prolific Italian opera composers. In
1784, Mazzinghi became musical director of
the King's Theatre, where he composed and
produced the operas La bella Arsena
(1795) and Il Tesoro (1796). He wrote
extensively for the piano, and in addition
to over 70 sonatas for that instrument, he
composed many glees, trios, and numerous
songs and short vocal pieces.

MOLLER, JOHN CHRISTOPHER.

Born, ?, ?

Died, New York, September 21, 1803.

German composer and organist. He appeared
briefly in New York in 1790 as harpsichordist, but soon left for Philadelphia
where he participated as manager and
performer with Alexander Reinagle and,
later, Henri Capron, in the City Concerts.
In 1793, he was organist of the Zion
Church in Philadelphia. Three years later,
in 1796, Moller succeeded James Hewitt
in the operation of the New York City
Concerts in a joint management with the
Von Hagens. His chief compositions include
six quartets, six piano or harpsichord
sonatas "with a violin or violoncello
accompaniment," keyboard rondos, overtures,
variations, and a "Duetti" for clarinet
and piano. He also wrote a piano method
entitled, <u>Compleat book of instruction
for the pianoforte</u>, published in London.

MORE, ISABELLA THEAKER.

> Little-known English composer, active
> from c1785.

MOULDS, JOHN.

> Born, ?, ?
>
> Died, ?, 1801 (?)
>
> English composer of the latter eighteenth
> century. Composer to the Ranelagh Gardens
> in London, and his dramatic music includes
> the two operas, The Phisiognomist (1795)
> and The Sultan (1796).

MOZART, WOLFGANG AMADEUS.

> Born, Salzburg, January 27, 1756.
>
> Died, Vienna, December 5, 1791.
>
> Austrian composer, son of Leopold Mozart
> (1719-1787). *See Grove, v. 5,*
> *p. 923-983.*

NICHOLS, THOMAS.

> Biographical information not available.

NICOLAI, VALENTIN.

> Born, ?, ?
>
> Died, ?, c1799.

Popular composer for the piano forte who
resided for a number of years in Paris.
His works were popular, but "This, however,"
noted Dr. Burney, "may probably have been more
owing to the sprightliness and pleasantry
of his style, than to the depth or orthodoxy
of his knowledge." His piano sonatas were
particularly well-received and achieved an
extensive sale. He died about the year 1799.

OSWALD, JAMES.

Born, ?, ?

Died, ?, January 1769 (buried at Knebworth
  on January 9, 1769)

Scottish violinist, composer, organist, and
dancing-master. *See Grove, v. 6,*
p. 461-462.

PAISIELLO, GIOVANNI.

Born, Taranto, May 8, 1740.

Died, Naples, June 5, 1816.

Italian composer. *See Grove, v. 6,*
p. 497-499.

PELISSIER, VICTOR.

> Flourished, 18th-19th centuries.
> Horn player and performer. In 1793,
> Pelissier settled in New York as the
> first horn player, composer, and
> arranger for the Old American Company.
> His operas include <u>Ariadne abandoned</u>
> <u>by Theseus in the Isle of Naxos</u> (1797)
> and <u>Edwin and Angelina, or The Banditti</u>
> (1796). In addition to operas, he also
> composed music for pantomimes and some
> chamber music.

PERCY, JOHN.

> Born, ?, 1749.
> Died, London, January 24, 1797.
> Although all but forgotten today, Percy's
> ballads were quite popular during the
> last part of the eighteenth century.
> Perhaps the most well-known is "Wapping
> Old Stairs," but he is also the composer
> of such songs as "Gaffer Gray" and "How
> Sweet the Moonlight," the latter based on

Shakespeare's <u>Merchant of Venice</u>. Percy
was also an accomplished tenor and
organist.

PHILE, PHILIP.

Born, ?, c1734.

Died, Philadelphia, 1793.

Violinist and composer. Active in Philadelphia
as a violinist from about 1784, when he became
conductor of the Old American Company orchestra.
After considerable travel, Phile finally
settled in Philadelphia in 1789, and died
there in 1793. His most famous composition
is <u>The President's March</u>, also known as
<u>Hail Columbia!</u>, which received numerous
printings and was subject to frequent
arrangements until well after his death.

PICCINNI, NICCOLO.

Born, Bari, Italy, January 16, 1728.

Died, Passy, France, May 7, 1800.

Italian opera composer, representative of
the Neapolitan school. Piccinni's early
musical training was received in Naples, and
in 1754 his first opera buffa was produced

there. Two years later, his first opera seria, <u>Zenobio</u>, was performed in Naples, but his greatest success was <u>La buona figliuola</u> (1760). During his life, he composed about 140 operas, and seemed equally conversant with both the comic and serious operatic styles. In 1773, Pasquale Anfossi, the first of Piccinni's rivals, arrived in Naples, moving to Paris in 1776. Piccinni was thereby involved in the "Guerre des Bouffons." His operas were subjected to comparison with the French operas of Gluck, and real controversy was sparked when both Piccinni and Gluck were commissioned to compose operas on the same subject, <u>Iphigenie en Tauride</u>. Gluck had the advantage in that his opera was performed in 1779, two years before Piccinni's opera appeared. Despite the journalistic war waged on behalf of both composers, Piccinni had the greatest respect and admiration for Gluck and his works.

Piccinni returned to Naples during the
Revolution, and then to Paris when he
found his health failing. He died at
Passy, near Paris, at the age of 73.

PILSBURY, AMOS.

Flourished, 1799.

American psalmodist and music publisher.
Pilsbury's chief musical compilation,
The United States' Sacred Harmony,
published in Boston in 1799, was very
popular and gained wide acceptance even
in the Southern states, particularly in
South Carolina. Virtually nothing is
known of Pilsbury's life and early
musical activities.

PIRSSON, WILLIAM.

Music teacher, engraver, and composer,
active in New York from c1799 until 1812,
possibly even later. He apparently
settled either in Brooklyn or Long Island
subsequent to 1812. No records are
available regarding Pirsson's death.

PLEYEL, IGNAZ JOSEPH.

Born, Ruppersthal, Austria, June 1, 1757.
Died, near Paris, November 14, 1831.
Composer and founder of French firm of
piano makers. Pleyel studied piano
under J. B. Vanhal, and had the good
fortune to receive instruction in composition under Haydn, with whom Pleyel became
a close friend. In 1776, Pleyel produced
his puppet opera, Die Fee Urgele, at
Esterhaz, and in 1783 his opera Ifigenia in
Aulide (Iphigenie in Aulide) was produced
in Naples. In 1789, he accepted the post
of maitre de chapelle at the cathedral in
Strasbourg. It was here that, in 1791, he
became involved in the French Revolution and
only narrowly escaped death. In 1795, he
moved to Paris, where he was responsible
for the first complete edition of Haydn's
string quartets, and in 1807 he founded the
piano factory still bearing his name.

Pleyel was a prolific composer, and his many
works include symphonies, concertos, string
quartets, serenades, and songs. Some of his
works were revived toward the middle of
the present century.

POOR, JOHN.

Born, Plaistow, New Hampshire, July 8, 1752.
Died, York Haven, Pennsylvania, December 5,
1829.
John Poor was prepared for Harvard by a
rigorous classical education, and he graduated
in 1775. In 1784, after the death of his
first wife, he moved to Pennsylvania, where he
spent the rest of his life. After settling
in Philadelphia, Poor became director of the
famous Young Ladies' Academy. This institution
soon outstripped in importance many of its
predecessors, including the Moravian school at
Bethlehem, Pennsylvania. Although failing to
gain sufficient financial aid, the institution
granted diplomas of merit, and did much for
expanding educational possibilities for women.

The curriculum comprised, among other courses
of study, training in the performance of
vocal music. Poor was head of the Academy
for more than twenty years. Throughout
his life, Poor was active in the Presbyterian
Church, and served as elder while residing
in New Hope, Pennsylvania, where he lived
until the death of his second wife in 1827.
He then moved to York Haven, where he died
two years later.

POWNALL, MARY ANN.

Born, ?, 1751.

Died, Charleston, South Carolina, August 11,
1796.

English actress and singer. Mrs. Pownall
was known first as Mrs. Wrighten, and her
first husband was a prompter in a London
theatre. In 1770, she made her debut in
The Recruiting Officer in London, and
from 1776 to 1788 was heard at Vauxhall
Gardens. She was a leading artist in
Boston's Old American Company, and later

sang in subscription concerts in New York.
She composed the lyrics and music of many
songs, some of which appeared in a book
compiled by her and James Hewitt and
published in New York in 1794.

READ, DANIEL.

Born, Rehoboth (now Attleboro), Massachusetts,
November 16, 1757.

Died, New Haven, Connecticut, December 4,
1836.

During the Revolutionary War, Daniel Read
served in the Continental Army, and at 21
settled in New Stratford, Connecticut, and
finally in New Haven, where he entered the
comb-making business. Read's first
publication containing music was The American
Singing Book (1785). This tune book went
through four editions, the last dated 1793,
and achieved extensive use throughout New
England. The American Musical Magazine,
also published by Read, was the first
periodical of its kind in the United States,

and its monthly issues contained sacred music
by popular American and European composers.
Other works appearing before 1800 include
An Introduction to Psalmody (1790) and
The Columbian Harmonist (four editions,
1793-1810). His last manuscripts
were completed in 1832, but were never
published before his death four years later.

REEVE, WILLIAM.

Born, London, 1757.

Died, London, June 22, 1815.

Reeve was organist at Totnes, Devonshire,
from 1781 until 1783, and from 1792 organist
of St. Martin's at Ludgate. He held the post
of composer to Covent Gardens and Astley's
Circus (1791), and was joint owner of Sadler's
Wells Theatre (1802). He composed incidental
music to some forty plays, many pantomimes
and operettas, some in collaboration with
Joseph Mazzinghi, and numerous songs.
Perhaps his most popular work is "I am a
friar in orders grey," which was heard in
the play The Merry Sherwood (1795).

REICHARDT, JOHANN FRIEDRICH.

Born, Königsberg, November 25, 1752.

Died, Giebichenstein, near Halle, June 26,

1814.

German composer and writer on music.

See Grove, v. 7, p. 108-110.

REINAGLE, ALEXANDER.

Born, Portsmouth, England, 1756.

Died, Baltimore, September 21, 1809.

Composer, conductor, pianist, and theatrical

manager. Before Reinagle had reached his

eighteenth birthday, he and his family moved

to Edinburgh, Scotland, where he received

much of his earliest musical training from

Raynor Taylor. In 1785, Reinagle had the good

fortune to visit the celebrated composer,

C. P. E. Bach, at Hamburg. In the following

year, Reinagle arrived in New York, soon

afterward settling in Philadelphia, where he

conducted and performed in numerous concerts.

In 1793, he and Thomas Wignell founded the

Philadelphia New Theatre which, after being

closed for a year, reopened on February 17,

1794, with a performance of Samuel Arnold's

The Castle of Andalusia. Thereafter,

regular concerts were given until 1809,

the year of Reinagle's death. His

compositions include instrumental works

for pianoforte and string ensembles,

as well as stage plays and many short

popular songs.

RELFE, JOHN.

Born, Greenwich, 1763.

Died, London, c1837.

English composer. *See Grove, v. 7,*

p. 121.

RÖSSLER, FRANZ ANTON.

See Rosetti, Francesco Antonio.

ROGERSON, DR. [ROBERT?]

Flourished, c1789.

American vocalist and composer, early

President of the Handel and Haydn Society.

Little is known of Rogerson's personal

life and activities. However, it is known

that in October, 1789, George Washington
visited Boston, where he was greeted with a
concert to celebrate his arrival. The first
part of the concert consisted of, among others,
airs from Handel's Messiah. The last half of
the concert featured Felsted's oratorio, Jonah,
with the solo vocalists including Dr. Rogerson.
His chief original composition is Anthem, Sacred
to the Memory of his Excellency John Hancock
(Boston, 1793).

ROSETTI, FRANCESCO ANTONIO.

Born, Niemes, Bohemia, October 26, 1746.
Died, Ludwigslust, Germany, June 30, 1792.
Bohemian composer, conductor, and double-
bass player. Real name: Franz Anton
Rössler. *See Grove, v. 7, p. 256.*

ROSS, JOHN.

Born, Newcastle-on-Tyne, October 12, 1764.
Died, Aberdeen, July 28, 1837.
English organist and composer of Scottish
extraction. *See Grove, v. 7, p. 239.*

ROWE, J.

Little-known compiler of sacred music; virtually
nothing known of his life or musical activities.

RUSS, D.

>An unidentified composer, Russ may have lived
>in the vicinity of Wilmington, Delaware.
>His <u>Uranian Harmony</u> was issued from Philadelphia
>in 1791. He and Raynor Taylor also collaborated
>in composing the song, "Friendship," found in
><u>The Philadelphia Repository and Weekly Register</u>
>(Philadelphia, 1801, vol. 1, no. 17).

SALIMENT, GEORGE EDWARD.

>Flutist and composer, first mentioned in 1791
>in New York newspapers. He resided in New
>York until 1800, at which time his name
>disappears from the directories.

SARTI, GIUSEPPE.

>Born, Faenza (baptized December 1), 1729.
>Died, Berlin, July 28, 1802.
>Italian composer. *See Grove, v. 7,*
>*p. 412-415.*

SCHETKY, JOHANN GEORG CHRISTOFF.

>Born, Darmstadt, 1740.
>Died, Edinburgh, November 29, 1824.
>German composer and cellist. *See Grove,*
>*v. 7, p. 482.*

SCHUBART, CHRISTIAN FRIEDRICH DANIEL.

> Born, Obersontheim, Swabia, March 24, 1739.
>
> Died, Stuttgart, October 10, 1791.
>
> Although lacking outstanding musical training, Schubart's gifts were sufficient to secure an organ post at Ludwigsburg in 1769. His middle years were spent chiefly in Mannheim and Ulm, and his Deutsche Chronik, founded in 1774 and published until 1777, immediately preceded his imprisonment at Hohenasperg for his free-thinking and liberal writings; he was not to be released until ten years later. Schubart's works were few, but include many compositions for piano and numerous variations. His work on the aesthetics of music, Ideen zu einer Aesthetik der Tonkunst, was published in Vienna after his death (1806). Perhaps Schubart's fame today rests on his words to four of Schubert's songs: Die Forelle, An mein Clavier, An der Tod, and Grablied auf einen Soldaten.

SELBY, WILLIAM.

>Born, England, 1738.

>Died, Boston, December 1798.

>Organist and composer. Selby settled in the
United States around 1771, and was appointed
organist of Trinity Church, Newport, Rhode
Island, in 1774. After 1777, he served as
organist at King's Chapel in Boston. His
compositions include anthems, songs, and
some instrumental works.

SHAW, ROBERT.

>Little-known compiler of vocal and
instrumental collections; flourished
c1794.

SHIELD, WILLIAM.

>Born, Durham, England, March 5, 1748.

>Died, London, January 25, 1829.

>Although Shield received his first musical
instruction from his parents, he was fortunate
enough to study with the prominent organist
in Newcastle, Charles Avison (1710-1770), and
he received instruction in violin from the

Italian violinist, Felice de Giardini (1716-1796). In 1772, Giardini engaged Shield as second violin with the opera orchestra in London, and a year later promoted him to principal viola, a position which he maintained for eighteen years. Shield's first opera, The Flitch of Bacon (1778) was so successful that he was appointed composer at Covent Garden. In 1817, he was appointed to the highly-esteemed post of Master of the King's Music, which he retained until his death in 1829. Such was his renown that Shield was buried in Westminster Abbey in the same grave as Clementi, and in 1891 a memorial cross was erected by public subscription in his hometown churchyard in Durham. Shield composed at least fifty dramatic pieces, including operas, pantomimes, and other stage works, six trio sonatas, six violin duos, and numerous short songs which gained wide popularity during his own lifetime.

SHUMWAY, NEHEMIAH.

Born, ?, 1761.

Died, ?, 1843.

Little-known composer and compiler of sacred music.

SICARD, STEPHEN.

Flourished, 1788.

Composer and dancing master. He came to Philadelphia about 1785, and the following year advertised himself as a pupil of Mr. Vestries, "assistant master of Mr. Gardelle, the first dancing master of the opera at Paris." Sicard may be traced in Philadelphia for a number of years.

SKINNER, THOMAS.

Little-known compiler of sacred music; flourished c1800.

SMITH, JOSHUA.

Biographical information not available.

SMITH, THEODORE.

Flourished 1770-1810.

English pianist, known chiefly for his opera Alfred. Composer of church music, piano concertos and sonatas, harp and piano duos, and numerous songs.

SPOFFORD, REGINALD.

Born, Southwell, Nottinghamshire, England, 1770.

Died, London, September 8, 1827.

Most of Spofford's [also Spofforth] musical
instruction was received from his uncle
Thomas Spofford, organist of Southwell
Minster. His interests turned to vocal
music, and his first glees were composed
around the year 1788. In 1795, he began
composing theatrical music, and a year later
wrote the music to The Witch of the Wood, a
farce produced at Covent Garden. Spofford's
most famous works include "Come, bounteous
May," "Health to my dear," and "How calm
the evening." Being a competent pianist,
he often accompanied at Covent Garden under
the direction of William Shield. He is best
represented, however, by his glees, numbering
about seventy, and marked by a lively and
fanciful style. His health failed during
the last years of his life, and in 1827 he
was buried in Kensington parish church, and
the Brompton cemetery there bears a plaque to
his memory.

STAES, FERDINAND PHILIPPE JOSEPH.

>Born, Brussels, December 16, 1748.

>Died, Brussels, March 23, 1809.

>Netherlands harpsichordist, organist, and composer. *See Grove, v. 8, p. 36.*

STAMITZ, KARL.

>Born, Mannheim, May 7, 1745.

>Died, Jena, November 9, 1801.

>Bohemian composer, violinist, and violist, son of Johann Stamitz. *See Grove, v. 8, p. 43.*

STEVENSON, JOHN ANDREW.

>Born, Dublin, November 1761.

>Died, Kells, co. Meath, September 14, 1833.

>Irish composer. *See Grove, v. 8, p. 85.*

STICKNEY, JOHN.

>Born, Stoughton, Massachusetts, March 31, 1744.

>Died, South Hadley, Massachusetts, April 23, 1827.

>At the age of fifteen, Stickney learned from the lawyer William Dunbar much of the new style of music being introduced by William Billings, also a resident of Stoughton. He was also a member of one of the singing societies established there by Billings. Stickney spent much of his life teaching music in several towns of the Connecticut Valley,

including Northampton, Hartford, and New Haven. He continued to conduct singing schools until about age 65, and was partially successful in his attempt to displace the traditional rote method of singing, advocating learning to read and sing by note. His chief publications is The Gentleman and Lady's Musical Companion (1774), containing music engraved and written in four clefs, with a revised and greatly altered edition appearing nine years later under the editorship of Daniel Bayley.

STONE, JOSEPH C.

Born, Ward, Massachusetts, c1758.

Died, Ward, Massachusetts, February 22, 1837.

Little-known composer and compiler and sacred music.

STORACE, STEPHEN.

Born, London, January 4, 1763.

Died, London, March 19, 1796.

The son of Stefano Storace, a double-bass player of Italian descent, Stephen was placed

in the St. Onofrio Conservatorio in Naples
at the age of twelve, where he studied
violin for a number of years. After having
met Mozart while traveling through Vienna,
Storace returned to England in 1787 and
soon produced his first opera, The Haunted
Tower (1789). His initial success led to
other operas, including No Song No Supper
(1790), The Pirates (1792), and The Prize
(1793). In all, he wrote about twenty operas,
several ballads and songs, and a string
quartet. The quartet had the distinction of
having been performed in Vienna by Haydn,
Dittersdorf, Mozart, and Johann Baptist
Vanhal. The anxiety and pressures brought
about by the stringent demands in his work
at Drury Lane no doubt contributed to his
untimely death in 1796 at the age of 33.

SWAN, TIMOTHY.

Born, Worcester, Massachusetts, July 23, 1758.
Died, Northfield, Massachusetts, July 23, 1842.

Composer and compiler of hymn tunes. Even though he received some rudimental instruction on the fife, Swan's musical education consisted of about three weeks at a singing school. He moved to Suffield, Connecticut, in 1782, where he lived for nearly thirty years. Very early in his career, he composed the hymn tune Poland, used in manuscript throughout New England. Such was the popularity of Swan's hymns that they were often included in the hymnals of Oliver Brownson, Simeon Jocelin, and Daniel Read. Swan was an admirer of poetry, and wrote much verse in the Scottish dialect. His chief publications issued before 1800 include The Songster's Assistant, a short pamphlet of two-part songs, many never before published. Although the authorship of The Federal Harmony (not to be confused with Asahel Benham's work of the same title) is questionable, recent scholarship indicates that it is perhaps one of Swan's earliest

publications. Four editions, all printed in
Boston, appeared between 1785 and 1792, and
contained two of his most popular early hymns,
"China" and "Lisbon."

TANS'UR, WILLIAM.

Baptised, Dunchurch, Warwickshire, November 6,
1706.

Died, St. Neot's, Huntingdonshire, October 7,
1783.

English organist, teacher, and composer.
Tans'ur (original German name: Tänzer)
appears to have been employed as a music
teacher at an early age, and held numerous
organ posts at such places as Ewell and
Barnes in Surrey (1737), Stamford in Lincoln-
shire (1756 and 1759), and Boston (1761).
The last forty years of his life were spent
at St. Neot's, where he was occupied as a
bookseller, stationer, and teacher of music.
Tans'ur died at St. Neot's in 1783 at the
approximate age of 83, for in the prefaces
to some of his publications of hymn tunes he

states that he was born in 1700, but not
baptized until six years later. In later
years, the appellation of "William Tans'ur,
senior, musico theorico" was adopted, and
his publications contain some of the earliest
printed examples of what were previously
only familiar hymn tunes learned by rote.
His chief works include The Royal Melody
Compleat (New Harmony of Zion, 1735 and 1755)
and Compleat Melody, with numerous editions
dating from c1724. Although actually a
British musician and composer, his collections
of psalm tunes attained wide popularity
and use in this country.

TAYLOR, RAYNOR.

Born, England, 1747
Died, Philadelphia, August 17, 1825.
Other than the fact that Raynor Taylor was
born in England probably in 1747, relatively
little is known of his early years. Much of
his musical training was received in London
at the King's Singing School, and in 1765 he

was appointed organist in Chelmsford.
In the same year he became musical director
of the famed Sadler's Wells Theatre.
Taylor settled in Philadelphia in 1793,
where he became organist of St. Peter's
Church, and in 1820 was instrumental in
founding the Musical Fund Society,
designed to further the cause of chamber
music in America. Taylor was an accomplished
singer, and composed many operetta-like
burlesques or farces which he called "olios."
In 1799, he joined with Alexander Reinagle
to publish a "Monody" lamenting the recently-
departed General George Washington.
Taylor's chief compositions include the
ballad-operas The Iron Chest (1797) and
The Shipwreck'd Mariner Preserved (1797).
Among his many shorter songs are "The
Wounded Sailor," "The Merry Piping Lad,"
and "The Wand'ring Village Maid." Taylor
died in 1825 at the age of 78, and is buried,
along with Benjamin Carr, in St. Peter's
churchyard, Philadelphia.

THOMAS, ISAIAH.

Born, Boston, January 19, 1749.

Died, ?, April 4, 1831.

American printer and founder of the American
Antiquarian Society, Thomas' introduction
to the art of printing began at the age of
six. In 1756, he was apprenticed to
Zechariah Fowle of Boston, and while in his
teens Thomas took over Fowle's trade. In
1766, he went to Halifax, hoping to learn
still more of the printing business. After
unsuccessful attempts to reach England, he
returned to Boston in 1770, where he and
Fowle established the Massachusetts Spy,
which was printed until 1904. As a minute-
man, he took part in the skirmishes at
Lexington and Concord and, together with Paul
Revere and others, helped warn of the approach
of the British. In 1812, he founded the
American Antiquarian Society and became its
first president. He also was the first printer
of Worcester, the first in Massachusetts to

deliver to a group the Declaration of Independence
(July 24, 1776), and he received an honorary
degree from Dartmouth in 1814 and from Allegheny
College in 1818. His personal friends included
Washington, Franklin, the Adamses, Jefferson,
Hancock, and other leaders of the time. As a
book publisher, he was noted for the fine
typography and for the popularity and importance
of the published work. His folio Bible was the
first printed in English in the United States,
and he is the first to publish the first
dictionary in America, Perry's Dictionary.
Thomas was the first American publisher to
do extensive publishing from musical type,
and his popular children's book, Mother
Goose Melody, contains an example of musical
notation.

TRISOBIO, FILIPPO.

Born, ?, ?

Died, Philadelphia (?), 1798.

Singing teacher, composer, and music publisher.

In 1796, Trisobio left London for America,

arriving in Baltimore in July of that year.
After appearing in a concert, he moved to
Charleston, South Carolina, finally settling
in Philadelphia where he published some of
his own compositions, as well as those of
others. His works include <u>Scuola del
Canto</u>, a collection of Italian songs of the
greatest composers of the time, and <u>The
Clock of Lombardy</u>, a "capriccio" for piano
solo. On January 12, 1798, he gave a concert
with Miss Broadhurst in which they sang
favorite Italian duets. Trisobio died in
poverty in 1798, presumably in Philadelphia.

TUFTS, JOHN.

Born, Medford, Massachusetts, May 5, 1689.
Died, Amesbury, Massachusetts, August 17, 1752.
Congregational minister and pioneer compiler
of sacred tune books. Graduated from Harvard
College in 1708, and was ordained minister
of the Second Church of Christ in West Newbury,
1714, a post which he held until his retirement
in 1738. His <u>A Very Plain and Easy Introduction</u>

<u>to the Art of Singing Psalm Tunes</u> (1714 or
1715), in which letters rather than notes were
used as musical notation, was considered a "daring
and unjustifiable innovation" by some critics.
Nevertheless, the work gained wide popularity and,
through varying titles, underwent at least eleven
editions, the last in 1774. Tufts retired in 1738
to Amesbury, where he became a shopkeeper and
died in 1752.

VANHAL, JAN KRTITEL.

Born, Nechanice near Hradec Kralove, May 22, 1739.
Died, Vienna, August 26, 1813.
Austrian composer of Bohemian origin. *See
Grove, v. 8, p. 668-669.*

VICTOR, H. B.

Composer, editor, and teacher. In 1759, Victor
arrived in London from Germany, and in 1774 came
to Philadelphia, remaining there for at least four
years. He credits himself with the invention of a
"tromba doppia, con tympana," in which he was able
play simultaneously two trumpets and two kettle
drums, the latter with his feet.

VIOTTI, GIOVANNI BATTISTA.

Born, Fontanetto Po, Vercelli, May 12, 1755.
Died, London, March 3, 1824.
Italian composer and violinist. *See Grove,
v. 8, p. 824-828.*

VOGLER, GERARD.

    Born, ?, ?

    Died, ?, ?

    Little-known German eighteenth-century music

    publisher, possibly brother of the Abbe

    Georg Joseph Vogler. *See Grove, v. 9,*

    p. 42-43.

WALTER, THOMAS.

    Born, Roxbury, Massachusetts, December 13, 1696.

    Died, Roxbury, Massachusetts, January 10, 1725.

    Clergyman and nephew of the Reverend Cotton

    Mather. In 1713, Walter graduated from

    Harvard College with an A. M. degree, and five

    years later was ordained as minister in Roxbury;

    his grandfather, Increase Mather, delivered

    the ordination sermon. Walter's Grounds and

    Rules of Musick Explained (1721), which went

    through numerous editions, was designed to

    improve the state of psalm singing in the New

    England churches. Only four years later, at the

    age of twenty-nine, Thomas Walter died of

    consumption in his home town of Roxbury.

WATTS, ISAAC.

    Born, Southampton, England, July 17, 1674.

    Died, Stoke Newington, London, November 25, 1748.

English Nonconformist theologian and hymnist. Watts was educated for the ministry at the Dissenting Academy at Stoke Newington, London, and in 1699 was chosen assistant minister of the Independent Congregation in Mark Lane, becoming full pastor in 1702. He suffered from ill health all his life, and from 1712 lived in partial retirement, spending most of his time writing. He died at the home of the English judge Thomas Abney in Stoke Newington, and a monument to his memory was erected in Westminster Abbey. Watts was the author of more than 600 hymns, some of which are still found in Protestant hymnals. His first publication, Horae Lyricae, issued in 1706, was followed by his Hymns and Spiritual Songs (1709, second ed.) and a hymnal for children, Divine Songs (1715), later issued under the title Divine and Moral Songs (1729).

WEBBE, SAMUEL, SR.

Born, London (?), 1740.

Died, London, May 25, 1816.

English composer and organist. Webbe's early
music instruction was received from a Mr.
Barbandt, organist of the Bavarian ambassador's
chapel in London. In 1763, he first appeared
as composer of unaccompanied vocal music, chiefly
glees, canons, and catches. Upon the death
of Thomas Warren Horne in 1794, Webbe became
secretary to the Catch Club, an office which
he retained for over twenty years until his
death in 1816. He was also librarian of the
Glee Club from 1787. Webbe's works include
nine volumes of catches and glees, a "Cecilian
Ode" for six voices, a harpsichord concerto, a
divertimento for wind band, and numerous
collections of masses and motets.

WHEATLEY, WILLIAM.

Little-known English song composer, active
from c1760.

WILLSON, JOSEPH.

Musician, music teacher, music publisher, and
composer. Probably lived in London up to 1800,
when he came to America, settling in New

Brunswick, New Jersey. His first appearance
as a vocalist was in New York in 1802.
From about 1804 until 1809 he served as
organist of Trinity Church, and three years
later opened a music store from which he
issued music until 1820, when his son
succeeded him. Although it is possible that
he may have returned to England in the mid-
1820s, nothing was heard from Willson after
1824.

WOOD, ABRAHAM.

Born, Northboro, Massachusetts, July 30, 1752.
Died, Northboro, Massachusetts, August 6, 1804.
During much of his life, Wood was greatly
involved in military duties: he was a militia
clerk during the Revolution, served as drummer
at Cambridge, and was one of the Committee of
Correspondence in 1777 and 1780. Nevertheless,
he was vitally interested in music, and was
chorister of Northboro Church and a respected
musician. He died suddenly of apoplexy at his
home in Northboro, where he spent his entire

life, in 1804. His <u>Columbian Harmony</u> was a joint compilation of Wood and Joseph Stone, the former contributing 26 tunes and the latter 42. Wood also published a <u>Hymn of Peace</u> (1784), <u>Divine Songs</u> (1789), and a <u>Funeral Elegy</u> (1800), composed on the death of General George Washington. With President Harrison's death in 1840, this <u>Elegy</u> was republished and used on that occasion.

WOODRUFF, MERIT N.

Born, Watertown, Connecticut, June 17, 1780. Died, Watertown, Connecticut, June 26, 1799. Son of Isaac Woodruff, head of an old and highly respected family in Milford, Connecticut. When Merit was only two years old, his father died suddenly of smallpox. Being one of eight children, Merit was not able to obtain even a perfunctory education. His love for music, however, was not stifled, and by the age of fourteen he had composed numerous hymn tunes. He was not athletically inclined

and, not being a swimmer, drowned at the age
of 19 when he waded too deeply in a small
wading pool near his home.

WRIGHT, THOMAS.

Born, Stockton-on-Tees, September 18, 1763.
Died, near Barnard Castle, November 24, 1829.
English organist and composer. Wright received
his first instruction in music from his
father, Robert Wright, and by the age of
eleven began studying organ with John Garth
at Sedgefield; he succeeded Garth in 1784.
Wright soon was famous for his organ improvi-
sations, and was also a respected teacher of
piano and violin in addition to organ. He
composed several hymn tunes, a concerto for
piano or harpsichord (1795), an "Anthem for
Thanksgiving for Peace" (1802), and numerous
overtures and songs. Wright was also an
amateur inventor, and designed a simple
pocket metronome, a mechanical device
allowing organ pipes to be played from an
organ keyboard, and a machine which was

designed to elevate coal, an invention for
which the Society of Arts offered him a
respectable premium.

YOUNG, JOHN.

17th-18th century.

Practically nothing is known of John Young
except that he was an English music publisher
active in London from about 1698 to 1730.
His son, Talbot Young, established a music
society with Maurice Green (c1695-1755),
the English organist and composer, and was
also an accomplished violinist.

PART FOUR

COMPOSER-COMPILER INDEX

Note: Titles preceded by an asterisk (*) are not yet
available in microtext form in the Early American
Imprints, 1639-1800 microprint series. Such items
are included in Part Two of his Bibliography.

Composer & title	Evans no.	Page
Abrams, Harriet		
Crazy Jane	48996	1
Adgate, Andrew		
*Mechanics lecture	21627	224-225
Philadelphia harmony (1789)	21629	2
Philadelphia harmony (1790)	22299	2
Philadelphia harmony (1791)	46110	3
Philadelphia harmony (1796)	29953	3
Philadelphia songster	21628	3-4
Rudiments of music (1788)	20916	4
Rudiments of music (1788)	45212	4
Rudiments of music (1799)	35083	5
Selection of sacred harmony (1788)	45213	5
Selection of sacred harmony (1790)	22884	5
Selection of sacred harmony (1794)	47212	5
Selection of sacred harmony (1797)	32818	5

Composer & title	Evans no.	Page
Aitken, John		
Compilation of the litanies (1787)	20186	6
Compilation of the litanies (1791)	23106	6
Scots musical museum	31701	6-14
Arne, Michael		
Cymon		
Quick march	37643	93
Sweet passion of love	32041	24
Homeward bound	30383	64
Homeward bound	32926	23
Homeward bound	33294	20
Quick march in Cymon	37643	93
Sweet passion of love	32041	24
Arne, Thomas Augustine		
Artaxerxes		
Celebrated duett [Fair Aurora]	47704	24
Soldier tir'd	45572	163
Celebrated duett in Artaxerxes		
(Fair Aurora)	47704	24
*Columbia and liberty	33602	227
The Echoing horn	33294	14
Fair Aurora	47704	24

Composer & title	Evans no.	Page

Arne, Thomas Augustine (continued)

  Love in a village

There was a jolly miller	33294	17
The Soldier tir'd	45572	163

  Sweet passion of love [See

    Arne, Michael]

There was a jolly miller	33294	17

  Thomas and Sally

The Echoing horn	33294	14

Arnold, Samuel

And hear her sigh adieu!	33314	25

  At the dead of night [See his

    Cupid benighted]

Braes of Ballendine	19750	112
Braes of Ballendine	31701	11

  The Castle of Andalusia

Braes of Ballendine	19750	112
Braes of Ballendine	31701	11
Flowers of the forest	31701	12

  Love soft illusion [arr. from

    Bertoni]

	35891	139
Scotch air	31701	11

Composer & title	Evans no.	Page
Arnold, Samuel (continued)		
Death and burial of Cock Robin	37107	49
Dorothy Dump	29498	184
-----. Walters sweethearts	30832	135
Favorite duett sung in the opera of the Children in the Wood [Young Simon in his lovely Sue]	29121	24
Favorite song in the opera of the Spanish Barber	35981	139
Finale to Inkle and Yarico	27694	180
Finale to Inkle and Yarico	30396	72
Flowers of the forest	31701	12
Fresh and strong the breeze is blowing	30383	64
Fresh and strong the breeze is blowing	33294	18
Fresh and strong the breeze is blowing	47823	124
Fresh and strong the breeze is blowing	49008	25
The Gipsy's song	26522	221
The Gipsy's song	29498	183

404

Composer & title	Evans no.	Page
Arnold, Samuel (continued)		
The Little gipsey	33667	66
Little Sally	31754	25
-----.	48776	25
Lorade in the tower	30832	137
Love soft illusion	35981	139
Maid of the Mill		
The gipsy's song	26522	221
-----.	29498	183
Medley duetto	27694	177
Moorish march	30832	136
The Mountaineers		
Happy tawny Moor	27694	179
-----.	30242	25
Lorade in the tower	30832	137
Moorish march	30832	136
Think your tawny Moor is true	30832	135
The way worn traveller	26783	27
-----.	27694	180
-----.	47705	27
When the hollow drum	31954	27
The Negro boy	30243	26
A New song for a serenade [Rise		
my Delia]	33294	21

Composer & title	Evans no.	Page
Arnold, Samuel (continued)		
O say bonny lass	35981	138
Oh say simple maid	30383	63
-----.	33294	22
Pauvre Madelon	25314	26
-----.	33536	26
Peeping Tom		
The Rush light	27661	26
Rise my Delia	33294	21
The Rush light	27661	26
Scotch air from Inkle and Yarico	31701	11
Scotch air from the Castle of		
Andalusia	31701	11
See brother see	29119	27
The Shipwreck		
And hear her sigh adieu!	33314	25
In dear little Ireland	48775	25
Little Sally	31754	25
-----.	48776	25
When on the ocean	48777	27
Sister, see, on yonder bough	30832	134
The Spanish barber, a favorite		
song in	35981	139

Composer & title	Evans no.	Page
Arnold, Samuel (continued)		
The Surrender of Calais		
Go with you all the world over	26522	217
Pauvre Madelon	25314	26
Pauvre Madelon	33536	26
Think your tawny Moor is true	30832	135
Walters sweethearts [see his		
Dorothy Dump]		
The Way worn traveller	26783	27
The Way worn traveller	27694	180
The Way worn traveller	47705	27
When first to Helen's lute	30832	134
When nights were cold [composed		
by Benjamin Carr, but introduced		
in Arnold's Children in the		
Wood; see Carr, Benjamin]		
When on the ocean	48777	27
When the hollow drum	31954	27
Young Simon in his lovely Sue	29121	24
Zorinski		
At the dead of the night [See		
his Cupid benighted]		
Courteous stranger	37106	47
Courteous stranger	37107	49

Composer & title	Evans no.	Page
Attwood, Thomas (continued)		
The Sea boys duett	27517	149
Tears that exhale	27694	178
Young Carlos sued a beauteous maid	27694	179
Young Carlos sued a beauteous maid	31701	8
Atwell, Thomas H.		
New York collection of sacred harmony	28216	28
Babcock, Samuel		
Middlesex harmony	28221	29
Bach, Johann Christian		
Ah seek to know [arr. Reinagle]	45572	162
Cease a while ye winds to blow	28222	29
No 'twas neither shape nor feature	33667	66
Barnard, John		
New version of the psalms of David	6820	29
Barthelemon, Francois Hippolite		
The Boatman	31701	8
Three favorite duetts	49016	30
Bayley, Daniel		
*Collection of anthems and hymn tunes	18341	229

Composer & title	Evans no.	Page
Bayley, Daniel (continued)		
Essex harmony (1770)	11560	30
Essex harmony (1771)	11979	30
Essex harmony (1772)	12319	30
Essex harmony, or musical miscellany (1785)	18925	30
New and compleat introduction to the grounds and rules of musick		
[1st ed.] 1764	9598	31
[2nd ed.] 1764	9599	31
*[3rd ed.] 1764	9600	229-230
1765	41518	31
1766	10236	32
1768	10829	32
New harmony of Zion; or complete melody	20956	32
New universal harmony	12664	32
Psalm singer's assistant (n.d.)	18926	33
Psalm singer's assistant (1767)	41691	33
Beissel, Johann Conrad		
Paradisisches Wunder-Spiel	7147	33-34
Belcher, Supply		
Harmony of Maine	26636	34-35
*Ordination anthem	31791	230-231

Composer & title	Evans no.	Page
Belknap, Daniel		
Autumn	36939	35
East Needham	36939	36
Evangelical harmony	36939	35
Funeral ode	36939	36
*Harmonist's companion (1794)	28255	231
Harmonist's companion (1797)	31792	36-37
Milton	36939	36
Summer	36939	35
View of the Temple--a Masonic ode	36939	36
Winter	36939	36
Benham, Asahel		
Federal harmony		
1790 ed.	22340	37
1792 ed.	24092	37
*1793 ed.	25159	231
1794 ed.	26640	37
*1795 ed.	28261	232
1796 ed.	30054	37
Social harmony (1798)	33398	38
Social harmony (1799)	36331	38
Benjamin, Jonathan		
Harmonia Coelestis	35179	38

Composer & title	Evans no.	Page
Billings, William		
*Anthem for Thanksgiving	25196	232
*Bird and the lark	22362	232
Continental harmony	26673	39
*Easter anthem	28301	232
Massachusetts harmony (1784)	18366	39
-----. (1786)	18933	39
Music in miniature	16205	39
New-England psalm-singer	11572	39-40
Psalm-singer's amusement	17104	40
*Republican harmony	28300	233
Singing master's assistant		
1778 ed.	15744	40
1778 ed.	43416	40
*1779 ed.	16206	233
*1780 ed.	16716	233
1781 ed.	43943	40
Suffolk harmony	19512	40
*Universal praise	25196	232
Billington, Thomas		
Sylvia	45572	162
Boccherini, Luigi		
Andantino tire	37107	51

Composer & title	Evans no.	Page
Carr, Benjamin (continued)		
The Italian monk		
Poor Mary	37106	47
-----.	37107	50
Little Boy Blew	37106	47
-----.	37107	50
Little sailor boy	34489	46
Mary will smile	35283	52
Medley duetto	27694	176
Medley duetto...from the Federal		
Overture	29498	185
*The Musical journal	30822	234
Musical journal for the flute	37106	46-48
Musical journal for the pianoforte	37107	49-52
The New somebody	35283	52
Poor Mary	37106	47
-----.	37107	50
*Poor Richard	25265	234
-----.	27517	149
-----.	35283	52
Shakespeare's willow	37106	47
-----.	37107	50
Six imitations of English...airs	37107	52
Take oh! take those lips away	46998	46

Composer & title	Evans no.	Page
Carr, Benjamin (continued)		
Tell me where is fancy bred	46998	46
Three ballads	35283	52
3 divertimentos	37107	52
Two favourite strathpey reels	27694	172
When icicles hang by the wall	46998	45
When nights were cold	27694	181
When nights were cold	33667	67
When nights were cold	35981	139
When nights were cold	46998	46
When nights were cold	46999	53
*Why huntress why	30370	235
The widow	37107	51
Cherubini, Maria Luigi		
Overture de Demophon	28412	53
Cibber, Colley (supposed composer)		
She Wou'd & she wou'd not		
Ye chearful virgins	27694	176
Ye chearful virgins	27694	176
Cleaveland, Benjamin		
*Hymns on different spiritual subjects (1786)	19562	236
*Hymns on different spiritual subjects (1788)	21002	236
*Hymns on different subjects (1793)	25304	236

418

Composer & title	Evans no.	Page
Dibdin, Charles (continued)		
Pastorale	45573	168
*Songs in the Deserter	26882	240
Dibdin's fancy	26522	218
-----.	33667	67
Father and mother and Suke	48105	56
Favorite country dance	27694	177
Flowing can	33294	14
-----. [As sung in Storace's No		
Song No Supper]	26522	220
Great News, or a trip to the Antipodes		
The smile of benevolence	33667	67
Tom Trueloves knell	33667	67
The Vet[e]rans	27694	179
*-----.	30345	240
Homes home	33667	68
I lock'd up all my treasure	27694	179
*Jack at the windlass	25392	240
Jacks fidelity [same as Polly Ply]	30383	65
-----.	33294	22
The Jolly ringers	26522	221
The Lamplighter	26522	217
Lovely Nan	27694	181
-----.	33667	65
The Lucky escape	26522	220
-----.	26878	56
-----	26936	62

Composer & title	Evans no.	Page
Dibdin, Charles (continued)		
The Oddities (continued)		
Poor Tom Bowling	30383	65
-----. Poor Tom, or the Sailor's epitaph.	33294	14
-----. Poor Tom Bowling, or the Sailor's epitaph.	26879	57
-----. Tom Bowling.	26522	217
Overture to the Deserter	45573	168
Pastorale [from the Deserter]	45573	168
The Patent coffin	48106	57
Polly Ply [same as Jacks fidelity]	30383	65
-----.	33294	22
Poor Jack	26936	61
-----.	33294	15
Poor Tom Bowling	30383	65
-----. Poor Tom, or the Sailor's epitaph.	33294	14
-----. Poor Tom Bowling, or the Sailor's epitaph.	26879	57
-----. Tom Bowling.	26522	217
Private theatricals		
The Lucky escape	26522	220
-----.	26878	56
-----.	26936	62

Composer & title	Evans no.	Page
Dibdin, Charles (continued)		
Private theatricals (continued)		
The Lucky escape	27694	175
-----.	33294	14
The Sailor's consolation	26936	62
-----.	33294	18
The Quaker		
I lock'd up all my treasure	27694	179
The Sailor's consolation	26936	62
-----.	33294	18
The Sailor's journal [alternate title of Nancy, or the Sailor's journal, q.v.]		
The Smile of benevolence	33667	67
The Soldier's adieu	26881	57
-----.	30383	63
*Songs in the Deserter	26882	240
The Token	26883	57
Tom Bowling [see his Poor Tom Bowling]		
Tom Tackle	30383	63
-----.	33294	22
-----.	35981	138

Composer & title	Evans no.	Page
Dibdin, Charles (continued)		
Tom Trueloves knell	33667	67
'Twas in the good ship Rover, or the		
Greenwich pensioner	26884	58
*The Vet[e]rans	30345	240
-----.	27694	179
The Waggoner	26885	58
-----.	29498	184
The Wags		
Death or victory	26936	62
-----.	33294	22
Will of the wisp		
Nancy, or the Sailor's journal	32040	57
-----.	33294	16
*-----.	34166	239-240
-----.	35981	139
-----. The Sailor's journal.	33667	67
-----. -----.	48107	57
Dignum, Charles		
Fair Rosal[i]e	32104	58
Dubois, William		
Free Mason's march	33649	59
-----.	37643	92
Duport, Pierre Landrin		
*United States country dances	37336	240-242

424

Composer & title	Evans no.	Page
French, Jacob		
New American melody	21841	74
Psalmodist's companion	25513	74
Frith, Edward		
The Contented cottager	47789	75
Galli, Signora _____		
Graceful move	21628	4
-----.	33294	19
Garnet, Horatio		
Ode for the fourth of July	33294	19
Garth, John		
Favorite rondo	45573	168
Gauline, John Baptiste		
So sweet her face	48453	76
Gaveaux, Pierre		
Le Reveil du Peuple	30396	69
Gehot, Jean		
The Reconsaliation [sic]	26522	215
Gilman, John Ward		
New introduction to psalmody	42240	77
Giordani, Giuseppe		
Altho heavn's good pleasure	22095	164
Amintas		
Altho heavn's good pleasure	22095	164

Composer & title	Evans no.	Page
Gram, Hans		
Death song of an Indian chief	25848	78
*Resurrection, an anthem for Easter	47067	245
Sacred lines for Thanksgiving-Day	25562	78
-----.	47066	79
Shape alone let others prize	33294	23
Sonnet. For the fourteenth of October, 1793 [See Graun, Carl Heinrich]		
Graun, Carl Heinrich		
Sonnet. For the fourteenth of October, 1793	25563	79
Griffiths, John		
*Collection of the newest cotillions (1794)	28774	245
*-----. (1797)	32213	245
Griswold, Elijah		
Connecticut harmony	30521	79-80
H., S. M.		
Paul and Virginia		
The Wretched slave	32374	81
-----.	39151	81

Composer & title	Evans no.	Page
Harington, Henry		
Damon and Clora	19750	112
-----.	27091	82-83
Harrison, Ralph		
Sacred harmony	22615	83
Hart, Joseph		
*Hymns, &c.	20405	247
*-----.	20406	247
Hawkins, John J.		
The Beauties of creation	38203	59
Dirge	38203	58
Ode on the death of Titian Peale	38203	59
Haydn, Franz Joseph		
Air by Haydn	30396	71
Andante d'Haydn	37107	52
Andante for the pianoforte	45573	168
Favorite easy sonata	48872	84
Favorite rondo in the gipsy style	35606	84
Haydns minuet	30396	71
Hurly burly	37106	48
Minuet	30396	71
Overture by Haydn	32241	84
Romance by Haydn	29498	183
Rondo	27694	178
Sonatina...opera 71	33863	84

Composer & title	Evans no.	Page
Hewitt, James		
Advice to the ladies	27542	154
Battle of Trenton	33381	84
La Chasse	27542	153
-----.	45573	168
*Collin's ode on the passions	28444	247-248
Federal Constitution & liberty		
forever	34113	84
Flash in the pan		
*O had it been my happy lot	34263	248
*When the old heathen gods	34114	248
-----.	34115	85
How happy was my humble lot	35618	85
*Lass of Lucerne Lake	28949	248
*O had it been my happy lot	34263	248
Overture de Demophon [see Cherubini,		
Maria Luigi]		
The Patriot		
*Lass of Lucerne Lake	28949	248
Primrose girl	27542	154
-----.	33294	21
-----. Primroses.	33667	66
A Rural life	27542	154

Composer & title	Evans no.	Page
Hewitt, James (continued)		
Six songs for the harpsichord [See Pownall, Mary Ann Wrighten]		
Sonata I [D major]	47449	85
Sonata II [C major]	47449	85
Sonata III [F major]	47449	85
Three sonatas for the piano forte	47449	85
Time, a favorite rondo	47450	85
*When the old heathen gods	34114	248
-----.	34115	85
When the shades of night pursuing	37106	48
-----.	37107	51
The Wish	47805	86
The Wounded Hussar	37614	86
Hodgkinson, John		
Let Washington be our boast	37633	86
Hoffmeister, Franz Anton		
Duetto	27694	173
Holden, Oliver		
American harmony	24403	86
A Dirge, or sepulchral service	39106	86-87
Massachusetts compiler	28848	87

Composer & title	Evans no.	Page
Holden, Oliver (continued)		
Sacred dirges, hymns, and anthems	37635	87-88
*-----.	38445	249
Union harmony (1793)	25619	88
-----. (1796)	30573	89
Worcester collection of sacred		
harmony [See Laus Deo!... in		
title index]		
Holyoke, Samuel		
The Essex harmony [See Kimball,		
Jacob]		
Exeter: for Thanksgiving	33893	89
Hark! From the tomb	37642	89
Harmonia Americana	23446	89-90
Instrumental assistant	37643	90-93
Washington	33294	22
Hook, James		
Alone by the light of the moon	26936	62
-----.	30581	94
-----.	32270	93
-----.	33294	16
Anna; or, the adieu	48147	94
As bringing home, the other day	19750	113
Bonny Charley	26522	217

Composer & title	Evans no.	Page
Hook, James (continued)		
Bonny Charley	31701	12
Bright Phoebus	33294	17
-----.	45572	162
-----.	48148	94
By baby bunting	37106	48
The Caledonian laddy	31701	11
Come rouse brother sportsman	33294	19
The Cottage in the grove	30582	94
Dear little cottage maiden	30383	63
-----.	33294	20
Donna donna donna Della	32271	94
Evening	35633	95
The Flower of Yarrow	48149	94
The Girl of my heart	35981	140
He loves his winsome Kate	32272	94
Here's the pretty girl I love	32273	94
Hither Mary	25626	95
Hoot awa ye loon	32274	95
The Hours of love	35633	95
I never lov'd any dear Mary but you	33667	67
I sigh for the girl I adore	30383	65
-----.	33294	19

Composer & title	Evans no.	Page
Hook, James (continued)		
Lucy or Selim's complaint	27136	97
-----.	27694	182
-----.	33667	67
Ma belle coquette	25628	97
-----.	47076	97
Ma chere amie	45572	162
*May day morn	48152	249
May I never be married [alternate title of The Kiss, q.v.]		
Mens fate deserves a tear	35981	140
Morning	35633	95
My heart is devoted dear Mary to thee [alternate title of The Indigent peasant, q.v.]		
Night	35633	95
Noon	35633	95
*Now's the time to sing and play	48153	249
O whither can my William stray	48474	97
Pretty maids all in a row	37106	47
-----.	37107	49
Rise Cynthia rise	26092	97
*Rondo	49089	250

Composer & title	Evans no.	Page
Hook, James (continued)		
*'Twas pretty Poll and honest Jack	29664	250
'Twas with in a mile of Edinburgh Town [See Within...]		
Two bunches a penny primroses	27517	148
The Unfortunate sailor	48887	99
The Way to get married	33583	100
The Wedding-day	25630	100
-----.	48888	100
What can a lassy do	32278	100
When Lucy was kind	30383	64
-----.	30586	100
Where Liffey rolls its silver streams	32279	100
Where's the harm of that	32280	101
William of the ferry	30587	101
Willy of the dale	47456	101
Winsome Kate	27694	179
-----.	31701	12
Within a mile of Edinburgh		
Within a mile of Edinburgh	33294	21
Within a mile of Edinboro' town	33667	66
Within a mile of Edinbourgh	27694	177-178
Within a mile of Edinburgh	31701	11

Composer & title	Evans no.	Page
Hook, James (continued)		
Within a mile of Edinburgh	47457	101
-----. 'Twas within a mile of		
Edinburgh town.	32067	99
*-----. 'Twas with in a mile of		
Edinburgh town.	30371	250
Ye sluggards	22095	165
Hopkinson, Francis		
*The Battle of the kegs	16305	250
[Beneath a weeping willows shade]	21152	102
Collection of psalm tunes	9406	101
[Come fair Rosina, come away]	21152	102
[Enraptur'd I gaze]	21152	102
[My gen'rous heart disdains]	21152	102
[My love is gone to sea]	21152	102
[O'er the hills far away]	21152	102
[See down Maria's blushing cheek]	21152	102
Seven songs for the harpsichord	21152	101-102
[The Trav'ler benighted and lost]	21152	101-102
Washington's march [See Washington's		
March in title index]		
Howard, Samuel		
Farewell ye green fields	19750	113
-----.	22095	164

Composer & title	Evans no.	Page
Howe, Solomon		
Worshipper's assistant	35643	103
Huntington, Jonathan		
Albany collection of sacred harmony	37667	103-104
J., H.		
The Charming creature	33294	20
Jackson, George K.		
One kind kiss	30383	64
-----.	30931	106
Jackson, William, of Exeter		
Canzonet	27542	154
Canzonett	37106	47
The Heavy hours	33294	15
The Lord of the Manor		
When first this humble roof		
I knew	26522	220
*-----.	30140	251
Jenks, Stephen		
*Laus Deo. The New-England harmonist		
(1799)	35667	251
-----. (1800)	37707	106-107
Jocelin, Simeon		
The Chorister's companion		
[1st ed.] (1782)	17567	107
2nd ed. (1788)	21177	107

Composer & title	Evans no.	Page
Krumpholtz, Johann Baptist		
Louisa's complaint	47093	110
Lane, Isaac		
An Anthem, suitable to be per-		
formed at an Ordination	33977	111
Christmas anthem	47671	111
Langdon, Chauncy		
Beauties of psalmody	19749	111
The Charms of nature	33294	22
Romping rosy Nell	33294	19
The Select songster	19750	111-114
Law, Andrew		
The Art of singing (1794)	27204	116
The Art of singing (1800)	37787	117
The Christian harmony (1794)	27205	117
The Christian harmony (1796)	30680	117
Collection of hymn tunes (1782)	17571	117
*Collection of hymn tunes (1786)	19753	254
*Collection of hymn tunes (1792)	24463	255
Collection of hymns, for social		
worship	17996	117

Composer & title	Evans no.	Page
Law, Andrew (continued)		
Collection of the best and most		
approved tunes		
*1779 ed.	16317	255
*1781 ed.	17201	255
*1782 ed.	17572	255
The Musical Magazine		
Number first (1792)	24464	118
Number second (1793)	25708	118
*Number third (1794)	27206	255-256
*Number fifth (1799)	35719	256
The Musical Primer		
*1780 ed.	16816	256
1793 ed.	25709	118
1800 ed.	49106	118
The Rudiments of Music		
1st ed., 1783	17997	119
2nd ed., 1785	19057	119
3rd ed., 1791	23491	119
4th ed., 1792	24466	119
*[unnumbered ed.] 1792	24465	256-257
4th ed., 1793	46806	120
*[unnumbered ed.] 1794	27207	257

Composer & title	Evans no.	Page
Law, Andrew (continued)		
Select harmony		
1779 ed.	16318	120
1784 ed.	18553	120
*1786 ed.	19754	257
1791 ed.	23492	120
*1792 ed.	24467	257
Select number of plain tunes		
1767 ed.	10662	121
*1772 ed.	12427	258
1781 ed.	17098	157
1785 ed.	18930	158
*1794 ed.	27208	258
Lee, Chauncey		
Ode for the Fourth of July 1799	36436	121
Lee, Thomas		
Sacred harmony	38446	121
Lesueur, Jean Francois		
The Wretched slave. Sung in the new		
opera of Paul and Virginia		
[See H., S. M.]		

Composer & title	Evans no.	Page
Linley, Francis		
Let life us cherish	47823	124
Linley's assistant for the piano-forte (1796)	47823	123-124
-----. A New assistant for the piano-forte (1796)	30695	121-123
Preludes	30695	122
-----.	47823	124
-----. Second set of preludes.	30695	122
Walzer	47823	124
Linley, Thomas		
Carnival of Venice		
Young Lubin was a shepherd boy	26522	220
For tenderness form'd [See Paisiello, Giovanni]		
Primroses deck	27562	124
The Spanish rivals		
Still the lark finds repose	26522	216
*Still the lark [finds] repose	34002	258
Young Lubin was a shepherd boy	26522	220
Little, William		
*The Easy instructor	34004	258-260

Composer & title	Evans no.	Page
Lyon, James		
A Dialogue on peace	9386	125
*Friendship: anthem	21578	260
Urania: or a choice collection of psalm tunes		
1761 ed.	8908	125
*1767 ed.	10666	261
1773 ed.	12839	126
Mann, Elias		
Marlborough's ghost	33294	15
Northampton collection of sacred harmony	32416	127
Markordt, J.		
Tom Thumb		
That petty fogging grizzle	27694	177
We kings who are in our senses	27694	178
Martini il Tedesco		
Henry the IV		
Martini's march	30396	72
The Mariners		
The sea boys duett	27517	149
Ronde. Chantee a la reine par Monseigneur le Dauphin.	27694	180

Composer & title	Evans no.	Page
Mazzinghi, Joseph		
The Magician no conjurer		
A Blessing on brandy & beer	30832	135
The Maid with a bosom of snow	35762	128-129
Moller, John Christopher		
The First [-third] number	25831	131-133
Meddley with the most favorite airs	47835	131
Rondo	25831	131
Sinfonia	25831	131
More, Isabella Theaker		
The Walls of my prison	26522	219
Moulds, John		
The Caledonian maid	29498	184
-----.	33667	66
-----.	47495	133
-----. The Much admired song of		
Arabella the Caledonian maid	47498	134
I sold a guiltless Negro boy	30832	136
-----.	33294	16
She dropt a tear and cried be true	37106	48
-----.	37107	50
-----.	47496	134
Sterne's Maria	30832	137
-----.	33294	16

Composer & title	Evans no.	Page
Paisiello, Giovanni (continued)		
How can I forget	47873	146
*Recitativo e rondo	48212	267
Whither my love	25309	195
-----.	26936	61
Pelissier, Victor		
Washington and Independence	34959	146
Pennsylvania. University.		
An exercise, performed at the		
public commencement...1790	22798	147
Percy, John		
The Captive	48223	147
A Wand'ring gipsey	37106	48
-----.	37107	51
Phile, Philip		
The Favorite new federal song [See		
The President's March]		
Hail Columbia [See The President's		
March]		
The New federal song [See The		
President's March]		
The President's march	27694	172
-----.	29609	150
-----.	30795	129

Composer & title	Evans no.	Page
Phile, Philip (continued)		
-----.	31044	150
-----.	33902	150
-----.	37643	92
-----. The Favorite new federal song.	33896	150
*-----. New federal song.	33897	268
*-----. The Truly federal song Hail Columbia!	33898	268-269
The Truly federal song Hail Columbia!		
[See The President's March]		
Philo-Musico		
[See Langdon, Chauncy]		
Piccinni, Niccolo.		
Overture La Buona Figliuola	31009	151
La Schiava. Overture.	22069	151
-----.	45573	168
Pilsbury, Amos		
The United States' sacred harmony	36119	151-152
Pirsson, William		
A Duetto for two flutes	27694	181
Pleyel, Ignaz		
Air	27517	148
Braw lads on Yarrow braes	31701	7

Composer & title	Evans no.	Page
Pleyel, Ignaz (continued)		
Chanson ecossoise	31701	7
Come blushing rose	47183	152
Danse ecossoise	31701	8, 10
Duetto	27694	175
-----.	29498	182
From thee Eliza I must go	31701	10
German hymn, with variations	49136	152
Henry's cottage maid	26522	218
-----.	27694	173
-----.	31017	152
Minuetto	37107	52
Minuetto & trio	37107	52
Oh, open the door	31701	7
One morning very early	31701	7
Pleyel's German hymn, with variations	49136	152
Rondo	37107	52
Shepherds I have lost my love	31701	7
Sonata	37107	51
*Twelve duets for 2 clarinets	27528	269

Composer & title	Evans no.	Page
Poor, John		
Collection of psalms and hymns	27533	153
Pownall, Mary Ann (Wrighten)		
Jemmy of the glen	27542	154
Jemmy of the glen	34409	153
Kisses sue'd for	28933	153
Lavinia	27542	154
Six songs for the harpsichord or		
piano forte	27542	153-154
The Straw bonnet	27542	154
Read, Daniel		
The American singing-book		
[1st ed.] 1785	19213	159
*2nd ed., 1788	21416	271
2nd ed., corrected, 1786	44957	159
3rd ed., 1787	20673	159
4th ed., 1793	26056	159
*5th ed., 1795	29388	272
The Columbian harmonist		
No. 1, 1793	26057	160
No. 1 [-3] 1795?	29389	160
No. II, 1795	29390	160
No. III, 1795	29391	161

Composer & title	Evans no.	Page
Reeve, William (continued)		
Oscar and Malvina		
A Favorite air	30832	135
From Oscar and Malvina	27694	179
The Jolly gay pedlar	27694	180
Oh ever in my bosom live	35981	138
Quick march	30832	137
*Our country is our ship	34287	274
A Picture of Paris		
Paddy Bull's expedition	26522	218
The Purse, or benevolent tar		
The Galley slave	33294	15
-----.	30383	64
How sweet when the silver moon	27694	177
When a little merry he	26522	221
-----.	29498	184
When seated with Sal	28503	161
*-----.	28504	274
-----.	29498	183
Quick march in the pantomime of		
Oscar & Malvina	30832	137
The Tinker	27694	182
When a little merry he	26522	221
-----.	29498	184

Composer & title	Evans no.	Page
Reeve, William (continued)		
When seated with Sal	28503	161
*-----.	28504	274
-----.	29498	183
The Witch	48239	161
Reichardt, Johann Friedrich		
The Angler	37106	48
Reinagle, Alexander		
America, commerce and freedom	27647	161
-----.	30396	71
Blaise et Babet, Overture de	45573	169
A Chorus, sung before Gen.		
Washington	22093	161
*Collection of favorite songs (1788)	21420	274
-----. (1789)	45572	162-163
-----. (1789)	22095	163-166
Federal march	21421	166
-----. Faederal march.	45573	168
Indian march	48240	167
Marian. Overture. [See Shield, William]		
*[The Music of the historical play of Columbus]	36194	275
Overture de Blaise et Babet	45573	169

Composer & title	Evans no.	Page
Reinagle, Alexander (continued)		
Rosa	37106	47
-----.	37107	49
The Sailor's landlady		
America, commerce and freedom	27647	161
-----.	30396	71
La Schiava [See Piccinni, Niccolo]		
The Secret		
Rosa	37106	47
-----.	37107	49
Selection of the most favorite		
Scots tunes	20674	167
Tantivy hark forward huzza	22097	167
'Tis not the bloom on Damons cheek		
[See Hook, James]		
Twelve favorite pieces	45573	168-169
The Volunteers	29440	169
Relfe, John		
Mary's dream, or Sandy's ghost	26067	169
Mary's dream [or Sandy's ghost]	31701	10
-----.	33294	20
Rössler, Franz Anton [See Rosetti, Francesco Antonio]		

Composer & title	Evans no.	Page
Selby, William		
*Apollo and the muses musical composition	22881	275-276
Ode for the New Year [1789]	33294	20
*Two anthems, for three and four voices	22882	276
Shaw, Robert		
The Gentleman's amusement (1794)	27694	171-182
-----. No. 4 [-5] (1795)	29498	182-185
*-----. No. 6 [-7] (1796)	31181	185, 277
*-----. (1796)	31182	185-186, 277-278
Shield, William		
Ah weladay my poor heart	27694	174
Air in Rosina	37643	93
Amidst the illusions	27694	180
-----.	29501	187
-----.	30969	189
The Bleak wind wistles [sic] o'er the main	26522	216
Boys when I play, cry oh crimini	30396	71
The Cheering rosary	25966	187
-----. The Rosary.	30832	135
-----. The Rosary.	33294	17
Court me not to scenes of pleasure	28591	187

Composer & title	Evans no.	Page
Shield, William (continued)		
Dans votre lit	27694	180
-----.	30396	71
Dear wanderer	30832	136
Ere around the huge oak	27694	172
E're around the huge oak	30383	64
*Fame, let thy trumpet sound	16523	278
The Farmer		
Ere around the huge oak	27694	172
E're around the huge oak	30383	64
No more I'll court the town bred fair	26522	218
Send him to me	26522	215
Whilst happy in my native land	27694	181
A Favorite song in...The Travellers in Switzerland	35981	139
Follies of a day		
Ah weladay my poor heart	27694	174
From night till morn	26522	216
-----.	30383	65
Good morrow to your night cap	22095	165
The Green Mountain farmer	34302	188

Composer & title	Evans no.	Page
Shield, William (continued)		
The Hartford Bridge, or Skirts of a Camp		
Amidst the illusions	27694	180
Amidst the illusions	29501	187
Amidst the illusions	30969	187
The Heaving of the lead	25967	188
The Heaving [of] the lead	26522	218
The Heaving of the lead	26936	61
The Heaving of the lead	33294	19
The Heaving of the lead	25967	188
The Heaving [of] the lead	26522	218
The Heaving of the lead	26936	61
The Heaving of the lead	33294	19
Hey dance to the fiddle & tabor	32261	188
Hey dance to the fiddle & tabor	35981	141
The Highland laddie	27694	176
The Highland Reel		
The bleak wind wistles [sic] o'er the main	26522	216
The Highland laddie	27694	176
Scotch melody	27694	174
Scots air	30396	71
Such pure delight	26522	216
Tho I am now a very little lad	27694	174

Composer & title	Evans no.	Page
Shield, William (continued)		
How can I forget [As found in Shield's opera Marian, composed by Paisiello. See also under Paisiello]	29502	146, 188
How happy the soldier	22095	164
-----.	33294	17
I travers'd Judah's barren sand	27694	172
I've kissed and I've prattled	22095	164
The Je ne scai quoi	27694	174
Johnny and Mary	22095	165
-----.	34539	188
The Lasses of Dublin	31701	10
-----.	33294	17
The Lock and Key		
Hey dance to the fiddle & tabor	32261	188
-----.	35981	141
Love in a camp, or Patrick in Prussia		
Dans votre lit	27694	180
-----.	30396	71
My soul is thine sweet Norah	22096	189
Marian [See also under Paisiello]		
Overture	22142	189
-----.	45573	169
Patty Clover	27694	172

Composer & title	Evans no.	Page
Shield, William (continued)		
Midnight wanderers		
The Cheering rosary	25966	187
-----. The Rosary.	30832	135
-----. -----.	33294	17
Dear wanderer	30832	136
The Seamans home	27517	149
*The Morning is up	34540	278
My friend and pitcher	22095	165
My soul is thine sweet Norah	22096	189
No more I'll court the town bred fair	26522	218
Noble peasant		
When scorching suns	27694	179
Norah the theme of my song	22095	164
O come away my soldier bonny	34262	189
O come sweet Mary come to me	29498	184
Old Towler	33667	66
-----.	47915	189
Out of my sight or I'll box your ears	22095	165
Paddy Bull's expedition	26522	218
Patrick in Prussia [See Love in a Camp, or Patrick in Prussia]		

Composer & title	Evans no.	Page
Shield, William (continued)		
The Patriot [See The Farmer]		
Patty Clover	27694	172
A Picture of Paris		
Paddy Bull's expedition	26522	218
The Poor Soldier		
Good morrow to your night cap	22095	165
How happy the soldier	22095	164
-----.	33294	17
The Lasses of Dublin	31701	10
-----.	33294	17
My friend and pitcher	22095	165
Norah the theme of my song	22095	164
Out of my sight or I'll box		
your ears	22095	165
Rose tree	21628	4
-----.	22095	165
-----.	30396	70
The Spring with smiling face	22095	164
The Twins of Latona	22095	164
The Rival Soldiers, or sprigs of laurel		
O come away my soldier bonny	34262	189
O come sweet Mary come to me	29498	184
Robin Hood		
I travers'd Judah's barren sand	27694	172
The Je ne scai quoi	27694	174

Composer & title	Evans no.	Page
Shield, William (continued)		
The Trump of fame	26522	219
The Trump of fame	27694	173
When the men a courting came	26522	219
The Rosary [Alternate title of The		
Cheering Rosary by William		
Shield, q.v.]		
Rose tree	21628	4
Rose tree	22095	165
Rose tree	30396	70
Rosina		
Air in Rosina	37643	93
I've kissed and I've prattled	22095	164
Sweet transports, gentle wishes		
go	26522	217
When bidden to the wake	33294	16
When William at eve	22095	164
When William at eve	31873	190
Scotch medley	27694	174
Scots air from the Highland Reel	30396	71
The Seamans home	27517	149
Send him to me	26522	215
A Smile from the girl of my heart	26522	217
A Smile from the girl of my heart	33667	66

Composer & title	Evans no.	Page
Shield, William (continued)		
The Waxen doll [See his When first I slipp'd my leading strings]		
When first I slipp'd my leading strings	30832	136
-----.	33294	16
-----. The Waxen doll.	29498	183
Shumway, Nehemiah		
The American harmony	26162	190
Sicard, Stephen		
*Federal minuet	21462	279
*The New Constitution	21462	279
The President of the United States' march	45591	190
Skinner, Thomas		
Connecticut harmony [See Griswold, Elijah]		
Smith, Joshua		
Divine hymns		
*Exeter ed., 1791	23768	279
*Portsmouth ed., 1791	23769	279
*Norwich ed., 1795	29529	280
*Portsmouth ed., 1795	29530	280
*Poughkeepsie ed., 1796	31206	280
*Exeter ed., 1797	32848	280

469

Composer & title	Evans no.	Page
Storace, Stephen (continued)		
The Haunted tower		
My native land	29498	183
My native land	30383	64
Now all in preparation	29498	185
Tho pity I cannot deny	29498	184
Whither my love	25309	195
Whither my love	26936	61
How happily my life I led	30396	72
The Iron chest		
Sweet little Barbara	36375	195
*The Jealous don	25307	282
Lodoiska		
Ye streams that round my prison creep	30832	137
*Lullaby [From The Pirates]	25307	282
-----.	25308	193
-----.	26522	220
-----.	26936	63
-----.	27694	176
-----.	33294	21
-----.	47612	193

Composer & title	Evans no.	Page
Storace, Stephen (continued)		
The Much admired ballad of the willow	34608	194
My Grandmother		
Say how can words a passion feign	27694	177
Within a mile of Edinbourgh [adapted from Hook]	27694	177-178
My native land	29498	183
My native land	30383	64
No more his fears alarming	47613	194
No Song No Supper		
Across the downs this morning	26522	215
Across the downs this morning	27694	175
From aloft the sailor looks around	26522	216
Go George, I can't endure you	27694	174
How happily my life I led	30396	72
The Sailor boy [capering ashore]	25613	194
The Sailor boy capering ashore	26936	62
The Sailor boy capering ashore	33294	18
Now all in preparation	29498	185

472

Composer & title	Evans no.	Page
Storace, Stephen (continued)		
Poor black boy	26522	221
-----.	27694	176
-----. The Favorite ballad of the poor black boy.	27126	193
The Pretty creature	27517	148
The Prize		
Oh dear delightful skill	27694	178
Poor black boy	26522	221
-----.	27694	176
-----. The Favorite ballad of the poor black boy.	27126	193
The Sailor boy [capering ashore]	25613	194
The Sailor boy capering ashore	26936	62
-----.	33294	18
A Sailor lov'd a lass	30203	194
-----.	30383	63
Say how can words a passion feign	27694	177
*The Scotch air in...the Pirates	25307	282
*The Shipwreck'd seamans ghost	25307	282
-----.	26160	194
-----.	30832	135
The Siege of Belgrade		
Tho' you think by this to vex me	48260	195
Spirit of my sainted sire	47614	195

Composer & title	Evans no.	Page
Storace, Stephen (continued)		
Sweet little Barbara	36375	195
Tho pity I cannot deny	29498	184
Tho' you think by this to vex me	48260	195
Welch air [from the Cherokee]	27694	182
Whither my love	25309	195
-----.	26936	61
The Willow, the much admired ballad of	34608	194
Within a mile of Edinbourgh [adapted from Hook]	27694	177-178
Ye streams that round my prison creep	30832	137
Suett, Richard		
Canzonett	27517	149
Swan, Timothy		
The Federal harmony		
*1785 ed.	19268	282
1788 ed.	21485	195-196
1790 ed.	22919	196
1792 ed.	24831	196
1793 ed.	46884	196
*1794 ed.	27762	282-283
The Shepherd's complaint	19750	113

Composer & title	Evans no.	Page
Tans'ur, William		
The American harmony		
5th ed., 1769	11489	196-198
6th ed., 1771	12240	198
7th ed., 1771	12241	198
8th ed., 1773	13035	199
8th ed., 1774 [See note, p. 199]	13647	196
The Royal melody complete [compleat]		
*1761 ed.	9021	284
1767 ed.	10782	199-200
1768 ed.	11085	200
Taylor, Raynor		
The American tar		
Independent and free	47929	202
Amyntor, a pastoral song	47617	202
*An anthem, for public or private		
worship	27783	284
Cease a while ye winds to blow		
[See Bach, Johann Christian]		
Chelmer's banks	26522	218
Citizen soldiers	47618	202
*Divertimenti	32910	284
An Easy and familiar lesson	45796	202

Composer & title	Evans no.	Page
Taylor, Raynor (continued)		
The Faded lilly! or Louisa's woe	37107	51
Independent and free	47929	202
Jack the guinea pig	26522	219
The Kentucky volunteer	27186	203
-----.	30396	71
The Lass of the cott	29607	203
The Merry piping lad	29608	203
Nancy of the vale	47619	203
Never doubt that I love	37106	48
-----.	37107	50
Nobody	33294	22
-----.	48621	203
The Reconciliation	27091	83
Rustic festivity	29610	203
*-----.	34633	285
The Shepherds evening	26522	219
Silvan, the shepherd swain	33786	203
-----.	48622	204
Sonata for the piano forte	32911	204
*Summer, a pastorale song	34634	285
Viva la liberte	29611	204
The Wand'ring village maid	29612	204
The Wells	22095	165
The Wounded sailor	27784	204

PART FIVE

TITLE INDEX

Note: Titles preceded by an asterisk (*) are not yet
available in microtext form in the <u>Early American</u>
<u>Imprints, 1639-1800</u> microprint series. Such items
are included in Part Two of this Bibliography.

Title & composer	Evans no.	Page
A la Chasse	27542	154
Across the downs this morning		
(Storace)	26522	215
-----.	27694	175
Adams and liberty. The Boston		
patriotic song.	33294	21
-----.	34293	1
-----.	34294	2
-----.	34298	1
-----.	38177	2
-----.	48557	1

Title & composer	Evans no.	Page
*Baptismal hymns	23149	229
Baron Stuben's march	37643	92
Batchelor's hall (Dibdin)	26522	215
-----.	26936	62
-----.	33294	15
The Battle of Gemmappe (Devienne)	30341	55
The Battle of Prague (Kotzwara)	25698	110
-----.	28938	110
*-----.	45773	253
-----. March.	30396	72
-----. Quick march.	29498	185
-----. Quick step.	30795	129
-----. Slow march.	30396	72
-----. Slow march.	30795	129
-----. Battle of Prague [adapted by Benjamin Carr]	27694	181
*-----. When Delia on the plain appears.	33970	253
*The Battle of the kegs (Hopkinson)	16305	250
The Battle of Trenton (Hewitt)	33381	84
The Beauties of creation (Hawkins)	38203	59
The Beauties of fancy	37643	91
The Beauties of friendship	33294	21
Beauties of psalmody (Langdon)	19749	111

Title & composer	Evans no.	Page
The Bee	33294	20
La Belle Catherine with variations	25831	132
Belleisle march	30795	130
-----.	37643	90
Ben & Mary (Dibdin)	37106	48
*Ben Backstay (Dibdin)	26877	239
-----.	27694	173
[Beneath a weeping willows shade]		
(Hopkinson)	21152	102
Bess the Gawkie	31701	8
Bessy Bell and Mary Gray	31701	12
The Bird	19750	113
*The Bird and the lark (Billings)	22362	232
The Birks of Invermay	19750	114
-----.	31701	6
The Black cockade	37643	91
Blackrock	20674	167
Blaise et Babet, Overture de		
(Reinagle)	45573	169
The Blathrie o't	31701	7
The Bleak wind wistles o'er the main		
(Shield)	26522	216
A Blessing on brandy & beer		
(Mazzinghi)	30832	135

Title & composer	Evans no.	Page
Ca ira *[See Ah caira]*		
The Caledonian frolick (Carr)		
Two favourite strathpey reels	27694	172
The Caledonian hunt	27694	181
The Caledonian laddy (Hook)	31701	11
The Caledonian maid (Moulds)	29498	184
-----.	33667	66
-----.	47495	133
Canada farewell	37643	91
Canty body	31701	11
Canzonett (Wm. Jackson of Exeter)	27542	154
-----.	37106	47
Canzonett (Suett)	27517	149
Captain Mackintosh's march	31701	12
-----.	37643	91
Captn. Truxton, or Huzza! for the		
Constellation	36246	44
-----. Huzza for the Constellation	36247	44
The Captive (Percy)	48223	147
The Captive of Spilberg (Dussek)		
Good night	48836	59-60
Heigho!	48837	60

Title & composer	Evans no.	Page
Captivity (Storace)	26218	192
The Capture (Storace)	25306	193
*-----.	25307	282
Carmagnole	30396	70
Carnival of Venice (Linley)		
Young Lubin was a shepherd boy	26522	220
Caro bene (Sarti)	45572	163
The Castle of Andalusia (Arnold)		
Braes of Ballendine	19750	112
-----.	31701	11
Flowers of the forest	31701	12
Love soft illusion [arr. from		
Bertoni]	35981	139
Scotch air	31701	11
Castles in the air (Dibdin)		
Father and mother and Suke	48105	56
Jacks fidelity [same as Polly Ply]	30383	65
No good without exception	27694	173
Polly Ply [same as Jacks fidelity]	33294	22
Tom Tackle	30383	63
-----.	33294	22
-----.	35981	138
A Catch for three voices	21628	3

494

Title & composer	Evans no.	Page
A Compilation of the litanies and vespers (Aitken)		
1787 ed.	20186	6
1791 ed.	23106	6
*The Compleat instructor for the violin (Victor)	16152	287-288
*A Compleat tutor for the fife	14686	238
Conclusion of the Federal Overture (Carr)	27694	176
*Connecticut	37336	241
Connecticut harmony (Griswold)	30521	79-80
The Contented cottager (Frith)	47789	75
The Continental harmony (Billings)	26673	39
The Convent bell (Attwood)	47343	28
Corydon's ghost (Dwight?)	33294	21
The Cottage boy	48100	54
The Cottage in the grove (Hook)	30582	94
The Cottager (Wheatley)	33294	18
Count Brown's march	37643	92
Court me not to scenes of pleasure (Shield)	28591	187
Courteous stranger (Arnold)	37106	47
-----.	37107	49
Crazy Jane (Abrams)	48996	1
*Crazy Jane (Davy)	37269	238

500

Title & composer	Evans no.	Page
The Critic		
Air	30396	71
Mock Italian trio [I left my		
country and my friends]	27694	175
Crymbo oble	26522	216
Cupid benighted (Arnold)	30622	24
-----.	37106	47
-----.	37107	49
-----. At the dead of the night.	48040	24
*-----. In the dead of the night.	30829	228
Cymon (M. Arne)		
Quick march in Cymon	37643	93
Sweet passion of love	32041	24
Dainty Davie	20674	167
Damon and Clora (Harington)	19750	112
Damon & Clora (Harington)	27091	82-83
Dance for waltzing	28535	55
Dans votre lit (Shield)	27694	180
-----.	30396	71
Danse ecossoise (Pleyel)	31701	8, 10
The Dauphin	19750	114
Davie Rae	31701	12
The Day of marriage	48102	55
Dead march	30795	130
Dead march & monody (Carr)	37105	44-45

Title & composer	Evans no.	Page
Dear little cottage maiden (Hook)	30383	63
-----.	33294	20
Dear Mary, or adieu to Old England	33613	55
*Dear Walter (Arnold)	29118	228
Dear wanderer (Shield)	30832	136
Death and burial of Cock Robin (Arnold)	37107	49
The Death of Anna (Spofford)	35981	140
The Death of General Wolfe	19750	114
Death or victory (Dibdin)	26936	62
-----.	33294	22
The Death song of an Indian chief (Gram)	25848	78
*Delaware	37336	241
Delia (Capron)	19750	112
-----.	25831	132
Delvin side	31701	9
Demophon, Overture de (Cherubini)	28412	53
The Desert plains	19750	112
The Deserter (Dibdin)		
March	30795	130
Overture	45573	168
Pastorale	45573	168
*Songs in the Deserter	26882	240

Title & composer	Evans no.	Page
Divertimento	27517	149
*Divine and moral songs for the use of children (Watts) [See also Divine songs for children]	23040	291
Divine hymns, or spiritual songs (Smith)		
*Exeter ed., 1791	23768	279
*Portsmouth ed., 1791	23769	279
*Norwich ed., 1795	29529	280
*Portsmouth ed., 1795	29530	280
*Poughkeepsie ed., 1796	31206	280
*Exeter ed., 1797	32848	280
Divine songs (Wood)	21877	212
*Divine songs for children (Watts) [See also Divine and moral songs for the use of children]	20857	291
Dog and gun	37643	91
Donald of Dundee	47410	59
Donna donna donna Della (Hook)	32271	94
Dorothy Dump (Arnold)	29498	184
-----. Walters sweethearts.	30832	135
Dorsetshire march	37643	92
Drink to me only with thine eyes	21628	4
-----.	22095	163
-----.	26522	219

Title & composer	Evans no.	Page
East nook of Fife	20674	167
*Easter anthem (Billings)	28301	232
An Easy and familiar lesson for two performers (Taylor)	45796	202
*The Easy instructor (Little)	34004	258-260
Echo	37643	93
The Echoing horn (T. A. Arne)	33294	14
Elegant extracts for the German flute		
[Book the first] 1794	26936	61-63
Book the second 1796	30383	63-65
The third book 1798	33667	65-68
Ellen arise (Carr)	33855	45
Ellen of the Dee (Ross)	35981	140
Ellen the Richmond primrose girl (Spofford)	48256	191
-----.	48620	191
*Ellen's fate deserves a tear	33668	242
Eloisa's complaint	19750	112
Emblems of mem'ry are these tears	37365	68
Encyclopaedia...vol. XII	33687	68-69
[Enraptur'd I gaze] (Hopkinson)	21152	102
*Episcopalian harmony (Cole)	49049	237
E're around the huge oak (Shield)	27694	172
-----.	30383	64

Title & composer	Evans no.	Page
Fair Aurora (T. A. Arne)	47704	24
Fair Maria of the dale	47773	73
Fair Rosal[i]e (Dignum)	32104	58
Fal lal la (Storace)	48259	193
*Fame, let thy trumpet sound (Shield)	16523	278
The Fan	19750	113
Farewell ye green fields (Howard)	19750	113
-----.	22095	164
The Farmer (Shield)		
Ere around the huge oak	27694	172
-----.	30383	64
No more I'll court the town bred		
fair	26522	218
Send him to me	26522	215
Whilst happy in my native land	27694	181
Father and mother and Suke (Dibdin)	48105	56
Favorite air	37643	93
A Favorite air in the pantomime of		
Oscar and Malvina (Reeve)	30832	135
The Favorite ballad of the poor black		
boy (Storace)	27126	193
Favorite country dance (Dibdin)	27694	177
A Favorite duett [In thee each joy		
possessing]	33667	67

Title & composer	Evans no.	Page
A Favorite song. Translated from the Irish [Thou dear seducer of my heart]	35467	73
*The Favorite songs from the last new comic opera, called The Pirates (Storace)	25307	281-282
A Favourite French song [J'ai perdu mon Euridice] (Gluck)	26522	218
A Favourite rondo (Staes)	45573	169
The Federal Constitution & liberty forever (Hewitt)	34113	84
Federal harmony (Benham)		
[1st ed.] 1790.	22340	37
2nd ed. 1792.	24092	37
*3rd ed. 1793.	25159	231
4th ed. 1794.	26640	37
*5th ed. 1795.	28261	232
6th ed. 1796.	30054	37
The Federal harmony (Swan)		
*1785 ed.	19268	282
1788 ed.	21485	195-196
1790 ed.	22919	196
1792 ed.	24831	196
1793 ed.	46884	196
*1794 ed.	27762	282-283

Title & composer	Evans no.	Page
Friendship. An ode.	19750	113
*Friendship: anthem	21578	260
Friendship--by Bidwell	33294	22
Friendship. Words by Mr. Bidwell of		
Connecticut.	21628	4
The Frog and mouse	19750	114
From aloft the sailor looks around		
(Storace)	26522	216
From night till morn (Shield)	26522	216
-----.	30383	65
From Oscar and Malvina (Reeve)	27694	179
From thee Eliza I must go (Pleyel)	31701	10
-----.	35524	75
Funeral dirge on the death of		
General Washington (Hagen, Sr.)	37009	81
*Funeral dirge on the death of		
General Washington (Hagen, Sr.)	37481	245-246
A Funeral elegy on the death of		
General George Washington (Wood)	39131	213
Funeral ode (Belknap)	36939	36
The Galley slave (Reeve)	30383	64
-----.	33294	15

Title & composer	Evans no.	Page
Granby's march	30795	129
-----. Marquis of Granby's march.	37643	91
Grand march (Attwood, arr. from Mozart)	27694	174
Grano's march	37643	91
The Grasshopper	33294	15
Great news, or a trip to the Antipodes (Dibdin)		
The Smile of benevolence	33667	67
Tom Trueloves knell	33667	67
The Vet[e]rans	27694	179
*-----.	30345	240
The Green Mountain farmer (Shield)	34302	188
The Grounds and rules of musick explained (Walter)		
1721 ed.	2303	209
1723 ed.	2490	209
1740 ed.	4622	209
1746 ed.	5878	210
1760 ed.	8760	210
1764 ed.	41504	210
Hail! America hail!	33294	18
Hail Columbia (Phile) [See The President's march]		

Title & composer	Evans no.	Page
*Hail patriots all	33832	246
Handel's clarionett	37643	91
Handel's gavot	37643	92
Handels march	30795	130
Handel's water piece	37643	93
Handle's [sic] water music	33837	82
Handyside's march	37643	92
The Happy marriage	31701	14
Happy tawny Moor (Arnold)	27694	179
-----.	30242	25
Hark! From the tomb, &c. (Holyoke)	37642	89
Hark hark from the woodlands	25831	132
Hark the goddess Diana (Spofford)	48257	191
Hark the lark at heav'n's gate sings	26522	219
The Harmless shepherd	19750	114
Harmonia Americana (Holyoke)	23446	89-90
Harmonia coelestis (Benjamin)	35179	38
The Harmonist's companion (Belknap)		
*1794 ed.	28255	231
1797 ed.	31792	36-37
The Harmony of Maine (Belcher)	26636	34-35
The Hartford Bridge, or Skirts of a		
Camp (Shield)		
Amidst the illusions	27694	180
-----.	29501	187
-----.	30969	187

Title & composer	Evans no.	Page
Heigho! In the new opera of the		
Captive of Spilberg (Dussek)	48837	60
The Heiress (Paisiello)		
For tenderness form'd	26720	146
-----.	45572	163
Henry the IV (Martini il tedesco)		
Martini's march	30396	72
Henrys cottage maid (Pleyel)	26522	218
-----.	27694	173
-----.	31017	152
Her absence will not alter me	33294	19
Here awa', Willie	31701	8
Here's the pretty girl I love (Hook)	32273	94
The Hermit	33294	21
Hero and Leander	33294	21
Hey dance to the fiddle & tabor		
(Shield)	32261	188
-----.	35981	141
The Highland character	31701	13
The Highland laddie (Shield)	27694	176
Highland queen	31701	13

Title & composer	Evans no.	Page
How charming a camp is (Attwood)	27694	178
How cold it is. A winter song.	33294	23
How happily my life I led (Storace)	30396	72
How happy the soldier (Shield)	22095	164
-----.	33294	17
How happy was my humble lot (Hewitt)	35618	85
How imperfect is expression	19750	113
-----.	22095	165
How sweet when the silver moon (Reeve)	27694	177
*Humming bird, or a collection of		
fashionable songs	23456	250
Hurly burly (Haydn)	37106	48
Huzza for the Constellation [See		
Captn. Truxton, or Huzza! for the		
Constellation]		
A Hymn on peace (Wood)	18890	213
Hymns, &c. Composed on various		
subjects (Hart)		
*Middletown ed., 1787.	20405	247
*Philadelphia ed., 1787.	20406	247
*Hymns and divine songs (Nichols)	23632	266

Title & composer	Evans no.	Page
Hymns and spiritual songs		
20th ed., 1762.	41323	104
21st ed., 1767.	41776	104
*[Unnumbered ed.] 1773.	13068	250-251
*[Unnumbered ed.] 1790.	23042	251
Hymns on different spiritual		
subjects (Cleveland)		
*1786 ed.	19562	236
*1788 ed.	21002	236
*1793 ed.	25304	236
I am a brisk & sprightly lad	27694	173
I have a silent sorrow here (Devon-		
shire)	48410	56
I left my country and my friends	27694	175
I lock'd up all my treasure		
(Dibdin)	27694	179
I love my Jean	31701	13
I love them all	48157	105
I never lov'd any dear Mary but you		
(Hook)	33667	67
I sigh for the girl I adore (Hook)	30383	65
-----.	33294	19

Title & composer	Evans no.	Page
Indian march (Reinagle)	48240	167
The Indian philosopher	33294	21
The Indigent peasant (Hook)	25627	96
-----.	29498	183
-----. My heart is devoted dear Mary to thee.	26936	62
Inkle and Yarico (Arnold)		
Finale	27694	180
-----.	30396	72
Fresh and strong the breeze is blowing	30383	64
Fresh and strong [the breeze is blowing]	33294	18
Fresh and strong the breeze is blowing	47823	124
Fresh and strong the breeze is blowing	49008	25
The Negro boy	30243	26
A New song for a serenade [Rise my Delia]	33294	21
O say bonny lass	35981	138

Title & composer	Evans no.	Page
The Irishman	33667	68
The Iron chest (Storace)		
Sweet little Barbara	36375	195
The Italian monk (Carr)		
Poor Mary	37106	47
-----.	37107	50
I've kissed and I've prattled		
(Shield)	22095	164
*Jack at the windlass (Dibdin)	25392	240
Jack of Grissipoly	31701	12
Jack of Newberry (Hook)		
Where Liffey rolls its silver		
streams	32279	100
Jack the guinea pig (Taylor)	26522	219
Jacks fidelity [same as Polly Ply]		
(Dibdin)	30383	65
-----.	33294	22
J'ai perdu mon Euridice (Gluck)	26522	218
Janizary's march	30795	129
Javotte or the maid of the Alps		
(Willson)	35569	212
The Je ne scai quoi (Shield)	27694	174
*The Jealous don (Storace)	25307	282

527

Title & composer	Evans no.	Page
Jemmy of the glen (Pownall)	27542	154
-----.	34409	153
Jockey to the fair	31701	14
John Anderson my jo John	31701	13
Johnny and Mary (Shield)	22095	165
-----.	34539	188
Johnny fa'	31701	9
The Jolly gay pedlar (Reeve)	27694	180
The Jolly ringers (Dibdin)	26522	221
The Jolly sailor	33294	19
*The Jovial songster	25675	252
Kath'rine Ogie	31701	9
Keep your distance (Hook)	47452	96
*Kentucky. French country dance.	37336	241
The Kentucky volunteers (Taylor)	27186	203
-----.	30396	71
The Kiss (Hook)	48150	96
-----. May I never be married.	22095	164
-----. -----.	34087	97
Kisses sue'd for (Pownall)	28933	153
Klaglied: Ich habe viel gelitten (Schubart)	48961	171

Title & composer	Evans no.	Page
Laddie lie near me	20674	167
*Ladies patriotic song	33973	253
Lady Anne Bothwell's lament	31701	8
Lafayette	26522	216
The Lamplighter (Dibdin)	26522	217
*A Large collection of cotillions		
and country dances	32352	253
*Lash'd to the helm (Hook)	48151	249
Lass gin ye lo'e me	31701	9
*The Lass of Lucerne Lake (Hewitt)	28949	248
The Lass of Peaty's mill	31701	7
The Lass of the cott (Taylor)	29607	203
The Lasses of Dublin (Shield)	31701	10
-----.	33294	17
The Last time I came o'er the Moor	31701	9
Laus Deo. The New-England harmonist		
(Jenks)		
*1799 ed.	35667	251
1800 ed.	37707	106-107
Laus Deo! The Worcester collection		
of sacred harmony		
[1st ed.] 1786	19752	114-115
2nd ed., 1788	21193	115

Title & composer	Evans no.	Page
Love in a village (T. A. Arne)		
There was a jolly miller	33294	17
Love shall be my guide (Hook)	47454	97
Love soft illusion (Bertoni as		
adapted by Arnold in The Castle of		
Andalusia)	35981	139
Lovely Nan (Dibdin)	27694	181
-----.	33667	65
Lovely nymph	19750	113
[Lovely nymph now cease to languish]	19750	113
A Lovely rose	25831	132
Lovely Stella	33294	21
Love's frailties		
Matilda	35805	128
Love's march	37643	92
Low down in the broom	31701	11
Lubins rural cot	27517	148
The Lucky escape (Dibdin)	26522	220
-----.	26878	56
-----.	26936	62
-----.	27694	175
-----.	33294	14
Lucy Gray of Allendale (Hook)	30383	64

Title & composer	Evans no.	Page
Lucy or Selim's complaint (Hook)	27136	97
-----.	27694	182
-----.	33667	67
*Lullaby [from the Pirates] (Storace)	25307	282
-----.	25308	193
-----.	26522	220
-----.	26936	63
-----.	27694	176
-----.	33294	21
-----.	47612	193
Ma belle coquette (Hook)	25628	97
-----.	47076	97
Ma chere amie (Hook)	45572	162
MacDonald's reel	31701	13
Madrigal	30396	72
Maggy Lauder	20674	167
The Magician no conjurer (Mazzinghi)		
A Blessing on brandy & beer	30832	135
Maid of the mill (Arnold)		
The Gipsy's song	26522	221
-----.	29498	183
The Maid with a bosom of snow		
(Mazzinghi)	35762	128-129

Title & composer	Evans no.	Page
Mary will smile (Carr)	35283	52
*Maryland	37336	241
Mary's dream (Relfe)	26067	169
-----.	31701	10
-----.	33294	20
The Massachusetts compiler (Holden)	28848	87
The Massachusetts harmony (Billings)		
1784 ed.	18366	39
1786 ed.	18933	39
*Massachusetts hop	37336	241
The Match-girl	25796	128
Matilda	35805	128
*May day morn (Hook)	48152	249
May I never be married (Hook) [alternate		
title of The Kiss, q.v.]		
*The Mechanics lecture (Adgate)	21627	224-225
Meddley with the most favorite airs		
(Moller)	47835	131
Medley-duetto (Arnold)	27694	177
Medley duetto from the Federal		
Overture (Carr)	27694	176
-----.	29498	185
Mens fate deserves a tear (Hook)	35981	140
The Merry piping lad (Taylor)	29608	203
Merry Sherwood (Reeve)		
The Tinker	27694	182

Title & composer	Evans no.	Page
The Middlesex harmony (Babcock)	28221	29
Midnight wanderers (Shield)		
The Cheering rosary	25966	187
-----. The Rosary.	30832	135
-----. The Rosary.	33294	17
Dear wanderer	30832	136
The Seamans home	27517	149
Military amusement	30795	129-130
The Military glory of Great-Britain	9188	130
The Mill mill o	31701	13
Milton (Belknap)	36939	36
*Minuet (Fischer)	28673	242
Minuet (Haydn)	30396	71
Minuet de la cour	30396	72
Minuet with new variations (Fischer)	29498	183, 184
Minuetto	27517	149
Minuetto (Pleyel)	37107	52
Minuetto & trio (Pleyel)	37107	52
Minuetto with eight variations		
(Saliment)	27694	180
*-----.	31154	275
*Miss Ashmore's favorite collection		
of songs	11969	262-263
*-----.	13124	262

Title & composer	Evans no.	Page
The Mountaineers (Arnold)		
Happy tawny Moor	27694	179
-----.	30242	25
Lorade in the tower	30832	137
Moorish march	30832	136
Think your tawny Moor is true	30832	135
The Way worn traveller	26783	27
-----.	27694	180
-----.	47705	27
When the hollow drum	31954	27
Mozarts march	30795	130
The Much admired ballad of the willow (Storace)	34608	194
The Much admired song of Arabella the Caledonian maid (Moulds)	47498	134
Music in miniature (Billings)	16205	39
*[The Music of the historical play of Columbus] (Reinagle)	36194	275
*The Musical journal (Carr)	38022	234
The Musical journal for the flute, or violin (Carr)	37106	46-48
The Musical journal for the piano-forte (Carr)	37107	49-52

Title & composer	Evans no.	Page
The Musical magazine (Law)		
Number first, 1792	24464	118
Number second, 1793	25708	118
*Number third, 1794	27206	255-256
*Number fifth, 1799	35719	256
The Musical primer (Law)		
*1780 ed.	16816	256
1793 ed.	25709	118
1800 ed.	49106	118
The Musical repertory [repository]		
1796 ed.	30832	134-137
1799 ed.	35981	138-141
The Musical society	33294	20
My fond shepherds	31701	13
My friend and pitcher (Shield)	22095	165
[My gen'rous heart disdains]		
(Hopkinson)	21152	102
My Grandmother (Storace)		
Say how can words a passion feign	27694	177
Within a mile of Edinbourgh		
(adapted from Hook)	27694	177-178
My heart is devoted dear Mary to thee		
(Hook) [Alternate title of The		
Indigent peasant, q.v.]		

Title & composer	Evans no.	Page
[My love is gone to sea] (Hopkinson)	21152	102
My Nanny o	31701	12
My native land	29498	183
-----.	30383	64
My soul is thine sweet Norah (Shield)	22096	189
Myra	21628	4
Nancy of the vale (Taylor)	47619	203
Nancy, or the Sailor's journal (Dibdin)	33294	16
-----.	35981	139
-----. The Favorite song of Nancy, or the Sailor's journal.	32040	57
*-----. -------.	34166	239-240
-----. The Sailor's journal.	33667	67
-----. -------.	48107	57
The Negro boy (Arnold)	30243	26
Neighbour sly (Dibdin)	27694	179
Never doubt that I love (Taylor)	37106	48
-----.	37107	50
Never till now I knew love's smart	33294	14
The New American melody (French)	21841	74
*The New American mock-bird	8940	226-227
New Anacreontic song	33294	17

Title & composer	Evans no.	Page
*A New and beautiful collection of select hymns (Goddard)	35554	244
A New and compleat introduction to the grounds and rules of musick (Bayley)		
[1st ed.] 1764	9598	31
[2nd ed.] 1764	9599	31
*[3rd ed.] 1764	9600	229-230
1765	41518	31
1766	10236	32
1768	10829	32
*A New and select collection of the best English, Scots and Irish songs	16874	263-264
A New assistant for the piano-forte or harpsichord (F. Linley)	30695	121-123
The New bow wow	30396	70
A New collection of sacred harmony (Brownson)	31884	42
*The New Constitution march, and Federal minuet (Sicard)	21462	279
A New contredance (Capron)	25831	133

Title & composer	Evans no.	Page
The New-England harmonist (Jenks) [See Laus Deo. The New-England harmonist]		
The New-England psalm-singer (Billings)	11572	39-40
The New federal song (Phile) [See The President's march]		
New French march "Le reviel [sic] du Peuple"	30795	129
New German march	37643	93
*New Hampshire. Allemande.	37336	241
The New harmony of Zion (Bayley)	20956	32
*New instructions for the German flute	15925	264
A New introduction to psalmody (Gilman)	42240	77
*New Jersey	37336	241
New-Jersey harmony	32547	142
The New President's march [See Washington's march]		
The New somebody (Carr)	35283	52
*The New song book being Miss Ashmore's favorite collection of songs	11969	262-263

Title & composer	Evans no.	Page
A New song for a serenade [Rise my Delia] (Arnold)	33294	21
*A New song, to the tune of Hearts of oak...The Liberty song	10881	264-265
The New universal harmony (Bayley)	12664	32
A New version of the psalms of David		
1720 ed.	2094	142
1754 ed.	40680	142
1754 ed.	40681	142
1755 ed.	7358	142
1757 ed.	7846	143
*1762 ed.	9068	265
1762 ed.	9069	143
1763 ed.	9344	143
*1763 ed.	9345	265-266
1765 ed.	9913	143
1765 ed.	9914	143
1767 ed.	10558	143
1770 ed.	42063	144
*1773 ed.	12673	266
1773 ed.	12677	144
1774 ed.	13149	144

Title & composer	Evans no.	Page
Orphee et Euridice (Gluck)		
A Favorite French song [J'ai perdu mon Euridice]	26522	218
Oscar and Malvina (Reeve)		
A Favorite air	30832	135
From Oscar and Malvina	27694	179
The Jolly gay pedlar	27694	180
Oh ever in my bosom live	35981	138
Quick march	30832	137
*Our country is our ship (Reeve)	34287	274
Out of my sight or I'll box your ears (Shield)	22095	165
The Outlaws (Kelly)		
Young Henry lov'd his Emma well	48903	109
Ouverture d'Iphigenie [en Aulide] (Gluck)	28751	77
Overture by Haydn	32241	84
Overture de Blaise et Babet (Reinagle)	45573	169
Overture de Demophon (Cherubini, arr. Hewitt)	28412	53
Overture La Buona Figliuola (Piccinni)	31009	151
Overture. La Schiava (Piccinni)	45573	168
Overture to the Deserter (Dibdin)	45573	168
Paddy Bull's expedition (Reeve or Shield)	26522	218

Title & composer	Evans no.	Page
Pauvre Madelon (Arnold)	25314	26
-----.	33536	26
Peeping Tom (Arnold)		
The Rush light	27661	26
Peggy I must love thee	31701	11
*Pennsylvania	37336	241
*Peter Pindar's new gypsy song (Wright)	26495	291
Philadelphia harmony (Adgate)		
1789 ed.	21629	2
1790 ed.	22299	2
1791 ed.	46110	3
1796 ed.	29953	3
Philadelphia march	37643	92
*The Philadelphia pocket companion		
for the German flute or violin	27516	267-268
The Philadelphia pocket companion		
for the guittar [sic] or clarinette	27517	147-149
The Philadelphia songster (Adgate)	21628	3-4
A Picture of Paris (Reeve or Shield)		
Paddy Bull's expedition	26522	218
Pinkie house	31701	8

Title & composer	Evans no.	Page
Pleyel's German hymn, with variations	49136	152
Plow boy	30396	70
*A Pocket book for the German flute	16014	269-270
*A Pocket book for the guitar	16015	270
*A Pocket book for the violin	16016	270
Polly Ply [same as Jacks fidelity]		
(Dibdin)	30383	65
-----.	33294	22
Polly's answer	19750	112
Polwart on the green	31701	9
Poor black boy (Storace)	26522	221
-----.	27694	176
[See also The Favorite ballad of the		
poor black boy]		
The Poor blind girl (DeCleve)	34383	55
Poor Jack (Dibdin)	26936	61
-----.	33294	15
Poor Lima (Attwood)	37106	47
-----.	37107	49
The Poor mariner	26522	217
Poor Mary (Carr)	37106	47
-----.	37107	50
*Poor Richard (Carr)	25265	234
-----.	27517	149
-----.	35283	52

Title & composer	Evans no.	Page
The Poor Soldier (Shield)		
Good morrow to your night cap	22095	165
How happy the soldier	22095	164
-----.	33294	17
The Lasses of Dublin	31701	10
-----.	33294	17
My friend and pitcher	22095	165
Norah the theme of my song	22095	164
Out of my sight or I'll box your ears	22095	165
Rose tree	21628	4
-----.	22095	165
-----.	30396	70
The Spring with smiling face	22095	164
The Twins of Latona	22095	164
Poor Tom Bowling, or the Sailor's epitaph (Dibdin)	26879	57
-----.	33294	14
-----. Poor Tom Bowling.	30383	65
-----. Tom Bowling.	26522	217
Portugueze hymn on the nativity [alternate title of Adeste Fideles]	37106	48
Prayer of the Sicilian mariners	27694	175

Title & composer	Evans no.	Page
Preludes (Linley)	30695	122
-----.	47823	124
-----. Second set of preludes.	30695	122
*A Present to children	23715	271
The President of the United States March (Sicard)	45591	190
The President's march (Phile)	27694	172
-----.	29609	150
-----.	30795	129
-----.	31044	150
-----.	33902	150
-----.	37643	92
-----. The Favorite new federal song.	33896	150
*-----. New federal song.	33897	268
*-----. The Truly federal song Hail Columbia!	33898	268-269
The President's new march [See Washington's march]		
The Pretty creature (Storace)	27517	148
Pretty maids all in a row (Hook)	37106	47
-----.	37107	49
The Primrose girl (Hewitt)	27542	154
-----.	33294	21
-----. Primroses.	33667	66

Title & composer	Evans no.	Page
The Prize (continued)		
Oh dear delightful skill	27694	178
Poor black boy	26522	221
-----.	27694	176
*Prussian march	34660	285
The Psalm-singer's amusement		
(Billings)	17104	40
The Psalm-singer's assistant (Bayley)		
1767 ed.	41691	33
n.d. [Evans gives 1785]	18926	33
The Psalmodist's companion (French)	25513	74
The Psalms, hymns, & spiritual songs		
9th ed., 1698.	817	154-155
12th ed., 1705.	39420	155
14th ed., 1709.	1381	155
15th ed., 1711.	39518	155
20th ed., 1720.	2095	155
20th [21st?] ed., 1722.	2317	155
22nd ed., 1729.	3134	156
25th ed., 1742.	4892	156
The Psalms, hymns, & spiritual songs		
[Edited by Thomas Prince, 1758]	8082	156

Title & composer	Evans no.	Page
Quick march	37643	91
Quick march from the Battle of Prague (Kotzwara)	29498	185
Quick march in Cymon (M. Arne)	37643	93
Quick march in the pantomime of Oscar & Malvina (Reeve)	30832	137
Quick step in the Battle of Prague (Kotzwara)	30795	129
The Race horse	26936	61
-----.	33294	19
Rakes of London	37643	91
*Recitativo e rondo (Paisiello)	48212	267
The Reconciliation (Taylor)	27091	83
The Reconsaliation (Gehot)	26522	215
La Recontre Imprevue (Gluck) [See La Recontre Luprette]		
La Recontre Luprette (Gluck) An Ode to sleep	30832	137
*The Republican harmony (Billings)	28300	233
The Request (Vogler)	26522	220
The Responsary (Bull)	28370	43
*Resurrection, an anthem for Easter (Gram)	47067	245

Title & composer	Evans no.	Page
Rondo (Pleyel)	37107	52
Rosa (Reinagle)	37106	47
-----.	37107	49
The Rosary (Shield) [See The Cheering rosary]		
Rose tree (Shield)	21628	4
-----.	22095	165
-----.	30396	70
Rosina (Shield)		
Air in Rosina	37643	93
I've kissed and I've prattled	22095	164
Sweet transports, gentle wishes go	26522	217
When bidden to the wake	33294	16
When William at eve	22095	164
-----.	31873	190
Roslin castle	30396	70
-----.	31701	6
Rosline castle, a favorite Scots song	48878	170
Rosy morn	21628	4
The Royal melody complete (Tans'ur)		
*1761 ed.	9021	284
1767 ed.	10782	199-200
1768 ed.	11085	200
Rudiments of music (Adgate) (1788)	20916	4
-----. (1788)	45212	4
-----. (1799)	35083	5

Title & composer	Evans no.	Page
Sacred lines for Thanksgiving-Day, November 7, 1793 (Gram)	25562	78
-----.	47066	79
The Sailor boy capering ashore (Storace)	25613	194
-----.	26936	62
-----.	33294	18
A Sailor lov'd a lass (Storace)	30203	194
-----.	30383	63
The Sailor's allegory	26522	218
The Sailor's consolation (Dibdin)	26936	62
-----.	33294	18
The Sailor's journal (Dibdin) [Alternate title of Nancy, or the Sailor's journal, q.v.]		
The Sailor's landlady (Reinagle) America, commerce and freedom	27647	161
-----.	30396	71
Sammlung Geistlicher Lieder	33625	171
Saturday night at sea	33294	18
Savage dance	30396	70
Say how can words a passion feign (Storace)	27694	177

Title & composer	Evans no.	Page
The Seamans home (Shield)	27517	149
Second set of preludes (Linley)	30695	122
The Secret (Reinagle)		
Rosa	37106	47
-----.	37107	49
See brother see (Arnold)	29119	27
[See down Maria's blushing cheek]		
(Hopkinson)	21152	102
Select harmony (Brownson)		
1783 ed.	17857	43
1791 ed.	23227	43
Select harmony (Law)		
1779 ed.	16318	120
1784 ed.	18553	120
*1786 ed.	19754	257
1791 ed.	23492	120
*1792 ed.	24467	257
A Select number of plain tunes (Law)	10662	121
*-----.	12427	258
-----.	17098	157
-----.	18930	158
*-----.	27208	258
The Select songster (Langdon)	19750	111-114

Title & composer	Evans no.	Page
*A Selection of hymns and spiritual songs (Broaddus)	33460	234
A Selection of sacred harmony (Adgate)		
[1st ed.] 1788	45213	5
3rd ed., 1790	22884	5
4th ed., 1794	47212	5
5th ed., 1797	32818	5
*A Selection of sacred harmony	21453	276-277
A Selection of the most favorite Scots tunes (Reinagle)	20674	167
Send him to me (Shield)	26522	215
Serenade	37643	90
*A Set of six songs (Juhan)	27176	252
Seven songs for the harpsichord or forte piano (Hopkinson)	21152	101-102
Shakespeare's willow (Carr)	37106	47
-----.	37107	50
A Shape alone let others prize (Gram)	33294	23
She dropt a tear (Moulds)	47496	134
-----. Ye lingring winds	37106	48
-----. Ye lingring winds	37107	50
She left me ah! for gold	31183	187

Title & composer	Evans no.	Page
She lives in the valley below (Hook)	48886	98
She wou'd & she wou'd not (Cibber)		
Ye chearful virgins	27694	176
Sheep in the clusters	33294	15
Shelty's song	31701	10
Shepherd I have lost my love		
[See Anna]		
The Shepherd's complaint (Swan)	19750	113
The Shepherd's evening (Taylor)	26522	219
The Shipwreck (Arnold)		
And hear her sigh adieu!	33314	25
In dear little Ireland	48775	25
Little Sally	31754	25
-----.	48776	25
When on the ocean	48777	27
*The Shipwreck'd seamans ghost		
(Storace)	25307	282
-----.	26160	194
-----.	30832	135
The Siege of Belgrade (Storace)		
Tho' you think by this to vex me	48260	195
Sigh no more ladies	27694	181
The Siller crown	31701	13

Title & composer	Evans no.	Page
Sixteen anthems (Flagg)	41612	73
Slow march [in the Battle of Prague] (Kotzwara)	30396	72
Slow march in the Battle of Prague (Kotzwara)	30795	129
A Smile from the girl of my heart (Shield)	26522	217
-----.	33667	66
A Smile from the youth that I love (Wright)	34552	214
The Smile of benevolence (Dibdin)	33667	67
So dearly I love Johnny o	47920	191
So sweet her face (Gauline)	48453	76
Social harmony (Benham)		
1798 ed.	33398	38
1799 ed.	36331	38
Softly as the breezes blowing (Capron)	25831	131
The Soldier tir'd (T. A. Arne)	45572	163
The Soldier's adieu (Dibdin)	26881	57
-----.	30383	63
Soldiers joy	30396	70
Somebody	33294	20
-----. Were I oblig'd to beg my bread.	27694	178

Title & composer	Evans no.	Page
Sonata	37643	93
Sonata (Pleyel)	37107	51
Sonata I [D major] (Hewitt)	47449	85
Sonata II [C major] (Hewitt)	47449	85
Sonata III [F major] (Hewitt)	47449	85
Sonata [C major] for the piano forte (Taylor)	32911	204
Sonatina...opera 71 (Haydn)	33863	84
*A Song book	34571	280
Song in the Spoil'd child [Since then I'm doomed]	33294	23
Song LI [Now let rich music sound] (words only)	33294	18
*[Songs for the amusement of children]	22894	281
*Songs in the Deserter (Dibdin)	26882	240
*Songs in the musical drama of the Adopted child (Hagen, Sr.)	33423	246
*The Songster's magazine	29542	281
Sonnet. For the fourteenth of October, 1793 (Graun)	25563	79
Sophronia	33294	20
*South Carolina	37336	241
The Spanish barber (Arnold) A Favorite song in the opera of the Spanish barber	35981	139

Title & composer	Evans no.	Page
Such pure delight (Shield)	26522	216
The Suffolk harmony (Billings)	19512	40
Suffolk march	37643	92
Summer (Belknap)	36939	35
*Summer, a pastorale song (Taylor)	34634	285
Supplement to the Chorister's companion (Jocelin)	24434	108
The Surrender of Calais (Arnold)		
Go with you all the world over	26522	217
Pauvre Madelon	25314	26
-----.	33536	26
Sweet Annie frae the sea-beach came	31701	8
Sweet lavender	33667	66
Sweet lilies of the valley (Hook)	26936	61
-----.	33294	19
Sweet lillies of the valley (Hook)	25629	98
Sweet little Barbara (Storace)	36375	195
Sweet little cottage (Graeff)	35981	140
Sweet little girl that I love (Hook)	26936	62
-----.	30584	98
-----.	33294	17
Sweet Martindale	33667	67

Title & composer	Evans no.	Page
Then say my sweet girl, can you love me? (Hook)	27789	99
-----.	30383	65
-----.	33294	20
There came a ghaist to Margret's door	31701	9
There was a jolly miller (T. A. Arne)	33294	17
There's my thumb	31701	8
There's nae luck about the house	31701	10
Thespian chaple	33627	204-205
Think your tawny Moor is true (Arnold)	30832	135
Third coldstream march	30795	129
This is no mine ain house	31701	13
Tho' Bacchus may boast of his care killing bowl (Shield)	33294	22
Tho I am now a very little lad (Shield)	27694	174
Tho pity I cannot deny (Storace)	29498	184
Tho prudence	30396	70
Tho' you think by this to vex me (Storace)	48260	195
Thomas and Sally (T. A. Arne) The Echoing horn	33294	14

Title & composer	Evans no.	Page
To me a smiling infant came	30832	137
To the ewe-bught's Marion	31701	10
To the maid I love best (Hook)	34912	99
The Token (Dibdin)	26883	57
Tom Bowling (Dibdin) [See Poor Tom Bowling, or the Sailor's epitaph]		
Tom Tackle (Dibdin)	30383	63
-----.	33294	22
-----.	35981	138
Tom Thumb (Markordt)		
That petty fogging grizzle	27694	177
We kings who are in our senses	27694	178
Tom Trueloves knell (Dibdin)	33667	67
[The Trav'ler benighted and lost] (Hopkinson)	21152	102
The Travellers in Switzerland (Shield)		
A Favorite song	35981	139
The Truly federal song Hail Columbia! (Phile) [See The President's march]		

Title & composer	Evans no.	Page
*The Vendue, on six month's credit	31484	287
*Vermont. French country dance.	37336	241
*A Very plain and easy introduction to the art of singing psalm tunes (Tufts)	2297	286-287
The Vet[e]rans (Dibdin)	27694	179
*-----. The Veterans.	30345	240
A View of the temple--a Masonic ode (Belknap)	36939	36
The Village harmony, or youth's assistant to sacred music		
*[unnumbered ed.] 1795	29793	288
2nd ed., 1796	31494	208
*3rd ed., 1797	33123	288
4th ed., 1798	34930	208-209
5th ed., 1800	38938	209
*The Village holiday	29794	289
-----. The Village holyday.	26522	221
The Village maid	27694	177
The Village spire (Giordani)	26522	217
*Virginia	37336	241
Viva la liberte	29611	204
*The Vocal charmer	26410	289

Title & composer	Evans no.	Page
*The Vocal muse; or ladies songster	24978	289-290
*The Vocal remembrancer	26411	290
*[The Volunteer songster, or vocal remembrances]	36662	290
The Volunteers (Reinagle)	29440	169
The Waggoner (Dibdin)	26885	58
-----.	29498	184
The Wags (Dibdin)		
Death or victory	26936	62
-----.	33294	22
The Walls of my prison (More)	26522	219
Walters sweethearts (Arnold)		
[See Dorothy Dump]		
Walzer (Linley)	47823	124
A Wand'ring gipsey (Percy)	37106	48
-----.	37107	51
The Wand'ring village maid (Taylor)	29612	204
Washington (Holyoke)	33294	22
Washington and independence (Pelissier)	34959	146
Washington's March		
General Washingtons march	27694	175
-----.	30396	70
-----. The New President's march.	35638	211

Title & composer	Evans no.	Page
Washington's March (continued)		
President's new march	30795	129
Washington's march	29834	210
-----.	30795	129
-----.	31554	210
-----.	37643	93
Washington's march at the Battle of Trenton	31555	210
*Washington's minuet and gavott	37336	241
Water music (Handel)	33837	82
Water music, March in the (Handel)	37643	93
Water piece (Handel)	37643	93
*The Waves were hush'd, the sky serene	34967	291
The Waxen doll (Shield) [See When first I slipp'd my leading strings]		
The Way to get married (Hook)	33583	100
The Way worn traveller (Arnold)	26783	27
-----.	27694	180
-----.	47705	27

Title & composer	Evans no.	Page
We kings who are in our senses		
(Markordt)	27694	178
The Wedding-day (Hook)	25630	100
-----.	48888	100
Welch air in the Cherokee (Storace)	27694	182
The Wells (Taylor)	22095	165
Were I oblig'd to beg my bread		
[See Somebody]		
*Werther to Charlotte (Callcott)	33483	234
What a beau your granny was	30396	70
What are the boasted joys of love		
(Shield)	34541	189
What can a lassy do (Hook)	32278	100
What med'cine can soften the bosom's		
keen smart (Boyce)	45572	163
What shepherd or nymph	26522	219
When a little merry he (Reeve)	26522	221
-----.	29498	184
When absent from the nymph I love	31701	9
When bidden to the wake (Shield)	33294	16
-----. When bidden to the wake or		
fair.	30396	71

Title & composer	Evans no.	Page
When on the ocean (Arnold)	48777	27
When pensive I thought on my love (Kelly)	33537	109
When rural lads and lasses gay	47680	212
When scorching suns (Shield)	27694	179
When seated with Sal (Reeve)	28503	161
*-----.	28504	274
-----.	29498	183
When the hollow drum (Arnold)	31954	27
When the men a courting came (Shield)	26522	219
When the mind is in tune	33214	212
*When the old heathen gods (Hewitt)	34114	248
-----.	34115	85
When the rosy morn appearing	30396	70
When the shades of night pursuing (Hewitt)	37106	48
-----.	37107	51
When wild wars deadly blast	31701	12
When William at eve (Shield)	22095	164
-----.	31873	190
Where Liffey rolls its silver stream (Hook)	32279	100
Where's the harm of that (Hook)	32280	101

Title & composer	Evans no.	Page
Winsome Kate (Hook)	27694	179
-----.	31701	12
Winter	33294	23
Winter (Belknap)	36939	36
Wisdom's favorite	19750	114
The Wish, or the sequel to Henry's cottage maid (Hewitt)	47805	86
The Witch (Reeve)	48239	161
Within a mile of Edinburgh (Hook)		
Within a mile of Edinburgh	33294	21
Within a mile of Edinboro' town	33667	66
Within a mile of Edinbourgh	27694	177-178
Within a mile of Edinburgh	31701	11
-----.	47457	101
-----. 'Twas within a mile of Edinburgh town.	32067	99
*-----. 'Twas with in a mile of Edinburgh town.	30371	250
Woe's my heart	31701	10
The Wonderful old man	19750	114
The Wood cutters	37643	91
The Wood robin	37107	50
-----.	49196	213

Title & composer	Evans no.	Page
The Woodman (Shield)		
Court me not to scenes of pleasure	28591	187
A Smile from the girl of my heart	26522	217
-----.	33667	66
The Streamlet that flow'd round		
her cot	26522	221
-----.	26936	61
-----.	27694	175
-----.	33294	20
-----. The Streamlet.	35981	141
-----. The Streamlet.	45572	162
The Waxen doll [See When first I		
slipp'd my leading strings]		
When first I slipp'd my leading		
strings	30832	136
-----.	33294	16
-----. The Waxen doll.	29498	183
Woolf's adieu	33294	15
The Worcester collection of sacred		
harmony (Holden) [See Laus Deo!		
The Worcester collection of sacred		
harmony]		
Worshipper's assistant (Howe)	35643	103
The Wounded Hussar (Hewitt)	37614	86
The Wounded sailor (Taylor)	27784	204

Title & composer	Evans no.	Page
The Wretched slave (H., S. M.)	32374	81
-----.	39151	81
Yankee Doodle	30396	70
-----.	31676	214
-----.	33902	150
*-----.	35063	292
-----.	37643	91
-----.	48535	214
Yarrimore. An Indian ballad.	28143	214
Ye chearful virgins (Cibber)	27694	176
Ye fair possessed	19750	113
Ye lingring winds (Moulds) [See		
She dropt a tear]		
Ye mortals whom fancies	33294	23
Ye sluggards (Hook)	22095	165
Ye streams that round my prison		
creep (Storace)	30832	137
Ye zephyrs where's my blushing rose		
(Stevenson)	25831	132
The Yellow-hair'd laddie [See		
The Yellow-hair'd lady]		
The Yellow-hair'd lady	25831	132
-----. The Yellow hair'd laddie	31701	6

Title & composer	Evans no.	Page
Young Carlos sue'd a beauteous maid		
(Attwood)	27694	179
-----.	31701	8
Young Henry lov'd his Emma well		
(Kelly)	48903	109
Young Jemmy is a pleasing youth	36747	221
The Young lover	19750	113
Young Lubin was a shepherd boy		
(Linley)	26522	220
Young Simon in his lovely Sue		
(Arnold)	29121	24
Young Willy for me	33252	222
Young's vocal and instrumental		
musical miscellany	26522	215-221
*The Youth's entertaining amusement		
(Dawson)	7181	238-239
Zorinski (Arnold)		
At the dead of the night [same as		
Cupid benighted]	48040	24
Courteous stranger	37106	47
-----.	37107	49
*In the dead of the night [same as		
Cupid benighted]	30829	228

PART SIX

NUMERICAL INDEX

Note: Titles preceded by an asterisk (*) are not yet
available in microtext form in the Early American
Imprints, 1639-1800 microprint series. Such items
are included in Part Two of this Bibliography.

Evans no.	Page	Evans no.	Page
22095	163-166	23446	89-90
22096	189	*23456	250
22097	167	23472	107
22098	99	23490	115
22142	189	23491	119
22299	2	23492	120
*22311	227	*23632	266
22340	37	*23634	266-267
*22362	232	*23715	271
*22588	252	*23749	275
22615	83	*23768	279
22798	147	*23769	279
*22829	272-273	24092	37
*22881	275-276	24403	86
*22882	276	*24433	251
22884	5	24434	108
*22894	281	24461	115
22919	196	*24463	255
*23040	291	24464	118
*23042	251	*24465	256-257
23106	6	24466	119
*23149	229	*24467	257
23227	43	24831	196

598

Evans no.	Page	Evans no.	Page
27621	127	28591	187
27647	161	*28673	242
27661	26	*28724	243
27694	171-182	*28725	243
27712	190	28751	77
*27762	282-283	*28774	245
*27783	284	28848	87
27784	204	28933	153
27789	99	28938	110
28143	214	*28949	248
28216	28	*29118	228
28221	29	29119	27
28222	29	29121	24
*28255	231	29122	133
*28261	232	*29328	269
*28300	233	*29388	272
*28301	232	29389	160
28370	43	29390	160
28412	53	29391	161
*28444	247-248	*29392	273
28503	161	29400	169
*28504	274	29498	182-185
28535	55	29501	187

74858

PRINTED
IN
U.S.A.